D1207957

BURT FRANKLIN SELECTED ESSAYS IN LITERATURE & CRITICISM #9

THE EVOLUTION *of* "THE FAERIE QUEENE"

THE EVOLUTION *of* "THE FAERIE QUEENE"

By

JOSEPHINE WATERS BENNETT

BURT FRANKLIN SELECTED ESSAYS IN LITERATURE & CRITICISM #9

BURT FRANKLIN

New York 25, N. Y.

1960

Published by
BURT FRANKLIN
514 West 113th Street
New York 25, N. Y.

The publication of this volume has been aided by a grant from the American Council of Learned Societies from a fund provided by the Carnegie Corporation of New York

PREFACE

IN THIS study I have undertaken to approach the problem of the structure of the *Faerie Queene* from the point of view of the actual process of composition. In the absence of manuscript materials, and even of an adequate account of Spenser's life, such an approach involves considerable temerity. But I believe that, whatever its limitations and defects, it brings us much nearer to the poet and to a full and active understanding of the poem than we can get by attacking the problem from the point of view of critical and theoretical principles, whether Spenser's or another's. It enables us to see the poem in the natural light of the poet's aims, his difficulties, and his uncertainties, rather than in the artificial light of critical theory and *post factum* apology.

I have surveyed the structure of the whole work and of each book in its relation to recognizable materials and techniques, in an effort to increase the reader's understanding of the poem by developing a rational theory of the probable method and progress of the composition. If this approach adds to the number of those who read the *Faerie Queene*, or to the understanding of those who have read it, I shall be well satisfied. The poet is as smooth of tongue and subtle in his tale as his own Guile, and the labor of following him through his spacious land of faery has been long and arduous, but it has also been full of pleasant surprises and fruitful discoveries.

All along the way I have been cheered on by friends and colleagues who have called my attention to pertinent materials or voiced challenging criticisms. A few of these I have been able to acknowledge in the text and notes. Others I take pleasure in mentioning here. Among my former colleagues I have to thank Professors R. M. Estrich, W. R. Parker, and F. L. Utley for suggestions and encouragement in the early stages of the work. Professor F. B. Williams looked up material for me in

England. Professor C. B. Millican read the manuscript at an early stage and gave me the benefit of his experience in Arthurian research. Professor Merritt Y. Hughes twice read and commented upon the whole work. I owe much to his challenging comments and to the enthusiastic support which he has given the undertaking. Professor Allan Gilbert reviewed one version of the study, and Professor Percy W. Long another. Both have given me detailed criticism and general encouragement, including the support of their recommendations. The late Professor H. S. V. Jones also read the manuscript and was most generous in his critical comments and his commendation of my results. It is with the deepest regret that I realize that he will never take the printed volume in his hands.

Among others to whom I am indebted for support and assistance in securing publication, I am privileged to count Professors Hoyt H. Hudson, Huntington Brown, and Don Cameron Allen. Professor George R. Coffman has been most helpful, and to him I owe permission to reprint part of the article from *Studies in Philology* which takes up most of chapter xv. That is the only part of this study which has previously been printed.

It has been my great good fortune to find help of another kind as I needed it. In 1934–35 the American Association of University Women awarded me their Dorothy Bridgman Atkinson traveling fellowship for a year's study in England, and, while I spent the year gathering materials for a very different work, it is a poor year's research indeed which cannot be turned to account in more than one direction. The resources of the Harvard College Library have been made available to me several times in the course of this study, and in 1940 a grant-in-aid from the American Council of Learned Societies gave me a most profitable summer at the Huntington Library and resulted in very substantially strengthening the chapters on the reputation of Arthur, the Virtues, and the background of Book I.

I have made the book the occasion for visits to the Folger and to the University of Illinois and the University of Chicago libraries, to each of which I owe an acknowledgment for courtesies extended to me. Finally, it has been my good fortune to live for the last five years within commuting distance of the Newberry Library, an institution whose resources and efficiency have been of constant assistance.

The publication of the book was assured by a grant from the American Council of Learned Societies, acting upon the recommendation of the Modern Language Association of America. The University of Chicago Press has given me prompt and effective support in all matters pertaining to publication, and I am deeply grateful to its able staff.

In connection with a task of as long duration as this has been it is impossible to acknowledge all debts, but it would be a major omission if I failed to mention the assistance given me by my husband, Dr. Roger E. Bennett, who has co-operated throughout by criticizing and suggesting, and who reviewed the whole manuscript for final revisions and read the proof.

JOSEPHINE WATERS BENNETT

EVANSTON, ILLINOIS
June 2, 1942

TABLE OF CONTENTS

I
THE BEGINNING

> Of Faerie lond yet if he more inquire,
> By certaine signes here set in sundry place
> He may it find; ne let him then admire,
> But yield his sence to be too blunt and bace,
> That n'ote without an hound fine footing trace.
>
> —II, Proem, 4.1-5

IT IS characteristic of great art that it conceals more than it reveals about the process of its creation. It appears as a complete whole in which the initial concept and the various stages of development have been absorbed, and only the finished work remains to give that illusion of miraculous origin which lies at the root of the theory of "poetic inspiration." The creative processes are more readily traced in less successful or less highly finished pieces, where uneven workmanship permits the reader to distinguish degrees of accomplishment and to pry into the method of composition and develop an understanding of the problems and aims of the creator through an appreciation of his failures as well as of his successes.

The *Faerie Queene* is a composition which both invites and resists such a study. Because of its great length, any attempt to examine it as a whole is necessarily arduous. Yet its unfinished state leaves the reader with a sense of unfulfilment which sets him to looking for clues to the author's intention and the direction of the poem's development. Once he begins to look, he discovers glaring fissures in the surface of the narrative and striking variations in method and technique which suggest that there is a history of struggle, of shifting aims and plans, to be discovered by anyone who can the poet's hound-fine footing trace.

But previous studies have centered on the probable ending of the poem, and only a few passing conjectures have been ventured as to how Spenser began. No one has undertaken to analyze the whole work in an effort to determine the guiding principles, the basic materials, and the inner history of its composition.[1] Critics have discussed Spenser's theories of epic and romance as these are apparent in his poem or are mentioned in the famous letter to Sir Walter Ralegh, and they have debated the soundness of his practice in various respects; but they have not attempted to imagine or reconstruct the actual process of composition as a basis for explaining the structure of the existing part of the poem.[2] In fact, Dean Church's dictum that Spenser wrote the poem according to a theoretical and preconceived plan has been generally accepted, and the letter to Ralegh, written in 1590, is commonly interpreted as a description of that hypothetical plan.[3] But we know that the poem had been under way for at least ten years when that letter was written. Why, then, should we imagine that it represents a pre-

[1] Janet Spens, *Spenser's Faerie Queene* (London: Edward Arnold & Co., 1934), chap. i, makes the first attempt to present a theory of a different beginning for the poem from that described in the letter to Ralegh. The present study was well under way before her book appeared. Her contention that Spenser began the poem as an illustration of the seven deadly sins seems to me to be very insufficiently supported by evidence, and I believe that she has not taken into account either all the evidence about Spenser's beginning or all the possible interpretations of the evidence adduced. Her arguments for a change of plan are useful, but they do not point necessarily to the change which she suggests.

[2] The history of criticism of the structure of the *Faerie Queene* has been surveyed by H. E. Cory in *The Critics of Edmund Spenser* ("University of California Publications in Modern Philology," Vol. II [Berkeley, 1911]), pp. 81–182, and *Edmund Spenser: A Critical Study* ("University of California Publications in Modern Philology," Vol. V [Berkeley, 1917]), chap. vii. Most of the pertinent criticism has been brought together in the new, variorum edition of *The Works of Edmund Spenser*, ed. Edwin Greenlaw, C. G. Osgood, and F. M. Padelford, I (Baltimore: Johns Hopkins Press, 1932), 314–62. Hereafter this work will be cited as *Variorum*.

[3] R. W. Church, *Spenser* ("English Men of Letters Series" [London, 1886]), pp. 120–30. See also W. J. Courthope, "The Poetry of Spenser," *Cambridge History of English Literature* (New York: Macmillan Co., 1933), III, 259–64; R. E. N. Dodge, *The Complete Poetical Works of Edmund Spenser* (Boston: Houghton Mifflin Co., 1908), p. 132 (hereafter cited as the *Cambridge Spenser*), and "Spenser's Imitations from Ariosto," *PMLA*, XII (1897), 191–97; E. de Sélincourt, *The Poetical Works of Edmund Spenser* (London: Humphrey Milford; Oxford: University Press, 1921), pp. xliii–li (hereafter cited as the *Oxford Spenser*); John W. Draper, "The Narrative-Technique of the *Faerie Queene*," *PMLA*, XXXIX (1924), 310–24, reprinted in *Variorum*, I, 348–51; W. L. Renwick, *Edmund Spenser: An Essay on Renaissance Poetry* (London: Edward Arnold & Co., 1925), pp. 52–54.

liminary sketch of what the poet was planning in 1580? On the contrary, it is much more probably a piece of apologetics, an attempt to rationalize what was being published and to sketch a plan which, in 1590, seemed to the poet a possible one for the completion of a poem which he had long ago begun, perhaps with very different plans in mind.

I propose, therefore, to treat the poem as a growing and developing conformation of ideas and to examine the meager external evidence, and the abundant but hitherto uncorrelated internal evidence, in an attempt to discover how it might have grown, in the course of many years, to its present state.

In order to approach the poem with a thoroughly open mind, we must not only put aside the notion that the letter to Ralegh describes Spenser's original plan but we must also try to rid ourselves of the idea that the poet began with the line, "A Gentle Knight was pricking on the plaine," and wrote straight ahead without alteration or rearrangement. The assumption of seriatim composition is not a reasonable one for so long and so complex a series of independent and semi-independent narratives. This fact has been recognized by several critics,[4] and yet practically all the existing discussions of Spenser's technique, of his allegory, and of his structure rest on the tacit assumption of seriatim composition, probably for no better reason than that no analysis of the poem has been offered which either established a different order of composition or even indicated all the evidences of rearrangement which the poem presents.[5]

Yet the *Faerie Queene* is a thoroughly experimental piece of

[4] J. C. Smith, *Spenser's Faerie Queene* (Oxford: Clarendon Press, 1909), I, xii, seems to be the first to suggest that "there is no reason to suppose that Spenser composed the whole of the *F. Q.* in the order in which he gave it to the world. It is more likely that he worked up many incidents and episodes as they occurred to him, and afterwards placed them in the poem." He goes no further than to cite some of the "lost" works which seem to have found their way into the poem. The first attempt to examine the poem in any other light than that of seriatim composition is that of Janet Spens.

[5] The assumption is inherent in Dodge's discussion of "Spenser's Imitations from Ariosto," pp. 151–204; and in J. J. Jusserand's "Spenser's 'Twelve Private Morall Vertues as Aristotle Hath Devised,' " *Modern Philology*, III (1905–6), 373–83. Dodge argues that, since Book I illustrates Holiness, Spenser began with the illustration of the virtues, while Jusserand points out that, since Holiness is not an Aristotelian virtue, the "twelve private morall vertues" must have been an afterthought. Courthope makes the

writing which betrays many evidences of changes both in intention and in arrangement of matter. Moreover, Spenser had no single story to tell, such as the wanderings of Aeneas, or the Fall of Man, which would help him to determine the order of events. He was putting together short, unrelated narratives derived from many different sources. Even if he had hit upon a satisfactory general plan at the start, a certain amount of rearrangement of such material would have been inevitable. Chaucer's problem, in the organization of the *Canterbury Tales*, was a very simple one in comparison, and yet recent studies have shown that Chaucer found it desirable to rearrange his stories.

The most constant purpose observable in Spenser's poem is the illustration of virtue. But he not only had to select the virtues which he wished to illustrate, and to arrange them in what he considered a suitable order, but he had to create a narrative with episodes illustrative of each virtue, and, in addition, he had to find a place for his general frame plot of Arthur and the Faery Queen. In the course of his search for material he would naturally find that the same story could be used to illustrate more than one virtue, and a shifting-about of episodes and narratives within a book, and even from one book to another, would be perfectly possible.

Our poet had other ends in view besides the illustration of virtue. He was celebrating Queen Elizabeth and trying to create the first English epic. He was wavering between Vergil and Ariosto as models of epic technique. He regarded Chaucer as his master of language. He was in search of a patron and in doubt as to whom to choose. The structure of the extant fragment clearly shows a shifting of emphases and intentions which would, in all probability, involve a shifting of plans and alteration of structure in the course of composition.

---

assumption of seriatim composition in his chapter in the *Cambridge History* already cited (see pp. 259–64); and A. B. Gough, in the Introduction to his edition of Book V (Oxford: Clarendon Press, 1918), pp. x ff., does the same. See also E. de Sélincourt, *Oxford Lectures on Poetry* (Oxford: Clarendon Press, 1934), p. 125. The further multiplication of instances is unnecessary. All discussions of Spenser's structure and plan, except that of Miss Spens, make the initial assumption of seriatim composition.

The lack of unity of plot, the confusion and inconsistency of parts of the narrative, and the magnitude of the undertaking in its final form, all suggest that the present poem developed along experimental lines, that it was written piecemeal and not seriatim in its present order, and that it was not begun and carried out according to a preconceived plan from which the poet drifted gradually, as his critics have assumed,[6] but that the plans grew as the poem grew. It is at least necessary to examine the possibility that the omnibus scheme outlined in the letter to Ralegh in 1590 represents an attempt to combine several beginnings, or several lines of development, into a plan which would conform to the epic theory of the day; that in 1590 it was not the original but the latest design; and that Spenser's beginning, if it is still preserved, must be looked for, not in the opening of Book I, but in some single element in the final, complex plot.

If we put aside the letter to Ralegh, as representing Spenser's plans in 1590 but not necessarily in 1580, we have left two very important pieces of evidence about the beginning of the poem. These are the *Shepheardes Calender*, especially the "October" eclogue, and the Spenser-Harvey letters. Since these were published in 1579 and 1580, what they tell us about the poet's epic ambitions and plans is of primary importance.

The "October" eclogue tells us, first of all, that Spenser had some ambition to be the English Vergil, for whom the writing of eclogues was a preparatory exercise for the loftier flight to come. It tells us also that the poet shared in the common Renaissance notion that the function of poetry is to teach morality (ll. 21–24). But, what is even more important, it indicates clearly the considerations which governed Spenser's choice of a subject for the heroic poem he was just beginning.

He says that the epic poet must "sing of bloody Mars, of wars, of giusts," that he must deal with the great, with "those that weld the awful crowne." But he is not content to confine himself to dead heroes. His primary aim is to make "antique praises vnto present persons fit." He sees his problem less in

[6] See *Variorum*, I, 314–62, and references in n. 3 above.

terms of the English equivalent for Aeneas than in terms of English equivalents for Augustus and Maecenas. The point is so important that we must see exactly what he says. Cuddie is lamenting that poetry does not pay, and Piers admonishes him (ll. 37–48):

> Abandon then the base and viler clowne,
> Lyft vp thy selfe out of the lowly dust:
> And sing of bloody Mars, of wars, of giusts,
> Turne thee to those, that weld the awful crowne.
> To doubted Knights, whose woundlesse armour rusts,
> And helmes vnbruzed wexen dayly browne.
>
> There may thy Muse display her fluttryng wing,
> And stretch her selfe at large from East to West:
> Whither thou list in fayre *Elisa* rest,
> Or if thee please in bigger notes to sing,
> Aduaunce the worthy whome shee loueth best,
> That first the white beare to the stake did bring.

To this speech Cuddie replies (ll. 55–64):

> Indeede the Romish *Tityrus*, I heare,
> Through his *Mecœnas* left his Oaten reede,
> Whereon he earst had taught his flocks to feede,
> And laboured lands to yield the timely eare,
> And eft did sing of warres and deadly drede,
> So as the Heauens did quake his verse to here.
>
> But ah *Mecœnas* is yclad in claye,
> And great *Augustus* long ygoe is dead:
> And all the worthies liggen wrapt in leade,
> That matter made for Poets on to play.

Here we have, expressly stated, Spenser's initial problem. He wished to play Vergil to an Augustus, and he was in doubt whether to choose for his Augustus the Earl of Leicester or the Queen. "E. K." seems to be very anxious that readers of the *Calender* understand this passage. He glosses "display" as follows:

> A poeticall metaphore: whereof the meaning is, that if the Poet list showe his skill in matter of more dignitie, then is the homely Æglogue, good occasion is him offered of higher veyne and more Heroicall argument, in the person of our most gratious soueraign, whom (as before) he calleth Elisa. Or if mater of knighthoode and cheualrie please him better, that there be many Noble and valiaunt men, that are both worthy of his payne in theyr deserued prayses, and also fauourers of hys skil and faculty.

To make clear just who are the "fauourers of hys skil," he glosses "The worthy" also:

> He meaneth (as I guesse) the most honorable and renowmed the Erle of Leycester, whom by his cognisance (although the same be also proper to other [i.e., to the Earl of Warwick]) rather then by his name he bewrayeth. . . . .

Finally, we learn that "the Romish Tityrus" is

> wel knowen to be Virgile, who by Mecænas means was brought into the fauour of the Emperor Augustus, and by him moued to write in loftier kinde, then he erst had doen.

Spenser's dilemma was a double one. He needed a patron and a subject. He could hardly hope to be the English Vergil if he chose for his Augustus a lesser figure than the reigning monarch; yet his sovereign was a woman, and the proper matter of epic was war, or at least "mater of knighthoode and cheualrie." The sex of his ruler created the primary difficulty which profoundly affected the whole course of his poem, as we shall see.

Spenser had written a graceful compliment to the Queen in his "Aprill" eclogue, where he employs the subject matter and tone of such courtly entertainments as those presented to Elizabeth at Kenilworth and Woodstock in 1575 and during her progress through Norfolk and Suffolk in 1578. Descriptions of these entertainments were circulating in print and so were known even to those who had not seen the rich pageantry.[7] But the problem of creating an epic out of graceful compliments to the beauty and chastity of the Queen was one which would have given pause to Vergil himself.

At the outset Spenser apparently did not see how he could attribute to Elizabeth the more heroic virtues. His choice, as he saw it, lay between praises of the "fayre Elisa" and an attempt to make military heroes of her courtiers, especially the Earl of Leicester. The very next notice that we have of his epic under-

[7] The influence of the pageants on Spenser has been discussed by C. R. Baskervill, "The Genesis of Spenser's Queen of Faerie," *Modern Philology*, XVIII (1920–21), 49–54. Gabriel Harvey seems to have been one of the followers of the progress of 1578. He attended at Audley End, near his home, and also at Mr. Capell's house in Hertfordshire (see his *Gratulationes Valdinenses* and the gloss to Spenser's "September"). For accounts of the entertainments see John Nichols, *The Progresses and Public Processions of Queen Elizabeth* (rev. ed.; London, 1823), Vols. I and II.

taking indicates that he had made up his mind in favor of the Queen as his Augustus. Early in 1580, so we learn from the letters to Gabriel Harvey, a poem called the *Faerie Queene* was already in existence in some state.

The association of the queen of fairies with Elizabeth makes its first appearance in the entertainment at Woodstock in 1575.[8] It seems to have developed out of the Renaissance notion that the English fairies were the equivalents of Diana and her band of nymphs. Such important translators as Phaer and Golding treated "fairies" as the nearest English equivalent to the classical wood deities, the "nymphs" of Vergil and Ovid.[9] Diana, as chief of the nymphs, was identified with the fairy queen,[10] and in the process of translation the fairy queen acquired Diana's attributes, including chastity, a virtue which she certainly did not exercise in medieval story. It seems to have been this identification of the fairy queen with Diana and chastity which opened the way for compliments to Queen Elizabeth as the fairy queen.

Miss I. E. Rathborne, in her study of *The Meaning of Spenser's Fairyland*,[11] draws upon medieval fairy lore and myths of the otherworld to illustrate the background of Spenser's fairyland. But the medieval queen of fairies was

[8] J. W. Cunliffe reprinted "The Queenes Majesties Entertainment at Woodstocke," *PMLA*, XXVI (1911), 92–141, from the edition of 1585. Baskervill (p. 53) thought that this entertainment launched the vogue for fairy lore in the royal entertainments. And Greenlaw discussed the Kenilworth entertainment in "Spenser's Fairy Mythology," *Studies in Philology*, XV (1918), 105–7.

[9] The pertinent passages are cited in M. W. Latham, *The Elizabethan Fairies* ("Columbia University Studies in English and Comparative Literature," No. 98 [New York, 1930]), pp. 48–52.

[10] Reginald Scot, in his *Discoverie of Witchcraft* (1584), calls the queen of fairies "the lady Sibylla, Minerva, or Diana," and Golding translates Diana as the fairy queen (see Latham, pp. 116 and 181). Lucy Allen Paton, in her *Studies in the Fairy Mythology of Arthurian Romance* ("Radcliffe College Monographs," No. XIII [Cambridge, Mass., 1903]), pp. 275 ff., shows that the classical Diana myths had a definite influence on medieval stories and were associated with the fairies; see also H. G. Lotspeich, *Classical Mythology in the Poetry of Edmund Spenser* ("Princeton Studies in English," No. IX [Princeton, N.J., 1932]), p. 92.

[11] "Columbia University Studies in English and Comparative Literature," No. 131 (New York, 1937).

identified with Proserpina, queen of the realms of the dead. Such an association would have been entirely unsuitable as a compliment to Queen Elizabeth. In fact, the author of the entertainment at Woodstock (1575), in which the fairy queen made her first appearance before Elizabeth, thought it necessary to make her say that she had transformed her face "then black" (as Proserpina) "now white" (as Luna or Diana) out of compliment to the Queen.[12] Spenser's Faery Queen is the English Queen and all the ideals she represented to him. She is chastity and immortal fame, queen not of the dead but of the ever living, bright Gloriana, or Belphoebe, not dark Proserpina. It remains to be shown that Spenser's acquaintance with medieval folk and fairy lore went beyond the most obvious current English sources.

The popularity of the fairy queen and Diana, of the fairies and the nymphs, in the royal entertainments from 1575 onward, indicates that a popular vein of courtly compliment had been opened up. Almost always, as in Churchyard's pageant of 1578,[13] a compliment to the Queen's chastity is involved. It is with Diana and chastity that the Queen is associated in Spenser's "Aprill" eclogue and in the Belphoebe passages of the *Faerie Queene*.[14]

The celebration of Elizabeth as the Diana-like fairy queen had contemporary literary precedent and suitable moral implications, but Spenser needed also a basic narrative on which to found his plot. This, according to contemporary critical theory,[15] should be "an historicall fiction," as Spenser says in his letter to Ralegh. In the English tradition the fairy queen was associated with King Arthur not only in Malory and the romances but also in Lydgate and Chaucer. Lydgate says of

[12] Baskervill, p. 52; Cunliffe, p. 98.

[13] Thomas Churchyard, *A Discourse of the Queenes Majesties Entertainment in Suffolk and Norfolk* (1578), reprinted in Nichols, *Progresses*, II, 179–213. The entertainment is discussed by Latham (p. 51) and by Baskervill.

[14] This was the usual association of ideas. See E. C. Wilson, *England's Eliza* ("Harvard Studies in English," Vol. XX [Cambridge, Mass., 1939]), chaps. iv and v.

[15] Draper, p. 319.

Arthur in his *Falls of Princes*, "He is a king y-crowned in Fairye,"[16] and Chaucer begins the *Wife of Bath's Tale:*

> In th' olde dayes of the Kyng Arthour,
> Of which that Britons speken greet honour,
> Al was this land fulfild of fayerye.
> The elf-queene, with hir joly compaignye,
> Daunced ful ofte in many a grene mede.[17]

It would have been quite natural, therefore, for Spenser to have turned to the Arthurian legend for his basic narrative. But his sovereign, his Augustus, was a woman, and the title of the 1580 beginning indicates that he had made his decision to celebrate her under the figure of the Faery Queen. It seems altogether probable that his first plot idea centered upon his titular heroine.

As the poem exists today, the Faery Queen is the center of two plot ideas. She is the object of Arthur's quest, and she is the mistress of a court whose chief ornament is the Order of Maidenhead. Since this order is clearly patterned on the Arthurian Round Table, it would seem that, to honor his female sovereign, Spenser had substituted the Faery Queen for Arthur. There would be no place for the legendary king in such a scheme, but the poet introduced Arthur "before he was king" in a set of nonlegendary adventures. This procedure had precedent in the medieval romances as well as in the treatment of Roland (Orlando) by both Boiardo and Ariosto. Nevertheless, it was in effect a rejection of the most suitable "historicall fiction" available to an English poet—a rejection which will be discussed more fully in a later chapter. Here we are concerned with the two plot ideas involving the Faery Queen.

Assuming that his title indicates that Spenser began with the intention of writing a poem about the Faery Queen, we must suppose that he began either with the court of Gloriana or with the love affair of Arthur. It has been asserted by several critics that the love affair was the kernel or starting-point of the whole

[16] Quoted in *Variorum*, I, 352. Greenlaw thinks that these lines give the clue to Spenser's association of Arthur with the fairy queen.

[17] *The Complete Works of Geoffrey Chaucer*, ed. F. N. Robinson (Boston: Houghton Mifflin Co., 1933), p. 101.

plot; so let us begin with this hypothesis and see where Spenser got the story and how he used it.

In the letter to Ralegh, Spenser says that he conceives Arthur "to haue seene in a dream or vision the Faery Queen, with whose excellent beauty rauished, he awaking resolued to seeke her out, and so . . . . he went to seeke her forth in Faerye land." The full poetic version of this story is to be found in Book I, Canto ix, stanzas 12–15, where Arthur tells of his experience. Arthur's story is little more than a paraphrase of Chaucer's burlesque *Tale of Sir Thopas*. Spenser's borrowing of this humorous tale for the basic frame of his ambitious poem is so surprising that several critics have expressed doubt of it and have cast about for some other source of Spenser's story. Miss Lucy Allen Paton, the late Professor Edwin Greenlaw, and Professor F. M. Padelford have reviewed the numerous medieval stories of fairy mistresses and have suggested that Spenser was merely following a well-known genre.[18] But they have failed to find a story which presents a close parallel to Spenser's. The only tale which has been produced involving a dream of a fairy mistress is *Arthur of Little Britain*, and Greenlaw argued that this was Spenser's source.[19] But the mistress of Arthur of Little Britain is not the queen of the fairies (who is regularly called Proserpyne) but only her protégée and double, named Florence. Moreover, Arthur's dream is not a direct and simple one, as in Chaucer and Spenser, but consists of an elabo-

[18] See *Variorum*, I, 267–68. Greenlaw ("Spenser's Fairy Mythology," p. 115) points out that Spenser's story is unlike the usual fairy mistress story because it ends, where the others begin, with the success of the lover. The stories which have been named as possible sources for Spenser are the *Sir Orfeo*, a medieval retelling of the *Orpheus and Euridice*, in which Pluto has become king of the fairies; and *Sir Launfal* and *Tomas of Ersseldoune*, neither of which involves a dream of a fairy. In both the fairy comes to a mortal lover and becomes his mistress immediately. See J. E. Wells, *Manual of the Writings in Middle English 1050–1400* (New Haven: Connecticut Academy of Arts and Sciences, 1926 ff.), pp. 128–29, 131–32, 224.

[19] "Britomart at the House of Busirane," *Studies in Philology*, XXVI (1929), 117–30, reprinted in *Variorum*, III, 359–66. Sarah Michie, "*The Faerie Queene* and *Arthur of Little Britain*," *Studies in Philology*, XXXVI (1939), 105–23, lists further parallels between the two works, but most of her citations are of elements common to the whole body of romance material, and, in any case, evidence that Spenser knew *Arthur of Little Britain* is not proof that he borrowed Arthur's dream from that source, when a better parallel exists in Chaucer.

rate allegory, like Britomart's dream at Isis Church, which the dreamer does not understand until it has been explained to him. Obviously we cannot accept this romance as Spenser's original when so complete a parallel as that provided by the *Sir Thopas* lay so close to his hand.

Spenser's admiration for Chaucer is well known. He acknowledged his discipleship in the "June" eclogue. He certainly knew the *Sir Thopas*, the meter of which he used in the "March" eclogue. Probably he could recite it from memory, as could many of his contemporaries.[20] Michael Drayton combined an imitation of it with allusive echoes of the *Shepheardes Calender* in the eighth eclogue of his *Shepheards Garland* (1593). Evidently he intended a good-natured satire on Spenser, for anyone who is thoroughly familiar with *Sir Thopas* can hardly fail to recognize Spenser's undisguised borrowing, and Drayton certainly intended to allude to Spenser in his eclogue.

Spenser's close and continuous debt to Chaucer can easily be established by a paralleling of the two texts. Both poets describe the knights as setting out on a hunting expedition. Arthur says:

> For on a day prickt forth with iollitie
> Of looser life, and heat of hardiment,
> Raunging the forest wide on courser free,
> The fields, the floods, the heauens with one consent
> Did seeme to laugh on me, and fauour mine intent [I, ix, 12].

Chaucer's knight also set out on a pleasant ride:

> And so bifel upon a day,
> For sothe, as I yow telle may,
> Sire Thopas wolde out ride . . . . [ll. 748–50].
>
> He priketh thurgh a fair forest,
> Therinne is many a wilde best,
> Ye, bothe bukke and hare . . . . [ll. 754–56].

[20] Warton cites *The Arte of English Poesie* for the statement that *Sir Thopas* was sung to the harp in Spenser's time (*Observations on the Fairy Queen of Spenser* [2d ed.; London, 1762], I, 52). Echoes of *Sir Thopas* are noted by W. L. Renwick in his edition of the *View of the Present State of Ireland* (London: Eric Partridge, Ltd., 1934), in *F. Q.*, II, iii, 27.3, and VI, ii, 6.1, as well as in the *View*, p. 91 (see his notes, p. 274). See also *Variorum* notes on III, vii, 48.2 and 58.4.

Ther spryngen herbes grete and smale . . . . [l. 760].
The briddes synge, it is no nay,
The sparhauk and the papejay,
That joye it was to heere . . . . [ll. 766–68].

Sire Thopas fil in love-longynge,
Al whan he herde the thrustel synge,
And pryked as he were wood . . . . [ll. 772–74].

Both knights grow weary of their sport and lie down to rest:

For-wearied with my sports, I did alight
From loftie steed, and downe to sleepe me layd;
The verdant gras my couch did goodly dight,
And pillow was my helmet faire displayd:
Whiles euery sence the humour sweet embayd,
And slombring soft my hart did steale away,
Me seemed, by my side a royall Mayd
Her daintie limbes full softly down did lay:
So faire a creature yet saw neuer sunny day [st. 13].

Sire Thopas eek so wery was
From prikyng on the softe gras,
So fiers was his corage,
That doun he leyde him in that plas
To make his steede som solas,
And yaf hym good forage.

"O seinte Marie, *benedicite!*
What eyleth this love at me
To bynde me so soore?
Me dremed al this nyght, pardee,
An elf-queene shal my lemman be
And slepe under my goore [ll. 778–89].

Arthur's dream is just the same except that the description is fuller:

Most goodly glee and louely blandishment
She to me made, and bad me loue her deare,
For dearely sure her loue was to me bent,
As when iust time expired should appeare.
But whether dreames delude, or true it were,
Was neuer hart so rauisht with delight,
Ne liuing man like words did euer heare,
As she to me deliuered all that night;
And at her parting said, She Queene of Faeries hight [st. 14].

Both knights immediately set out to seek their lovely visitor. Sir Thopas determines:

"An elf-queene wol I love, ywis,
For in this world no womman is
Worthy to be my make
In towne;
Alle othere wommen I forsake,
And to an elf-queene I me take
By dale and eek by downe!" [ll. 790–96].

Arthur has the same reaction:

When I awoke, and found her place deuoyd,
And nought but pressed gras, where she had lyen,
I sorrowed all so much, as earst I ioyd,
And washed all her place with watry eyen.
From that day forth I lou'd that face diuine;
From that day forth I cast in carefull mind,
To seeke her out with labour, and long tyne,
And neuer vow to rest, till her I find,
Nine monethes I seeke in vaine yet ni'll that vow vnbind [st. 15].

So he is on his way "to seeke her forth in Faerye land." Sir Thopas also sets out immediately for the same destination:

Into his sadel he clamb anon,
And priketh over stile and stoon
An elf-queene for t'espye,
Till he so longe hath riden and goon
That he foond, in a pryve woon,
The contree of Fairye
So wilde;
For in that contree was ther noon
That to him durste ride or goon,
Neither wyf ne childe;

Til that ther cam a greet geaunt,
His name was sire Olifaunt,
A perilous man of dede.
He seyde, "Child, by Termagaunt!
But if thou prike out of myn haunt,
Anon I sle thy steede
With mace.
Heere is the queene of Fayerye,
With harpe and pipe and symphonye,
Dwellynge in this place" [ll. 797–816].[21]

[21] *Chaucer*, ed. Robinson, pp. 198–99.

The parallel is unmistakable. And yet the difference in tone between Chaucer's burlesque and Spenser's heroic poem cannot be lightly passed over. It has been suggested that perhaps Spenser took Chaucer quite seriously.[22] But that suggestion is untenable in view of the evidence that the comic character of Sir Thopas was commonly recognized. Both Sir Thomas Wyatt and John Lyly, as well as Drayton, make familiar allusion to it.[23] Yet it does not seem probable, or even possible, that Spenser selected a well-known comic figure as the equivalent for Aeneas in a poem which was expected to make of its author the English Vergil. But there is the alternative possibility that when Spenser began a poem about the Faery Queen he had laid aside his Vergilian ambition and had taken Ariosto for his guide. The playful tone of Ariosto, with his gallantry and personal flattery, may well have seemed more suitable for a feminine Augustus than the solemnity of Vergil. And Ariosto's continuation of Boiardo may have suggested to Spenser that he continue Chaucer's unfinished *Tale*.

It will be remembered that we first hear of the *Faerie Queene* in the letters which Spenser and Gabriel Harvey exchanged in 1579–80. Spenser wrote:

> I wil in hande forthwith with my *Faery Queene*, whyche I praye you hartily send me with al expedition: and your frendly Letters, and long expected Iudgement wythal, whyche let not be shorte, but in all pointes suche, as you ordinarilye vse, and I extraordinarily desire.[24]

To this appeal Harvey replied:

> In good faith I had once againe nigh forgotten your *Faerie Queene:* howbeit by good chaunce, I haue nowe sent hir home at the laste, neither in better nor worse case, than I founde hir. And must you of necessitie haue my Iudgement of hir in deede? To be plaine, I am voyde of al iudgement, if your *Nine Comœdies*, whervnto in imitation of *Herodotus*, you giue the names of the

[22] Lilian Winstanley in the Introduction to her edition of Book I (Cambridge: University Press, 1915; reprinted, 1928), pp. lvii–lix.

[23] Wyatt contrasts the *Knight's Tale* with *Sir Thopas* in his satire "Of the Courtiers Life Written to Iohn Poins," in *Tottel's Miscellany*, ed. H. E. Rollins (Cambridge: Harvard University Press, 1928), I, 86, ll. 30–31. Lyly makes Sir Tophas (as he spells it) the leading comic character in *Endimion*, retaining the extravagant dress, the absurd hunting, and the ridiculous love affair of Chaucer's knight.

[24] *Oxford Spenser*, p. 612.

Nine Muses, (and in one mans fansie not vnworthily) come not neerer *Ariostoes Comœdies*, eyther for the finenesse of plausible Elocution, or the rarenesse of Poetical Inuention, than that *Eluish Queene* both [i.e., doth] to his *Orlando Furioso*, which notwithstanding, you wil needes seeme to emulate, and hope to ouergo, as you flatly professed your self in one of your last Letters. . . . . But I wil not stand greatly with you in your owne matters. If so be the *Faerye Queene* be fairer in your eie than the *Nine Muses*, and *Hobgoblin* runne away with the Garland from *Apollo:* Mark what I saye, and yet I will not say that I thought, but there an End for this once, and fare you well, till God or some good Aungell putte you in a better minde.[25]

Harvey's strictures are somewhat vague. We cannot be entirely sure that the contrast between Hobgoblin and Apollo is sincere criticism and not merely a desire to play on the tities of Spenser's poems, but the reference to "that *Eluish Queene*" sounds scornful and suggests that Harvey shared with "E. K." a lofty and somewhat puritanical contempt for fairy stories. It was a very common attitude before Shakespeare transformed the fairies into the playthings of the poets.[26] The ignorant and the superstitious believed in them, and therefore they probably had in Harvey's mind, as in "E. K.'s," associations not only with ignorance but with Roman Catholicism also. They were invented, says "E. K.," "by a sort of bald Friers and knauish shauelings" who "soughte to nousell the comen people in ignorounce."

Harvey's objection was to the contents of Spenser's poem and not to the model. He likes the *Nine Comedies* better than the *Faerie Queene* because they are nearer to Ariosto's comedies than the *Faerie Queene* is to the *Orlando Furioso* in "finenesse of plausible Elocution" and "rarenesse of Poetical Inuention." Some critics, taking it for granted that Harvey is talking about the legend of Redcrosse, and finding very little imitation of Ariosto there, have suggested that Harvey did not mean that Spenser was imitating Ariosto but only that he hoped to sur-

[25] *Ibid.*, p. 628.

[26] See the gloss for "June"; and Thomas Churchyard's comments about fairy lore in "A Handeful of Gladsome Verses, Giuen to the Queenes Maiesty at Woodstocke this Prograce, 1592," reprinted in *Fugitive Tracts Written in Verse, First Series* (1875), collected for Henry Huth. Baskervill (pp. 49 ff.) has some comments on this point, and Latham (*passim*) indicates the frequency with which fairies were associated with devils, witches, and evil spirits.

pass him by writing a better heroic poem. But the late Professor Dodge, in his study of "Spenser's Imitations from Ariosto," takes it for granted that the emulation took the form of imitation, and W. J. Courthope and J. W. Mackail express the opinion that Spenser began with an imitation of Ariosto.[27]

The usual Elizabethan sense of the word "emulate" was "to strive to equal or rival; to copy or imitate with the object of equalling or excelling."[28] Moreover, Harvey specifically compares the two works on the basis of "elocution" and "poetical invention." We know that Renaissance critical theory encouraged the closest kind of imitation, especially of subject matter.[29] Therefore, before we try to make something else out of Harvey's plain statement that Spenser would "seeme to emulate, and hope to ouergo" the *Orlando*, we ought to consider whether the poem about which Harvey was talking may not have been a thoroughly recognizable imitation of Ariosto.

In this connection G. L. Craik's remarks about the 1580 version of the poem are interesting because they are above suspicion of ex parte argument. He says:

> The Fairy Queen, it may be remembered, had not greatly taken Gabriel Harvey's fancy when he first read a part of it ten years before this [i.e., before 1589]. We cannot be sure that what he then saw was any portion of the poem as afterwards published; it is perhaps rather probable, from the length of time that had elapsed, and from the difference of manner between the Fairy Queen, as we actually have it, and such of Spenser's poetry as was certainly written before 1580, that the first attempt, upon which Harvey pronounced so discouraging a judgment, may have been something quite unlike any part of the poem in the shape it ultimately took.[30]

[27] Courthope thinks that imitation of Ariosto was the inspiring motive of the whole work (*A History of English Poetry* [London, 1897], II, 259), and Mackail interprets Harvey's censure as indicating "some foolish ambition in Spenser to outdo Ariosto on his own lines" (*The Springs of Helicon* [New York: Longmans, Green & Co., 1909], p. 127).

[28] See the *Oxford English Dictionary* for contemporary examples.

[29] See H. O. White, *Plagiarism and Imitation during the English Renaissance* ("Harvard Studies in English," Vol. XII [Cambridge, Mass., 1935]), esp. chap. i. W. S. Webb, "Vergil and Spenser's Epic Theory," *ELH*, IV (1937), 62–84, ably presents an interpretation of Spenser's theory as inferred from his practice, but the inference involves belief that the poet worked from theory to practice, whereas theory is often the justification of practice.

[30] *Spenser and His Poetry* (rev. ed.; 3 vols.; London, 1871), I, 104–5.

Mr. J. C. Smith, in the Introduction to his edition of the poem (I, xi, note), says that he finds it "hard to believe that Harvey, who though a pedant was no fool, can have seen anything like the whole of Book I without recognizing its superlative merits." There is another piece of evidence also that the early version which Harvey did not like was not the legend of Redcrosse. In the same paragraph in which he expresses his censure of the *Faerie Queene* he takes occasion to praise the Revelation of John as superlative in that kind. Now Book I draws extensively on the Revelation for major elements in its plot, and we can hardly suppose that Harvey would condemn a poem for its subject matter and at the same time praise the subject matter out of which it was constructed.

With the possibility that the first version of the *Faerie Queene* has entirely disappeared, we cannot deal. We must proceed on the hypothesis that it is still a part of the poem. Since it was called the *Faerie Queene*, it is justifiable to assume that it was about that character, and therefore it could not have consisted of the legend of Redcrosse because the Faery Queen plays only a very minor and offstage part in that book. It is hardly credible that Spenser planned from the first to write an epic of the Faery Queen in which his titular heroine never appeared at all.

We cannot suppose that he borrowed Chaucer's burlesque *Sir Thopas* as the basis of a grand heroic poem symbolizing the search of Virtue for Glory. He came to that in the end, but we need not suppose that he began there. Three pieces of evidence indicate that the 1580 beginning was not pitched in so high a key. There is the hard fact of the *Sir Thopas* borrowing; there is Harvey's comparison of Spenser's beginning with his *Nine Comedies* and the *Orlando Furioso;* and, finally, there is evidence that Spenser planned a fairly elaborate continuation of the *Sir Thopas*.

This last consists of a fragment of a continuation of *Sir Thopas* which has escaped notice because it is imbedded in Book III (vii, 47–61). It tells the following story:

Satyrane rescues a squire from a giantess, and the squire explains that she is Argante, twin sister of Ollyphant, the two being embodiments of male and female lust. They are pursued by male and female representatives of chastity, called Sir Thopas and Palladine.

The squire explains that his captivity in the hands of Argante was the result of a vow of obedience to his mistress. She had ordered him to "do seruice vnto gentle Dames"

> And at the twelue monethes end .... bring their names
> And pledges; as the spoiles of my victorious games.

He succeeded so well that his mistress was angry and sent him out again to find as many chaste women as he had found unchaste ones; but he has found only three in three years.

Sir John Harington was quick to recognize that the Squire's tale "is to the like effect" as Ariosto's tale of woman's unchastity as told by the Host.[31] But the much more immediate relationship to Chaucer's *Sir Thopas* has been ignored, except for Warton's remark that the giant Ollyphant is probably the same as the giant Sir Olifaunt whom Sir Thopas encounters in fairyland. He is certainly Chaucer's giant, as is proved by the fact that in the 1590 edition of Spenser's poem we are told that Ollyphant destroyed many knights "Till him Chylde *Thopas* to confusion brought" (st. 48.4). In the 1596 edition the line was changed to read, "And many hath to foule confusion brought."

But when Spenser created this humorous episode, he did more than borrow a piece of satire from Ariosto and a couple of names from Chaucer. The imitation of Ariosto is framed in a situation which constitutes an elaboration and continuation of *Sir Thopas*. The interpretation of Sir Thopas as the champion of chastity is suggested by Chaucer himself, who remarks that "he was chaast and no lechour" (l. 745). Gabriel Harvey designated the tale as "morall" in his copy of Chaucer,[32] and it was probably the combination of the fairy queen and the chastity motif which suggested to Spenser the possibility of turning Chaucer's lighthearted poem into a tribute to Queen Elizabeth.

Ollyphant, the giant who barred Sir Thopas' way into fairyland, becomes in Spenser's hands the embodiment of lust, and he is given a twin sister, Argante, who has for her chief enemy,

[31] *Orlando Furioso in English Heroical Verse .... Now Secondly Imprinted the Yeere 1607*, p. 373.

[32] Harvey's designation may have been influenced by Spenser, since he was annotating the 1598 edition of the *Canterbury Tales* (see G. C. Moore Smith, *Gabriel Harvey's Marginalia* [Stratford-upon-Avon: Shakespeare Head Press, 1913], p. 228).

Palladine, a lady knight. But beyond this situation we have nothing more of the story. It is introduced as an episode in Satyrane's pursuit of Florimell, where it is very imperfectly fitted in, probably for the sake of its bearing on the theme of the book, which is chastity. It is clearly a fragment of another story entirely. Two of the figures, Argante and Palladine, are never mentioned again. All mention of Sir Thopas was removed by the changing of a line in the second edition. Ollyphant is mentioned only once again—at the opening of Canto xi, where he is the object of pursuit by Satyrane and Britomart and where the passage in Canto vii is definitely alluded to. We might suspect that the maiden knight Palladine, who was "so chaste a wight," may have been a previous incarnation of Spenser's chief heroine. The giantess Argante has a "secret Ile," very like Acrasia's, where she holds her victims in slavery to lust. There is a giant embodiment of lust, like Ollyphant, who captures Amoret in Book IV. But none of these possible connections is made by the poet. The two giant symbols of lust and their two chaste pursuers are abandoned at the very moment of their creation—unless they represent a fragment of a discarded plot, the other parts of which have been altered to fit other stories and situations.

While Spenser leaves a good many loose ends, especially in Book III, he does not, anywhere else in the poem, leave this kind of unassimilated and uncompleted opening of a new story introducing a new set of characters. Its relation to *Sir Thopas* and its fragmentary condition suggest that it is a part of an old attempt to continue *Sir Thopas*, which Spenser imported bodily into his story of Satyrane because it had a bearing on the subject of chastity.

In spite of the implications of moral allegory in the plot, Spenser's tone in this passage is light and whimsical, as if he aimed at a continuation of *Sir Thopas*, not as burlesque, but in imitation of the tone of Ariosto. He borrows not only the plot but some of the linguistic mannerisms of Chaucer's *Thopas*, particularly the phrase "many a Jane" (st. 58.4), and such archaic makeweight words as "ywis" and "perdy." Indeed, this passage is in sharp contrast to the rest of Book III in the matter of archaic diction and seems to be nearer to the language of the *Shepheardes Calender* than to that of any other part of the *Faerie Queene*.[33]

Besides the archaic language, there are certain evidences of struggle for rhymes, which suggest that these stanzas were written quite early in the history of the composition.[34] R. E. N. Dodge comes very near suggesting that this passage is an early piece, for he remarks: "Though in 1580 . . . . he may have enjoyed the looser episodes of the *Orlando Furioso* much like Harington, by 1589, when the final touches were put to the first three books of his poem, his taste must have been decidedly more sober."[35]

There is very little in Book I to suggest Spenser's enjoyment of "the looser episodes of the *Orlando Furioso*," but it is evident that Dodge was thinking of the tale of the Squire of Dames in Book III and of the tale of Hellenore which follows it, for he goes on to cite these two tales as evidence that Spenser "never quite lost sympathy with Ariosto's scandalous *verve*." It is evident from his remarks on the development of the poem that

[33] We can hardly have an adequate study of Spenser's diction until we have a historical dictionary of Elizabethan English. According to B. R. McElderry, Jr., "Archaism and Innovation in Spenser's Poetic Diction," *PMLA*, XLVII (1932), 144–70, there are only 320 archaisms in Spenser, and half of these occur in the *Calender*. Sixty-seven of the rest are nonce words. In the short passage (135 lines) under discussion five of these words occur: *behight*, *whilome*, *yfere*, *mistreth* (dial.), and *avise*. *Eftsoons* he thinks was not really archaic. But, in addition to these words, Spenser uses several archaic phrases: *at vauntage*, *me lever*, *hent in hand*, the rare expression *have a do with*, the always colloquial *to chose*, and the Chaucerism *many a Jane*.

[34] E.g., he rhymes *bespake*, *behight*, *make*, *on hight*, *right*, where the first two rhymes are too much alike and the second and fourth are practically identical. In the series *were*, *yfere*, *appere*, the second word is obviously dragged in for the rhyme. *Behauioure* is rhymed with *deuoure; seruicis* is forced into line with *this*, *ywis*, *amis*, and *ywis* is a makeweight rhyme borrowed from Chaucer. *Desartes* is rhymed with *hartes*, and *stayd* with *strayd*, *sayd*, *denayd*. *Thirst* is contorted to *thrust* to rhyme with *luſt*, etc. In the absence of a dictionary of Spenser's rhymes it is not possible to say whether this list of bad rhymes is very unusual or not, but six bad rhymes in a series of fifteen stanzas indicates at least that the poet was far from his best in these stanzas. An attempt to study *Rime as a Criterion of the Pronunciation of Spenser*, *Pope*, *Byron*, *and Swinburne*, by Arvid Gabrielson (Uppsala: Almqvist & Wiksells Boktryckeri-A.-B., 1909), is of some interest.

[35] "Spenser's Imitations from Ariosto," p. 167.

Dodge thought of the *Faerie Queene* as written in the same order in which it was published, and therefore he did not draw the natural conclusion from his two observations. His intuition of the poet's progress from admiration of Ariosto's scandalous verve in 1580 to a "decidedly more sober" tone in 1589 seems to agree with the natural progress of a young man's development, but he does not attempt to account for the fact that Spenser's closest imitations of Ariosto appear, not in Book I, but in Book III.

We know so little about Spenser the man that we tend to recreate him from Spenser the poet and even to interpret the poet according to the order of publication of his works rather than the order of composition.[36] But a genuine glimpse of an ambitious young man at the threshold of what all young men hope for, a brilliant career, can be caught from the five Spenser-Harvey letters[37] and from the memorandum which Harvey made in his copy of *Howleglas:*

> This Howletglasse, with Skoggin, Skelton, and L[a]zarillo, giuen me at London, of Mr. Spensar xx Decembris [15]78 on condition [that I] shoold bestowe ye reading of them oue[r] before ye first of January [imme]diatly ensuing: otherwise to forfeit unto him my Lucian jn fower uolumes.[38]

The young poet who gave his former tutor jestbooks and coveted a copy of Lucian,[39] who hoped to travel, to be presented to the Queen, to secure the patronage of the greatest in the land,

[36] This, I believe, is the fundamental mistake of Cory's *Critical Study*, which is based on the usual assumption of seriatim composition of the *Faerie Queene*, and which finds a falling-off in the later books and attempts to account for it. Greenlaw, in his review (*Modern Language Notes*, XXXV [1920], 165–77), challenges the falling-off and the theory devised to explain it, but he does not challenge the fundamental assumption of seriatim composition.

[37] Miss Mary Parmenter, in a paper on "Immerito's Letters by Gabriel Harvey," read before the Modern Language Association in 1936, has raised the question of the authenticity of these letters printed in 1580. She argues that they were written entirely by Harvey. I believe it is very probable that Harvey selected and edited them, but I think it is going much too far to conclude that Spenser had no hand in the composition of the two ascribed to him or that the letters do not represent his interests and activities at the time when they purport to have been written.

[38] *Gabriel Harvey's Marginalia*, p. 23.

[39] Spenser read Lucian. He cites the *Toxaris* in the *View* (see Renwick's edition, p. 76). A possible echo of *The Runaways* in the story of Hellenore will be discussed in connection with the structure of Book III.

the young poet who had just acquired a wife, an *altera Rosalindula*, is a more genuine flesh-and-blood figure than the disconsolate lover and stern moralist of the *Calender*. It is this young man of the letters and the jestbooks who, I suggest, was struggling with the problem of whether to undertake a Vergilian epic celebrating a courtier or to choose the Queen as his Augustus and Ariosto as his model.

If what Harvey saw in 1580 was an attempt to continue *Sir Thopas* in such a way as to celebrate the chastity of the Faery Queen, then the English poet was imitating Ariosto, since Ariosto continued the love story of Orlando which had been left unfinished by Boiardo, converting it into flattery of his patron. But Harvey did not much admire "that *Eluish Queene*," and the difficulties in the way of adjustment of tone and subject matter are obvious enough. It is not surprising that Spenser abandoned the attempt. What is surprising is that he openly incorporated two bits of this material in the later and more serious and ambitious poem. Perhaps, in the Ariosto-like Books III and IV there are other parts of the *Sir Thopas* continuation, but they have been altered to fit other characters; and, if they are to be detected, it must be by methods other than simple anaylsis of the narrative.

II
THE LETTER TO RALEGH

Helpe then, O holy Virgin chiefe of nine,
Thy weaker Nouice to performe thy will,
Lay forth out of thine euerlasting scryne
The antique rolles, which there lye hidden still,
Of Faerie knights and fairest *Tanaquill.*

—I, Proem, 2.1–5

HAVING learned what we could about Spenser's aims in 1579–80 and having ventured a conjecture as to the nature of his earliest effort to celebrate the Faery Queen, we are now ready to turn to the plan published ten years later in a letter to Ralegh appended to the first instalment of the poem. In this letter Spenser puts forward, not the Faery Queen, but Arthur, as the chief subject of his poem. His moral purpose is "to fashion a gentleman or noble person in vertuous and gentle discipline," and his subject is "the historye of king Arthure . . . . before he was king." His models are Homer in his Agamemnon and Ulysses, Vergil in Aeneas, Ariosto in Orlando, and Tasso in Rinaldo and Godfredo.

This is all very proper and in accordance with the best literary criticism of his day. But it is the gloss and not the text. Arthur is not the chief hero of the poem. In fact, it is upon Spenser's failure to build a single unified action around a hero-in-chief that the *Faerie Queene* has been most often and most severely censured. His earliest critics seized upon this fact, and Dryden attempted a defense based on the letter. He says:

> Every one is most valiant in his own legend: only we must do him that justice to observe, that magnanimity, which is the character of Prince Arthur, shines throughout the whole poem; and succours the rest, when they are in distress.[1]

[1] "A Discourse concerning the Original and Progress of Satire," in *Essays of John Dryden*, ed. W. P. Ker (Oxford: Clarendon Press, 1900), II, 28.

But, as John Hughes observes,

Prince *Arthur* is indeed the principal Person, and has therefore a share given him in every Legend; but his Part is not considerable enough in any one of them: He appears and vanishes again like a Spirit; and we lose sight of him too soon to consider him as the Hero of the Poem.[2]

Thomas Warton objected at more length that if Arthur is to be the hero of all the virtues, he should have been the hero of each of the major adventures:

If the magnanimity of Arthur did, in reality, thus shine in every part of the poem with a superior and steady lustre, our author would fairly stand acquitted. At present it bursts forth but seldom, in obscure and interrupted flashes.[3]

The failure of Arthur to develop as the hero carries with it, as a necessary corollary, a failure in unity of action. On this point the lines of criticism are laid down by Hughes, Upton, and Hurd. Hughes says that "the several Books appear rather like so many several Poems, than one entire Fable."[4] Warton agrees that "Spenser perhaps would have embarrassed himself and the reader less, had he made every book one entire detached poem of twelve cantos, without any reference to the rest."[5] John Upton would hear none of this. He found in the story of Arthur the necessary "simplicity and unity" of character and action. He went so far as to compare Spenser with Homer, resolutely maintaining that the *Faerie Queene* fulfils all the requirements of classical epic.[6] But his apology is notable for blind loyalty rather than for sound judgment.

Richard Hurd, following a line of defense suggested by Hughes, put forward the theory that Spenser was writing a "Gothic," not a classical, epic and that he ought to be judged according to the rules of the form he aimed at. On that basis Hurd defends the whole structure as unified by the annual feast described in the letter to Ralegh. He treats Arthur as an unfortunate concession to the classicists—a concession which,

[2] *The Works of Mr. Edmund Spenser* (London, 1715), I, lix–lx.

[3] *Observations on the Fairy Queen of Spenser* (2d ed.; London, 1762), I, 7.

[4] *Works*, I, lix. [5] *Observations*, I, 10.

[6] Preface to his edition of *Spenser's Faerie Queene* (London, 1758), I, xx–xxvii.

"whatever the author pretended, and his critic too easily believed, was but an after thought."[7]

But whether or not Arthur was a concession to the classicists, Spenser put him forward in the letter as his chief hero and announced the models which he thought he ought to follow. Yet he was certainly aware that the part of Arthur which he was describing did not fit the poem as he was publishing it. Some apologists have insisted that this is because the poem was never finished and that in the later books the poet would, by some kind of retroactive magic, have made Arthur his chief hero.

The prominence given to Arthur is not the only discrepancy between the letter and the poem. In fact, the most surprising thing about the letter is that it describes two distinct sets of plot ideas imperfectly joined together, neither of which faithfully represents the actual structure of the existing poem. In order to make this point clear, it will be necessary to analyze the letter and to compare it with the poem. Spenser begins as follows:

> Sir knowing how doubtfully all Allegories may be construed, and this booke of mine, which I haue entituled the Faery Queene, being a continued Allegory, or darke conceit, I haue thought good aswell for auoyding of gealous opinions and misconstructions, as also for your better light in reading thereof, (being so by you commanded,) to discouer vnto you the general intention and meaning, which in the whole course therof I haue fashioned, without expressing of any particular purposes or by-accidents therein occasioned.

With this preamble he plunges immediately into his account of his intentions in regard to Arthur:

> [1] The generall end therefore of all the booke is to fashion a gentleman or noble person in vertuous and gentle discipline: Which for that I conceiued shoulde be most plausible and pleasing, being coloured with an historicall fiction, the which the most part of men delight to read, rather for variety of matter, then for profite of the ensample: I chose the historye of king Arthure, as most fitte for the excellency of his person, being made famous by many mens former workes, and also furthest from the daunger of enuy, and suspition of present time. In which I haue followed all the antique Poets historicall, first Homere, who in the Persons of Agamemnon and Vlysses hath ensampled a good gouernour and a vertuous man, the one in his Ilias, the other in his Odysseis: then Virgil, whose like intention was to doe in the person of Aeneas: after him Ariosto comprised them both in his Orlando: and

[7] *Letters on Chivalry and Romance* (2d ed.; London, 1762), pp. 56–75.

lately Tasso disseuered them againe, and formed both parts in two persons, namely that part which they in Philosophy called Ethice, or vertues of a priuate man, coloured in his Rinaldo: The other named Politice in his Godfredo. [2] By ensample of which excellente Poets, I labour to pourtraict in Arthure, before he was king, the image of a braue knight, perfected in the twelue priuate morall vertues, as Aristotle hath deuised, the which is the purpose of these first twelue bookes: which if I finde to be well accepted, I may be perhaps encoraged, to frame the other part of pollliticke vertues in his person, after that hee came to be king. To some I know this Methode will seeme displeasaunt, which had rather haue good discipline deliuered plainly in way of precepts, or sermoned at large, as they vse, then thus clowdily enwrapped in Allegoricall deuises. But such, me seeme, should be satisfide with the vse of these dayes, seeing all things accounted by their showes, and nothing esteemed of, that is not delightfull and pleasing to commune sence. For this cause is Xenophon preferred before Plato, for that the one in the exquisite depth of his iudgement, formed a Commune welth such as it should be, but the other in the person of Cyrus and the Persians fashioned a gouernement such as might best be: So much more profitable and gratious is doctrine by ensample, then by rule. [3] So haue I laboured to doe in the person of Arthure: whome I conceiue after his long education by Timon, to whom he was by Merlin deliuered to be brought vp, so soone as he was borne of the Lady Igrayne, to haue seene in a dream or vision the Faery Queen, with whose excellent beauty rauished, he awaking resolued to seeke her out, and so being by Merlin armed, and by Timon throughly instructed, he went to seeke her forth in Faerye land.

So much for his intentions regarding Arthur. Next he turns to the Faery Queen and her court:

[4] In that Faery Queene I meane glory in my generall intention, but in my particular I conceiue the most excellent and glorious person of our soueraine the Queene, and her kingdome in Faery land. And yet in some places els, I doe otherwise shadow her. For considering she beareth two persons, the one of a most royall Queene or Empresse, the other of a most vertuous and beautifull Lady, this latter part in some places I doe express in Belphœbe, fashioning her name according to your owne excellent conceipt of Cynthia, (Phœbe and Cynthia being both names of Diana.)

Then he gives us an account of his double representation of the twelve virtues by Arthur and the twelve knights:

[5] So in the person of Prince Arthure I sette forth magnificence in particular, which vertue for that (according to Aristotle and the rest) it is the perfection of all the rest, and conteineth in it them all, therefore in the whole course I mention the deedes of Arthure applyable to that vertue, which I write of in that booke. [6] But of the xii. other vertues, I make xii. other knights the patrones, for the more variety of the history: Of which these three bookes contayn three. The first of the knight of the Redcrosse, in whome I expresse Holynes: The seconde of Sir Guyon, in whome I sette forth Temperaunce: The third of Britomartis a Lady knight, in whome I picture Chastity.

Next he turns to a defense of his method:

But because the beginning of the whole worke seemeth abrupte and as depending vpon other antecedents, it needs that ye know the occasion of these three knights seuerall aduentures. For the Methode of a Poet historical is not such, as of an Historiographer. For an Historiographer discourseth of affayres orderly as they were donne, accounting as well the times as the actions, but a Poet thrusteth into the middest, euen where it most concerneth him, and there recoursing to the thinges forepaste, and diuining of thinges to come, maketh a pleasing Analysis of all.

So, having defended his conception of the critical dictum of beginning *in medias res*, he gives us the last item in his complex plot:

[7] The beginning therefore of my history, if it were to be told by an Historiographer, should be the twelfth booke, which is the last, where I deuise that the Faery Queene kept her Annuall feaste xii. dayes, vppon which xii. seuerall dayes, the occasions of the xii. seuerall aduentures hapned, [8] which being vndertaken by xii. seuerall knights, are in these xii. books seuerally handled and discoursed. The first was this. . . . .

It is apparent from this letter that Spenser understood the criteria of the epic "kind" as they were explained by various critics of his time. He believed, as did his contemporaries, that moral allegory was an essential part of poetry. He intended to teach morality by example, through the history of Arthur, following the best ancient and modern writers. He seems to recognize the need for a hero-in-chief and a simple and unified action, but he actually proposes two such actions: Arthur's search for the Faery Queen and the annual banquet where the quests of the twelve exemplary knights are initiated.

In fact, the plan consists of eight more or less distinct plot elements which group themselves about two nuclei. I have indicated these elements, as they occur in the letter, by a series of numbers. Arthur is to be the perfect gentleman who exemplifies the twelve moral virtues and magnificence which is the sum of all the virtues (1, 2, and 5). There are also twelve knights who represent the twelve virtues and who set out on twelve quests from the annual banquet (6, 7, 8). These two centers of plot are held together very loosely by the fact that Arthur is on the quest of the Faery Queen, who represents both Glory and Queen Elizabeth (3, 4). Arthur's quest and Gloriana's court are really two rival foci of the plot,[8] and the rivalry is emphasized by the fact that each has attached to it the illustration of the twelve virtues. These rival plot centers set up a cross-current in the flow and direction of the narrative, since Arthur should move toward the Faery Queen, while actually he moves away from her repeatedly as he meets and accompanies each of the knights in turn who sets out from her court on a quest.

These rival foci of the plot not only represent rival and opposing currents in the stream of the narrative but they also represent two different adaptations of the Arthurian legend. Arthur has these adventures at a period in his life before the legendary story begins. But the Faery Queen and her court represent another adaptation of the Arthurian matter, and this time the Faery Queen takes the place of King Arthur and becomes the mistress of an Order of Maidenhead which is substituted for the Order of the Round Table.

It hardly seems probable that Spenser initiated both of these adaptations of the Arthurian legend at the same time. It is rather the kind of thing which results from a cumulative process. If he began with the intention of celebrating Elizabeth as his Augustus under the guise of the Faery Queen, then it is natural to suppose that the Faery Queen nucleus is older than the idea of making Arthur the central figure in the plot. If Spenser began with the *Sir Thopas* continuation, it is not necessary to suppose that he substituted Arthur for Thopas at the very start. The name "Sir Thopas" survived in the 1590 version of the fragment of Chaucer continuation in III, vii. No name at all is mentioned in the redaction of the *Sir Thopas* in Book I (ix, 12–15), where Arthur tells of his experience in a first-person narrative. A comparison of the style of this passage with that of the passage in III, vii, seems to indicate that the story Arthur tells has received a polishing. Sidney frequently converted a third-person narrative in the old *Arcadia* into a first-person narrative in the redaction, and Spenser's revisionary elaborations probably followed the same course.

A very similar case is that of Britomart's story in Book III,

[8] This fact was noted by Dean Kitchin (see *Variorum*, II, 280).

which remains a narrative told in the third person, although it has been put into a setting which calls for a first-person narrative. Sidney, in his *Defense of Poesie*, explains that the poet, in beginning *in medias res*, must "recount things done in former time or other place . . . . by some *Nuntius*," or narrator.[9] The rule is laid down by Minturno, the best known of the Italian critics. It is a rule which Spenser follows not only in the story of Arthur in Book I, and imperfectly in the story of Britomart in Book III, but also in such shorter narratives as that of Sir Trevisan (I, ix, 21–54), and of Amavia (II, i, 35–61). It is not, however, the most natural way to tell a story, and it did not come naturally to Spenser, if we can judge by the openings of the stories of Redcrosse and Guyon. It was probably a sophisticated second thought with Spenser as it was with Sidney.

The step is a long one from continuing *Sir Thopas* in imitation of Ariosto and in graceful compliment to the Queen's chastity to beginning an epic of Arthur. As we shall see when we come to analyze Book I, Arthur is there a composite of Sir Thopas, the Redeemer of the Apocalypse, and the legendary Arthur. Such an incongruous amalgamation must surely have resulted from a process of development and gradual evolution. It could hardly have been deliberately planned on a theoretical basis before the poem was begun. But the place of Arthur in Spenser's plans is a large problem which must be left for later chapters. Let us return to the letter.

In the first three books of the poem more attention is given to the Faery Queen and her knights than to Arthur and either his virtues or his pursuit. The letter not only misrepresents the general theme and emphasis of the poem but it also misrepresents the subject matter of two out of the first three books. It says of Book I:

> In the beginning of the feast, there presented him selfe a tall clownishe younge man, who falling before the Queen of Faries desired a boone (as the manner then was) which during that feast she might not refuse: which was that hee might haue the atchieuement of any aduenture, which during that feaste should happen, that being graunted, he rested him on the floore, unfitte

[9] See K. O. Myrick, *Sir Philip Sidney as a Literary Craftsman* ("Harvard Studies in English," Vol. XIV [Cambridge, Mass., 1935]), p. 135.

through his rusticity for a better place. Soone after entred a faire Ladye in mourning weedes, riding on a white Asse, with a dwarfe behind her leading a warlike steed, that bore the Armes of a knight, and his speare in the dwarfes hand. Shee falling before the Queene of Faeries, complayned that her father and mother an ancient King and Queene, had bene by an huge dragon many years shut vp in a brasen Castle, who thence suffred them not to yssew: and therefore besought the Faery Queene to assygne her some one of her knights to take on him that exployt. Presently that clownish person vpstarting, desired that aduenture: whereat the Queene much wondering, and the Lady much gainesaying, yet he earnestly importuned his desire. In the end the Lady told him that vnlesse that armour which she brought, would serue him (that is the armour of a Christian man specified by Saint Paul, v. Ephes.) that he could not succeed in that enterprise, which being forthwith put vpon him with dewe furnitures thereunto, he seemed the goodliest man in al that company, and was well liked of the Lady. And eftesoones taking on him knighthood, and mounting on that straunge Courser, he went forth with her on that aduenture: where beginneth the first book, vz.

A gentle knight was pricking on the playne. &c.

This account is specific and detailed, and it fits so perfectly into the narrative of the first book that we might almost believe that Spenser had already written the first scene for the twelfth book before he began Book I. However, it should be observed that the introductory device which he sketches, the male-Cinderella story, belongs at the beginning of the narrative. Its chief function, that of creating suspense as to the knight's ability, is destroyed if the story is not told until after the knight has proved his worth. Either Spenser's plan to put this part of his story at the end of the poem was a serious error in narrative technique or the introductory scene was an afterthought.

Concerning the inception of the adventure of Sir Guyon, Spenser is much briefer and less satisfactory:

The second day ther came in a Palmer bearing an Infant with bloody hands, whose Parents he complained to haue bene slayn by an Enchaunteresse called Acrasia: and therfore craued of the Faery Queene, to appoint him some knight, to performe that aduenture, which being assigned to Sir Guyon, he presently went forth with that same Palmer: which is the beginning of the second booke and the whole subiect thereof.

This preliminary scene does not fit the narrative of the first canto of Book II.[10] In the poem both Guyon and the Palmer

[10] Janet Spens, *Spenser's Faerie Queene* (London, 1934), pp. 15–37, points out the most glaring difficulties, and I have gladly made use of her corroborative testimony,

are present at the death of Amavia, and it is Guyon himself who takes up the babe with the bloody hands and carries it, not to the court of the Faery Queen, but to Medina. It is usually assumed that the letter represents Spenser's original plan and that the poem is a departure from it. But this is most unlikely, since it involves the assumption that the poet concocted the present elaborate plan before he wrote Book I, then forgot or modified it when he began Book II (and it certainly was not in his mind when he wrote Book III), and then, in 1590, suddenly remembered or revived it again, describing it in the letter to Ralegh as if he had been following it all along. Neither is the discrepancy the product of a momentary failure of memory, because, when he wrote the letter, he must have been reading his proofs very recently,[11] and the scene at Amavia's death is a brilliant picture which its creator would not forget easily. We must conclude that, whenever the opening of Book II was written, the poet did not at that time have the annual feast in mind, nor was he planning to have each quest begin at the court of the Faery Queen.

The third book departs even further from the scheme set forth in the letter. The poet says of it:

> The third day there came in, a Groome who complained before the Faery Queene, that a vile Enchaunter called Busirane had in hand a most faire Lady called Amoretta, whom he kept in most grieuous torment, because she would not yield him the pleasure of her body. Whereupon Sir Scudamour the louer of that Lady presently tooke on him that aduenture. But being vnable to performe it by reason of the hard Enchauntments, after long sorrow, in the end met with Britomartis, who succoured him, and reskewed his loue.

This narrative, which Spenser describes as if it were the central plot of the whole book, is in fact merely the culminating episode, which is confined entirely to the last two cantos. Moreover, earlier in the letter, in naming the knights who are the heroes of the respective books, he names the third "of Brito-

although her theory of the evolution of the poem differs entirely from mine. Since this study was completed, J. H. Walter has published "'The Faerie Queene': Alterations and Structure," *Modern Language Review*, XXXVI (1941), 37–58.

[11] For evidence that Spenser read proofs on the first three books see the long list of "Faults Escaped," in the 1590 edition.

martis a Lady knight, in whome I picture Chastity," yet the quest is undertaken by Sir Scudamour. Virtue and quest have been separated and assigned to two different characters.

The poet shows himself to be uneasily aware that this book does not fit the plan he is describing, for he adds a further paragraph about it:

> But by occasion hereof, many other aduentures are intermedled, but rather as Accidents, then intendments. As the loue of Britomart, the ouerthrow of Marinell, the misery of Florimell, the vertuousnes of Belphœbe, the lasciuiousnes of Hellenora, and many the like.

Just what he means by "accidents" rather than "intendments" is not clear. Possibly he was distinguishing episodic intrusions from the main thread of the plot. But, even so, the exposition can hardly be made to square with the contents of the book. Britomart is the titular and exemplary knight; yet Scudamour sets out on the quest. And Scudamour's adventure, described in the letter as though it were the main plot, is entirely confined to the last two cantos. Since Britomart has never been to the court of the Faery Queen, nothing short of extensive re-writing could bring this book into harmony with the annual banquet and knightly quest elements in Spenser's announced plan.

Book IV departs even further than does Book III from the quest motif. It is called "The Legend of Cambel and Telamond (*sic!*), or of Friendship," yet Cambel and his friend play only a very minor part (in Cantos ii–iv) in a book which is chiefly concerned with the affairs of Florimell and Britomart, characters carried over from Book III.

The fact that this fourth book takes the poet even further from his announced plan has suggested to his critics that he had abandoned his formal scheme by the time he began to write the second instalment. But that could hardly have been the case, for Books V and VI return to the pattern of Books I and II. They are closely unified around a single knight who sets out on a quest assigned to him by the Faery Queen.

We cannot explain the structure of the poem by simply assuming, therefore, that the poet began in 1580 with the plan he described in 1590 and modified it as he got deeper into his poem.[12] If he had begun to introduce changes in a preconceived plan by the time he began Book II, why did he return to his original plan in Books V and VI? And why, if he had begun to modify his general structure in Book II and had wandered still farther away in Book III, did he describe his abandoned plan in the letter to Ralegh?

It has been suggested that Books III and IV differ from the others because of the nature of the virtues dealt with.[13] But, while this explanation might account for the change in allegorical method observable in these books, there is nothing in either chastity or friendship which prevented them from being illustrated by a knightly quest. Britomart's rescue of Amoret could have been made the central plot of Book III, instead of an isolated episode at the end of it, if Spenser had begun the book with such a plan in mind. The same is true of Book IV, where the poet had before him a medieval friendship story easily adaptable to the quest form, the story of *Amis and Amiloun;* but he chose to use it for a minor episode and not for his main plot.[14]

It has also been suggested that Spenser was trying to avoid

[12] Modern critics, beginning with Dean Church, have adopted this theory. Church calls the scheme outlined in the letter "his pre-arranged but too ambitious plan" (*Spenser* [London, 1886], p. 129). This is also the point of view of Courthope, Dodge, and De Sélincourt (see references in chap. i, n. 3). W. L. Renwick asserts that Spenser's "elaborate scheme based on critical principles" was coeval with the 1580 beginning, although "he may not have been very certain of his design, and may have changed his mind as the work progressed" (*Edmund Spenser* [London, 1925], pp. 46 and 54). Professor J. W. Draper asserts that the plan described in the letter "bears every impress of having been worked out beforehand" ("The Narrative-Technique of the *Faerie Queene*," *PMLA*, XXXIX [1924], 318). Lawrence Blair, in his examination of the relation of the poem to the announced plan, takes it for granted that the poem developed away from the plan ("The Plot of the *Faerie Queene*," *PMLA*, XLVII [1932], 81–88). R. H. Perkinson, in his reply (*PMLA*, XLVIII [1933], 295–301), puts forward H. Clement Notcutt's "The *Faerie Queene* and Its Critics," *Essays and Studies by Members of the English Association*, XII (1926), 63–86, as a satisfactory explanation of the structure of the poem, but Dr. Notcutt is concerned with defense and apology rather than with analysis and explanation. He argues: "If the *Faerie Queene* is as faulty in structure .... as the critics declare, then it is not a great poem," but they say it is a great poem; therefore, the structure is not faulty.

[13] De Sélincourt, Introduction to the *Oxford Spenser*, pp. xlv ff.; Greenlaw on Cory, *Variorum*, I, 344–48.

[14] The relation of the story of Amyas and Placidas to the medieval friendship story has been studied by H. M. Ayres, "The *Faerie Queene* and *Amis and Amiloun*," *MLN*, XXIII (1908), 177–80.

monotony of structure.[15] Certainly the monotony of twelve quests, described in twelve books, all of about the same length, and each illustrating a moral virtue, is obvious. In addition, there is evidence that the poet struggled with the problem of a lack of connection between the books. But these are not the considerations which produced the discrepancy between the letter and the opening of Book II. If the Palmer had appeared at Faery Court without the babe and made his complaint, then the finding of Amavia and her babe, in the first canto, would have become an incident in Guyon's quest rather than the starting-point for it, and poem and letter would be in perfect agreement. The adjustment of poem to plan would have been so easy that it seems obvious the first canto of Book II was written before the annual banquet was thought of.

The departure of Book III from the frame scheme of knightly quests is more serious because it divides virtue and quest between two characters and because it tells a story of the exemplary knight, Britomart, which puts her outside the circle of Faery Court entirely. It is curious that, of all the virtues, the representative of chastity should have least place in the court of the Faery Queen. Her quest is the search for her lover, but the quest in the illustration of chastity is undertaken by Scudamour. Surely, when Spenser created Britomart, he had a general structure for the poem in view different from the one described in the letter.

The contents of Books II and III do not fit into the frame plot of the annual banquet as the occasion for the twelve quests, and, indeed, this annual feast plays no part in the poem as it exists today. In spite of the elaborate use made of it in the letter and in spite of its importance as a device for unifying the plot, it is mentioned only once in the six extant books. In II, ii, 42, Guyon tells Medina that his mistress has a custom:

> An yearely solemne feast she wontes to make
> The day that first doth lead the yeare around;
> To which all knights of worth and courage bold
> Resort, to heare of straunge aduentures to be told.

[15] Courthope, in the *Cambridge History of English Literature*, III, 264.

We hear of quests initiated at the court of the Faery Queen in Books I, II, V, and VI,[16] but this is the only mention of the annual feast. And this account does not agree perfectly with what is said of the feast in the letter, because in the poem the feast is described as held on "the day that first doth lead the yeare around," while in the letter it is said to be a twelve days' feast.[17]

There is further and more serious difficulty involving time. Professor A. C. Sprague has pointed out that, since the opening of Books II and III show the knight who has finished his quest encountering the one whose quest is just beginning, the twelve sets of adventures must be successive rather than concomitant[18] and suggest successive annual feasts. The arrangement is that of a relay race rather than that of a mile run with twelve entries.

The natural inference seems to be that the annual feast was a very late embellishment of the plot; and this inference is strengthened by an examination of the changes made by the poet in his references to time in the 1596 edition of Part I. In 1590 Arthur tells Guyon that he has been looking for the Faery Queen for seven years (II, ix, 7.5–6). But in 1596 this indication of a lapse of years has been carefully removed. Again, in stanza 38.9 of the same canto, Arthur is reported, in the 1590 version, to have sought his lady for three years, but the time shrinks in 1596 to twelve months. Evidently the poet had some idea, when he revised the second book for the second edition, of

[16] For Redcrosse see I, i, 3; vii, 46; xii, 41; Guyon, II, ii, 43; III, i, 2; Artegall, V, i, 4; xi, 36; Calidore, VI, i, 7 and 10; x, 1; xii, 12.

[17] The Elizabethans celebrated twelve days of Christmas, including New Year's Day. G. W. Kitchin (*Variorum*, II, 203) suggests that Spenser had in mind not January 1 but March 25, but that is an unnecessary assumption. January 1 was celebrated as New Year's Day, with exchange of gifts. It was the beginning of the social and religious, as contrasted with the legal, year. See J. Nichols, *Progresses and Public Processions of Queen Elizabeth* (London, 1823), I, 108 ff. and *passim;* Thomas Naogeorgus [Kirchmeyer], *The Popish Kingdome or Reigne of Antichrist*, trans. Barnabe Googe, ed. R. C. Hope (London, 1880), fol. 45v; and "E. K.'s" defense of beginning the year with January, in the "Generall Argument" to the *Shepheardes Calender.*

[18] The suggestion that, the feast being an annual affair, the quests began in successive years is rejected by G. B. Parks, who shows that the annual chronology is not consistently followed ([London] *Times Literary Supplement*, April 27, 1933, p. 295, and June 29, 1933, p. 447).

bringing the action within the scope of twelve months[19] in accordance with current theories of the unity of time in epic action. But it is equally evident that no such limits were thought of when Arthur's part in Book II was first written.

We are forced to conclude that the idea of tying together the twelve sets of adventures by making them begin, and perhaps end, at a grand feast at Faery Court is a very late and superficial addition to the plot, and the management of Book IV suggests that it was never really made a part of the structure of the poem.

The omission of the letter to Ralegh from the 1596 edition of the poem may have been due to the exigencies of printing or to political considerations, since Ralegh was out of favor at that time. But it may also have been due to Spenser's wish to suppress some features of his plan, since by 1596 he must have realized that he was not going to be able to carry out that plan at all fully. Perhaps he saw that the annual banquet could only function as a unifying device if it appeared near the beginning of the poem, where it could provide the necessary account of the antecedent action. Put at the end, it could not operate retroactively.

It has been suggested that Spenser may have intended to convert the annual banquet into a grand finale in which all the knights should return with their trophies and Arthur should be united to his Faery Queen.[20] But it seems fruitless to speculate about how the poet might have solved his difficulties. At best, we have evidence only about his beginnings. From this evidence, provided by the existing books of the poem, it appears that the annual feast was not adopted as the starting-point of the quests until after the first three books were practically com-

[19] See footnotes in *Spenser's Faerie Queene*, ed. J. C. Smith (Oxford, 1909); and the note on II, ix, 7.5, in *Variorum*, II, 511.

[20] Draper (p. 311 n.) has suggested a plausible reconstruction. A more ambitious attempt to explain Spenser's whole meaning on the basis of a reconstruction of his ending is to be found in Isabel E. Rathborne's *The Meaning of Spenser's Fairyland* (New York, 1937), pp. 129, 189, 195, 221, 223, 224, 230, 233–34, and 239–40. She reconstructs the ending of the poem from fairy-tale analogues, but she has not shown that Spenser understood the nature or logic of folklore or that he had read the stories which she cites.

pleted.[21] The changes made in the calculation of time, the time sequence indicated by the links between the books, and the narrative discrepancies between the poem and the letter, all point to the very late addition of the annual feast to the plot.

On the other hand, the twelve quests, as distinct from the occasion of the annual feast, constitute one of the most well-defined elements in the plot. Redcrosse, Guyon, Arthegall, and Calidore are in their respective books all primarily and consistently knights on a quest. Only the third and fourth books depart from this pattern.

I have already pointed out that there are two distinct plot ideas in the poem which concern the Faery Queen: one is Spenser's adaptation of the *Sir Thopas* plot and the other makes her the center of a court and gives her an order of knighthood imitative of the Order of the Round Table and probably intended as a compliment to the Order of the Garter. If, as I suggested in the first chapter, Spenser began in the lighter vein of Ariosto-imitation indicated by the *Sir Thopas* continuation, that plot would naturally develop in the direction of the adventures of Sir Chastity. But between that beginning, characterized by the tale of the Squire of Dames, and the adventures of Redcrosse and Guyon there is either a very long step or a complete break and a fresh start.

Perhaps Harvey's disapproval, and other events of the spring of 1580 which made profound changes in the poet's personal plans, affected his epic plans also, and the books of Redcrosse and Guyon were begun with a different theme and plan in mind. If that was the case, then sometime later the poet sublimated his original Faery Queen plot and used it in an effort to tie together more firmly the books of his more serious and ambitious poem. There is, however, some evidence that the Ariosto-imitation continued through the creation of the Order of Maidenhead and that knights originally created in the lighter vein of the *Sir Thopas* continuation were later converted into exponents of particular virtues. This evidence lies in the character and treatment of the knights of the Order of Maidenhead.

[21] Miss Spens (pp. 16–17, 35–36) comes to the conclusion that the annual feast was never worked into the structure of the poem.

III
THE ORDER OF MAIDENHEAD

As last yledd with farre reported praise,
Which flying fame throughout the world had spred,
Of doughtie knights, whom Faery land did raise,
That noble order hight of Maidenhed,
Forthwith to court of *Gloriane* I sped.

—I, vii, 46.1–5

THE Order of Maidenhead forms the chief ornament of the court of the Faery Queen. It was clearly intended as a counterpart of the Order of the Garter, which in turn was commonly described as having been founded in imitation of the Arthurian Order of the Round Table,[1] so that Spenser's order may be regarded as shadowing both of these organizations.

Let us begin by observing certain general facts about the Order of Maidenhead. It is mentioned in every book except the sixth. Both Guyon and Arthegall are members of it, but Redcrosse and Britomart are not. It is, therefore, not coextensive with the twelve knights who represent the moral virtues. While it is mentioned in Books I and II, it functions chiefly in Books III, IV, and V, in parts of the plot which are derived from Ariosto. But the most curious fact about it is that it is one of the most important elements of the general structure of the poem, and yet it is not mentioned in the letter to Ralegh.

[1] See E. Greenlaw, *Studies in Spenser's Historical Allegory* ("Johns Hopkins Monographs in Literary History," Vol. II [Baltimore, 1932]), pp. 40, 46, 56; and *Variorum*, II, 202–3 and 280; see also N. H. Nicolas, "Observations on the Institution of the Most Noble Order of the Garter," *Archaeologia*, XXXI (1846), 104–63; L. F. Mott, "The Round Table," *PMLA*, XX (1905), 237; I. L. Schulze, "Notes on Elizabethan Chivalry and *The Faerie Queene*," *Studies in Philology*, XXX (1933), 148–59. Contemporary accounts of the Order of the Garter are included in Harison's "Description of Britaine," in Raphael Holinshed's *Chronicles* (1577, 1587), both editions of which Spenser knew (see 1587 ed., pp. 159–62).

The order is first named by Una (I, vii, 46) as an organization of knights of Faeryland at the court of Gloriana. Guyon mentions his membership in the order (II, ii, 42), and later in his book we learn that Arthegall and Sophy are famous members of it (ix, 2–6). In Book III we are told that many of its members are singularly devoted to the beautiful Florimell. Her lovers include Satyrane, Peridure, and Calidore (viii, 28). When she flees from Faery Court, they all set out in pursuit of her. Indeed, the pursuit of Florimell may very well be an earlier plot device than the twelve quests, just as the twelve successive quests seem to have been an earlier idea than the single annual banquet. Florimell's adventures are closely modeled on those of Ariosto's Angelica,[2] and, according to Harington, Angelica represents the honor that brave men seek.[3] The pursuit of Florimell by the knights of Maidenhead may, therefore, be an early version of the idea which ultimately became Arthur's search for Gloriana.

The quest of Florimell was undertaken by this group of knights when she fled from Faery Court in search of her wounded lover. Sir Satyrane, having picked up her lost girdle on the seashore, tells Paridell that "all the noble knights of *Maydenhead*, which her ador'd" must now mourn for her as dead. But Paridell is unwilling to abandon the pursuit of the fleeing beauty, and Satyrane decides to add his labors to those of "the rest, which in this Quest proceed." We might suppose that all, or a considerable number, of the knights of this order have set out in quest of her (III, viii, 46–50). Such expressions as "O ye braue knights, that boast this Ladies loue," "But sith that none of all her knights is nye" (viii, 27, 29), and "Full many knights, that loued her like deare" (IV, ii, 26) are used. Her flight is the one continuous thread of narrative in Book III. It is mentioned in the first canto (st. 15) and again in the fourth (sts. 46–51), and her subsequent adventures are taken up in Cantos vii and viii.

[2] See the chapters on Books III and IV below.

[3] *Orlando Furioso in English Heroical Verse* (2d ed., 1607), p. 151; and see p. 332, where Orlando's love for Angelica is said to be emblematic of a young man's love of pleasure or honor.

Florimell is "belov'd of meny a knight," and when Sir Satyrane finds her lost girdle (a symbol of chastity), he jumps to the conclusion that she has been devoured by the witch's beast and declares a tournament for the girdle (IV, ii, 25 ff.). This tournament is fought by the knights of Maidenhead on one side and challengers on the other (IV, iv). We learn the names of other knights of the order: Ferramont, Devon, Douglas, Paliumord, Sangliere, and Brianor. The whole three days' tournament is worked out so that the two sides remain definite and unconfused. On the third day Arthegall enters the lists in disguise as a challenger and overcomes two knights of his own order. His conduct is like that of Lancelot and other knights of medieval romance who frequently sought honor in this way.[4] Britomart, as a stranger, enters the lists and wins the tournament:

> So did the warlike *Britomart* restore
> The prize, to knights of Maydenhead that day.

In Book V (iv, 21 ff.) we are told that the Amazon queen has challenged the Order of Maidenhead *in toto*. Sir Terpin has taken up the challenge and has been defeated, and Artegall, in an attempt to rescue him, is captured and imprisoned and is finally rescued by Britomart. Book VI is the only one in which the order is not mentioned.

In view of the extensive use of the Order of Maidenhead in Books III, IV, and V, it is remarkable that it is not mentioned at all in Spenser's account of his plans for the poem set down at the end of Book III. If it was a new device, taken up as an alternative for the knightly quest of Books I and II, we might reasonably expect the poet to mention it in the letter to Ralegh. But it forms no part of the illustration of the twelve moral virtues by twelve knightly quests which Spenser puts forward in his letter as one of the two main elements in his plot. This fail-

[4] See Jessie L. Weston, *The Three Days' Tournament* (London: David Nutt, 1902), where many instances of this kind are noticed. Sir Henry Lee, the Queen's official champion, appeared as an unknown knight in the Accession Day tournament in 1581 and on other occasions, and other contemporary examples of "unknown" knights could be cited (see E. K. Chambers, *Sir Henry Lee* [Oxford: Clarendon Press, 1936], pp. 135, etc.).

ure to mention the order in his account of the complicated plot and his handling of it in Books III and IV and in the central part of Book V suggest that it was not a new plot idea but an old and largely abandoned one. This impression is borne out by an examination of Spenser's treatment of the various knights of the order.

These knights are often handled in a very inconsistent manner. Paridell is first mentioned as a devoted follower of Florimell (III, viii); yet two cantos later he has turned his attention to the seduction of Hellenore, and in the fourth book he is one of the loose companions of Duessa and Ate. Finally, in V, ix, 41, he is named, along with Blandamour, as a conspirator against Mercilla. Sir Terpin is an unfortunate but honorable knight who answered the challenge of the Amazon queen in Book V. But in Book VI a knight of the same name displays all the knightly vices.[5] Sir Sangliere takes an honorable part in the tournament on the side of the knights of Maidenhead in Book IV; but he appears as a particularly vicious individual in the opening canto of Book V. Sir Calidore's defection is not so serious. He is first mentioned in III, viii, 28, as one of the devoted followers of Florimell. He does not appear, however, until the opening of Book VI. In the meantime he seems to have quite forgotten Florimell, leaving the way open for a more successful devotion to Pastorella.

Sir Satyrane preserves a noble character throughout, but when we meet him in Book III, at the seashore, picking up Florimell's lost girdle, we hardly recognize him as the knight who rescued Una from the satyrs. Moreover, some change of plan about him seems to be indicated by the fact that in III, vii, 30.6, he bears a satyr's head upon his shield but that in IV, iv, 17.4, he carries a "maidenheaded" shield. The satyr's head suggests his name and agrees with the story of his origin in Book I; the "maidenheaded" shield fits better with his activities as a member of the Order of Maidenhead and the cult of Florimell in Books III and IV.

It has been pointed out that the name of Blandamour, one of

[5] The first Terpin is apparently executed in V, v, 18.

these knights, probably comes from *Sir Thopas*.[6] The suggestion is interesting in view of Spenser's use of Chaucer's *Tale*. Blandamour is not said to be a member of the Order of Maidenhead, but he is a close associate of Paridell, who is. He appears in Books IV and V as a paramour of Duessa and the false Florimell.

Even Arthegall presents a dual character. He is first mentioned in II, ix, 6, as a knight of Maidenhead high in the favor of the Faery Queen. In Book III, in the first three cantos, his personal appearance, ancestry, and descendants are described. He is praised as a very famous knight, but nothing is said that remotely suggests his function in Book V as the exponent of justice. Merlin says that he is a changeling, brought up by the fairies, but really the son of Gorlois, king of Cornwall. Through his son by Britomart is traced the line of British kings.

In Book IV, Cantos iv–vi, Arthegall appears as the "Salvage knight" and fights against the knights of Maidenhead. His subsequent downfall at the hands of Britomart, his ambush of her, and the fight and recognition scene were hardly designed to illustrate justice. He behaves like a knight of the romances, but neither his motive nor his action in the ambushing of Britomart is in accord with justice. Book V takes a fresh start. From the first he is the champion of a definite virtue, brought up, not by the fairies, but by Astraea. By her he is armed with a magic sword, and we hear for the first time that he is on a quest, the rescue of Irena. There is even a respelling of his name, for in the earlier books he is usually called "Arthegall," but in Book V usually "Artegall."

The change in the conception of the character of so many knights of the Order of Maidenhead seems to indicate a change in the poet's plans. If the order was created early in the history of the poem, then it is easy to see how Spenser's plans developed in the direction of the more specific illustration of virtue and were finally formalized in the scheme of twelve exemplary

[6] Professor Skeat noted that Spenser's Blandamour (IV, i, 32, etc.) may be derived from Pleyndamour. Professor F. P. Magoun, Jr., points out that Pleyndamour was spelled Blandamour in the fifteenth- and sixteenth-century texts of *Sir Thopas* ("The Chaucer of Spenser and Milton," *Modern Philology*, XXV [1927], 129–31; cf. F. N. Robinson's *The Complete Works of Geoffrey Chaucer* [Boston, 1933], p. 846).

knights. If this is the direction of growth, then the poet did one of two things with his already created knights. He either metamorphosed them into examples of virtues, as in the case of Guyon, Artegall, and Calidore, or he reduced them to minor or villainous parts, as in the case of Paridell, Sangliere, and Terpin.

It seems very improbable that Spenser planned from the beginning to include wicked as well as exemplary knights in an order intended to compliment the chastity of the Queen and the Order of the Garter. But, on the other hand, if he created a band of knights while he was feeling his way, with Ariosto for his guide (none of whose knights is a model of virtue throughout), then the subsequent degradation of some knights, and the elevation of others to a higher plane of ethical significance, would be a natural process in the evolution of the poem. Some such process seems apparent in the openings of Books V and VI, where Artegall and Calidore are described all over again, as if they were new creations.

If Spenser's plans developed along the lines I have indicated, then it is evident that most of the early material is to be found in Books III and IV rather than in Books I and II. These (III and IV) are the books which, with the Britomart and Florimell sections in Book V, are most heavily and most directly indebted to Ariosto, both in narrative technique and in subject matter. If Gabriel Harvey's remarks indicate that Spenser was imitating Ariosto in 1580, we should expect to find traces of the early work among the more obvious borrowings. The legend of Redcrosse contains little that could be described as either direct emulation or imitation of the *Orlando*, either in matter or in manner. Even the second book has no more than a canto which is written in the manner of the Italian poet and which borrows extensively from him. It is not until we come to Books III and IV that emulation is apparent and imitations also begin to appear in impressive volume. These two books, which owe most, and most directly, to the *Orlando Furioso*, and which describe the activities of the knights of Maidenhead, are precisely the books which depart most completely from the general plan for the poem described in 1590. Not only do they depart furthest from the virtue-knight-quest formula but they imitate Ariosto's narrative technique[7] as well as his subject matter.

In his discussion of "Spenser's Imitations from Ariosto,"[8] R. E. N. Dodge observes that "the general character of Book III differs markedly from that of the preceding books, and approximates very distinctly to the type of the *Furioso*." In a very important passage he goes on to analyze the differences, pointing out that Book III represents a radical departure from Books I and II not only in its handling of narrative but also in the type of characters represented and in the management of the allegory. In all three the departure is in the direction of Ariosto. Professor Gilbert points out that Spenser employs Ariosto's method of ending his cantos chiefly in the last four books.

Proceeding on the assumption of seriatim composition, Dodge concludes:

> Having begun his poem with Ariosto in mind, therefore, he still found Ariosto his most convenient resource; indeed, as we have seen, during the very days of his early enthusiasm for the *Gerusalemme Liberata* [when he was writing the last canto of Book II] the *Faerie Queene* was drifting, as if irresistibly, towards the type of the *Furioso*, and was accumulating imitations in double volume.[9]

But is it reasonable to suppose that, when he had Ariosto chiefly in mind, Spenser's structure, tone, and subject matter were more formal (more like those of Vergil and Tasso) and produced Books I and II and that the *Faerie Queene* grew more like the *Orlando* when Spenser turned to Tasso for inspiration at the end of Book II and the opening of Book III? Surely it is better to abandon the hypothesis of seriatim composition, and to look in the more Ariosto-like books for evidence of Spenser's Ariosto-like beginning, and to look not so much in the exploits of Britomart, as in the "many other aduentures intermedled, but rather as Accidents, then intendments," such as the fragmentary story of the Squire of Dames and the plot idea of the pursuit of Florimell by the Order of Maidenhead.

As I pointed out in the first chapter, if Spenser began the

[7] See A. H. Gilbert, "Spenser's Imitations from Ariosto: Supplementary," *PMLA*, XXXIV (1919), 225–32.

[8] *PMLA*, XII (1897), 191.

[9] *Ibid.*, p. 197.

poem as a celebration of the "fayre Elisa" under the guise of a fairy queen, then he must have begun either with the *Sir Thopas* story or with that derived from the Order of the Round Table with its knightly quests. In either case he began with a native theme but turned to Ariosto for plot amplifications. Both devices center in the person of the Faery Queen, and both celebrate chastity, a virtue which no poet could afford to neglect if he wished to please Queen Elizabeth.[10] When the first three books were finally arranged for publication, the Book of Chastity was given an honorable place at the end of the first instalment, and that other great virtue of the Queen's, True Religion,[11] was put first. But we are not therefore justified in assuming that the Book of Redcrosse was begun in 1579–80 in emulation of Ariosto and under the title of the *Faerie Queene*. It seems instead to represent a different beginning—one designed in accordance with a more exalted theme and on the more formal model of Vergil. Eventually these two beginnings were combined in one poem, but the conception of Una remains quite distinct from that of the Faery Queen. The development of the latter seems to have been from a beginning in which she inspired the love of Sir Chastity and was given a court made up chiefly of knights dedicated to Maidenhead, to a formalized scheme in which all the virtues were to be included and each was to have a special knight as its exemplar.

[10] See E. C. Wilson, *England's Eliza* ("Harvard Studies in English," Vol. XX [Cambridge, Mass., 1939]), esp. chap. v.

[11] See Wilson, esp. chaps. i and ii.

IV
THE APOTHEOSIS OF THE FAERY QUEEN

> Ne let his fairest *Cynthia* refuse,
> In mirrours more then one her selfe to see,
> But either *Gloriana* let her chuse,
> Or in *Belphoebe* fashioned to bee:
> In th' one her rule, in th' other her rare chastitee.
>
> —III, Proem, 5.5–9

ACCORDING to the account of Spenser's beginnings contained in the preceding chapters, the order of development of the plot was, as we would expect it to be, in the direction of aggrandizement of the titular heroine.[1] She is simply an English Diana, or Venus, in the "Aprill" eclogue, and that character was probably carried over into the beginning of the *Sir Thopas* continuation. The first step in her apotheosis would then be the substitution of the Order of Maidenhead for the conventional band of nymphs who were Diana's attendants and a popular term of compliment to the court ladies.

From this beginning, Spenser's conception of his Faery Queen grew as the poem grew, for I believe that what is said of her in the letter to Ralegh, and in the proems to Books I and III, represents her last apotheosis, not her first incarnation. In the beginning the poet was doubtful whether "in fair Elisa rest, or if thee please in bigger notes to sing advance the worthy whom she loveth best." He did not, at first, see how he could raise his feminine subject to the heights of epic action. But ten years later he wrote:

> In that Faery Queene I meane glory in my generall intention, but in my particular I conceiue the most excellent and glorious person of our soueraine

[1] Because they have looked at the poem as composed in the same order in which it was published, critics have asserted that the poet became less serious and lofty as he proceeded. I. E. Rathborne, in her discussion of *The Meaning of Spenser's Fairyland*

the Queene, and her kingdome in Faery land. And yet in some places els, I doe otherwise shadow her. For considering she beareth two persons, the one of a most royall Queene or Empresse, the other of a most vertuous and beautifull Lady, this latter part in some places I doe express in Belphœbe, fashioning her name according to your owne excellent conceipt of Cynthia, (Phœbe and Cynthia being both names of Diana).

Between the writing of the "October" eclogue and the publication of the first part of the *Faerie Queene*, the Diana-like mistress of Sir Chastity had evolved into Gloriana, the "nurse of vertue" who bestows "due praise, that is the spur of dooing well." She has become a true Renaissance ideal and a suitable central figure for an epic. But in the process of idealization something has been lost, and this the poet restores to her in the character of Belphoebe, who takes the place of his earlier conception of her as a Diana.

If this was the process of evolution of the Faery Queen, then we should expect to find that the concept of the Faerie Queene as Gloriana was a late embellishment of the plan; and that is exactly what we do find. The name "Gloriana" appears only nine times in the entire poem. Four of these occurrences are in the second instalment, in matter which was certainly written after 1590.[2] Another is in the Proem of Book III, where the poet puts into verse the compliments to Ralegh's *Cynthia* which are expressed also in the letter written in 1589. There are several indications that the writing of proems was one of the finishing touches added to the several books just before publication. As G. L. Craik remarks: "These introductions to the several Books of the Fairy Queen, we may here observe, have all the appearance of having been written after the poem itself, and inserted, like the Dedicatory Sonnets, by the author when he was preparing it for the press."[3] Certainly the compliment to Ralegh in the Proem to Book III dates these stanzas as written in 1589.

(New York, 1937), assumes that the search of Arthur for Gloriana was an initial concept when she calls attention (pp. 16–17) to the resemblance between Poliziano's *Stanze* and the story of Arthur as told by Spenser.

[2] The name appears in the introductions to two cantos of Book V (viii, 3, and xii, 3) and in Colin's celebration of his love in Book VI (x, 4 and 28).

[3] *Spenser and His Poetry* (London, 1871), II, 6.

Of the other four uses of the name "Gloriana," two appear in the fairy genealogy in Book II, which was almost certainly a late addition to that book.[4] The other two are in stanzas (i, 3, and vii, 46) which there are other reasons for thinking belong to the final polishing of the highly finished first book. Six of these occurrences of the name are in introductory matter, and the other three are in passages which seem, for other reasons, to be very late additions to the poem. As Courthope observed, "If all mention of Gloriana were excised from the *Faery Queen*, the framework of the poem, as we have it, would be hardly disturbed."[5] In fact, it would not be disturbed at all.

Belphoebe has much more substance than Gloriana; she makes three personal appearances—in Books II, III, and IV. The Timias-Belphoebe story in Book III represents Ralegh's devotion to the Queen (v, 18–55) and mentions tobacco to enforce the identification, which is also pointed to in the Proem of the book. This passage was either written or revised to fit Ralegh in the late summer of 1589, after Ralegh had undertaken the sponsorship of the poem. The similar Timias-Belphoebe passage in Book IV clearly shadows Ralegh's disgrace in 1592. Both allegories are, therefore, very late additions to the poem.[6]

The appearance of Belphoebe in II, iii, presents a more complex problem. This is a humorous episode involving the theft of Guyon's horse. The chief actors in the canto are Braggadochio and Trompart, Spenser's leading comic characters, modeled on Ariosto. Braggadochio steals Guyon's horse and secures the services of Trompart. The pair encounter Archimage, who agrees to get Arthur's sword for Braggadochio if he will use it to attack Guyon. Then Archimage vanishes so suddenly that he frightens the two rogues into flight. While they are still quaking, they are further alarmed by the sudden arrival of Belphoebe. Braggadochio crawls under a bush to hide but is driven out. He recovers self-confidence while Belphoebe is delivering a

[4] One is in the argument to Canto x, the other in st. 76. The date of composition of the fairy genealogy will be discussed in chap. vii.

[5] W. J. Courthope, *History of English Poetry* (London, 1897), II, 259.

[6] They are discussed more fully in chaps. xi and xiii.

speech on the way to honor through toil, and attempts to seize her.

The comic situations are emphasized throughout this canto, and the boasting cowardice of Braggadochio is developed fully. In tone, type of incident, and characters involved the whole canto presents what I believe was the nature of Spenser's first attempt at Ariosto-like writing. Both the theft of the horse and the encounter with Belphoebe are imitated from humorous stories in Ariosto.[7] It could, of course, be argued that Spenser's humor was a development of maturity. But this canto does not seem to me to be in the vein of high seriousness which characterizes Spenser's mature plan, as described in the letter, and the incidents belong to a part of Guyon's story which I believe was written early.[8]

The appearance of Belphoebe, who seems otherwise to be a late addition to the poem, in this apparently "early" episode, constitutes the chief problem in any attempt to trace the history of this canto. The poet asserts, in his letter to Ralegh, that he fashioned the name "Belphoebe" "according to your owne excellent conceipt of Cynthia, (Phœbe and Cynthia being both names of Diana)." We have no reason to suppose that Spenser was acquainted with Ralegh's *Cynthia* before the two poets came together in the summer of 1589, so that we must either doubt Spenser's statement about his choice of the name or assume that this passage, like that in Book III, was written in 1589—or we must conclude that the poet rechristened in 1589 the heroine of a previously written passage. The last seems to be the most probable conclusion. The huntress who comes upon Braggadochio is a Diana-like figure, and the names "Diana" and "Belphoebe" are metrically interchangeable. If the poet brought his Faery Queen on the scene in the early version of the poem, as it seems natural that he should, then this is perhaps a revised version of an early appearance.

[7] Belphoebe and Braggadochio present a reversal of the situation in the first canto of the *Orlando*, where Angelica comes out of a bush to put herself under the protection of Sacripant, he promptly attempts to rape her, and she runs away. This parallel was not noted by Dodge, but a similar reversal of Angelica's part in the Timias-Belphoebe story in Book III has been noticed.

[8] See chap. vii and Index under "Guyon."

The passage is commonly interpreted as an allegory of Alençon's courtship of Queen Elizabeth. If that interpretation is correct, it fits best with an early date for the creation of the passage. Spenser's interest in the affair dated from 1578–80, when he was in Leicester's service, and certainly ceased with Alençon's death in 1584. However, we cannot be sure enough of the allusion to date the passage by it.

If the poet was making use of an old episode involving the Faery Queen in order to introduce more of Belphoebe into his first instalment, he certainly polished it carefully when the final version of the book was made. Much of the elaborate description of Belphoebe, with its echoes of Tasso, may have been worked up at this time;[9] but the humorous intent, evident in the activities of Braggadochio, the touch of burlesque in Belphoebe's greeting of Trompart, and his reply in words which echo Aeneas' greeting to Venus,[10] fit perfectly the tone and content of what I have postulated was Spenser's Ariosto-like beginning. Therefore, I believe that it is most probable that this canto represents early material which found its way into the Book of Guyon and then, in 1589, was embellished with the name "Belphoebe" as a substitute for some earlier designation of the Faery Queen, perhaps "Diana."

But while Gloriana and Belphoebe, at least in name, were late additions to the poem in 1589, the Faery Queen was, so far as we can tell, Spenser's starting-point. While she never appears in person, references to her are fairly frequent in Books I and II. Book III has only two, and Book IV has no references, but Books V and VI mention her in connection with the quests.[11]

[9] The line, "Upon her eyelids many Graces sate" (st. 25), echoes a line quoted by "E. K." from Spenser's early *Pageants* (see the gloss to "June"). But Spenser used the image in *Amoretti*, xl, 3–4, and in the second of the *Fowre Hymnes*, ll. 253–55, so that we cannot infer an early date for the passage from this echo. However, the description of Belphoebe is full of echoes from many sources, as if the passage had been worked over with great care, and perhaps more than once.

[10] See M. Y. Hughes, *Virgil and Spenser* ("University of California Publications in English," Vol. II [Berkeley, 1929]), pp. 359–61.

[11] References to the Faery Queen are as follows: I, vii, 36 (she brings Arthur's armor to fairyland); ix, 6–20 (Arthur falls in love with her); x, 58 (her city is Cleopolis); xi, 7, and xii, 18, 41 (she is at war with a Paynim king); II, i, 28, v, 11, and viii, 43 (references to her picture painted on Guyon's shield); ii, 40–43 (Guyon tells Medina about her); ix, 2–7 (Guyon tells Arthur about her); III, i, 2 (Acrasia has been sent to

The almost complete absence of mention of the Faery Queen in the Ariosto-like Books III and IV is compensated for by the activities of the knights of Maidenhead in the pursuit of Florimell, who has fled from Faery Court. Satyrane carries a "maidenheaded shield." The court of the Faery Queen forms the background for the action, much as the wars of Charlemagne form the setting for the *Orlando Furioso.*

Aside from references to her court and her Order of Maidenhead, the Faery Queen is mentioned several times in Book II as pictured on Guyon's shield. Otherwise, all reference to her is in connection either with the initiation of quests or with Arthur's search. If the love story is the oldest element in the plot, then we can trace three successive intentions: the search of Sir Thopas–Arthur for the Faery Queen; the creation of her court with its Order of Maidenhead; and, finally, the formal illustration of the virtues by twelve knights of her court. The series has the logic of progressive development to recommend it. The queen of fairies of whom Sir Thopas dreamed seems, at the beginning, if we can judge from the *Sir Thopas* continuation, to have been a symbol of chastity. The first step in her development was the acquisition of a court made up chiefly of a knightly order dedicated to virginity. The conversion of that order into a formal scheme to illustrate twelve moral virtues represents a further step in the idealization of Spenser's royal mistress. But the true reward of virtue, according to Renaissance ideals, was immortal glory; and so the Faery Queen became Gloriana, the final enlargement of a plan of adulation which was intended from the beginning for Queen Elizabeth, but which grew in magnificence as the poem grew. The "Idea of pure Glory" is the final exaltation of the Queen of Sir Chastity's dream and of Guyon's shield. What had been lost in the process, the personal flattery of the Maiden Queen, was restored to her in the person of Belphoebe, who is simply another incarnation of that first, Diana-like Faery Queen.

---

her court); iv, 54 (Arthur thinks of her); V, i, 4 (Eirena has gone to her court for aid); xi, 37 (reference to her court); VI, x, 1, and xii, 12 (she sends Calidore on his quest). In II, i, 1.6, she is called "Elfin Queene."

V

THE ROLE OF PRINCE ARTHUR

> Both shield, and sword, and armour all he wrought
> For this young Prince, when first to armes he fell;
> But when he dyde, the Faerie Queene it brought
> To Faerie lond, where yet it may be seene, if sought.
>
> —I, vii, 36.6–9

HAVING reviewed the development of Spenser's conception of Gloriana, our next task is to discover the place of Arthur in Spenser's growing plans. Several critics have taken it for granted that Arthur was Spenser's starting-point and that the nucleus of the plot is the search of Arthur for Gloriana. But if Spenser began with the love story, he began with the *Sir Thopas* plot, which is still the basis and whole substance of the love story. The problem then is: When did Arthur supplant Sir Thopas?

Gabriel Harvey had not liked the first version of the poem, which I believe was the *Sir Thopas* continuation, and early in the period of composition Spenser shifted his center of interest to the court of the Faery Queen, and the plot developed in the direction of the knights of Maidenhead. Apparently the lover who was in search of the Faery Queen dropped into the background or out of the story entirely. Some time much later, when he decided to add Arthur to his cast of characters, Spenser revived the part of the lover for him in order to give him a sufficiently important role for so august a figure. No poet would deliberately plan to present Arthur as a minor or subordinate character in an English national epic.

But, as Hurd concluded, "the adventure of Prince Arthur, whatever the author pretended . . . . was but an afterthought."[1] Warton says that Arthur is "only a subordinate or

[1] Richard Hurd, *Letters on Chivalry and Romance* (2d ed.; London, 1762), p. 70.

accessory character";[2] and, among more recent critics, Dodge remarks: "Arthur remains a mere figure-head, appearing but once in each book."[3] Professor W. L. Renwick observes that "the place of Arthur in the epic-romance was never quite clearly worked out; his appearances are fitful and unrelated."[4]

There are three difficulties in Spenser's presentation of Arthur: he "appears but seldom," his appearances are unrelated to one another, and in four of the six books he serves as a piece of machinery, introduced at a predetermined point (Canto viii) and dismissed in time to leave the culminating episode of the book for the hero of that book. Such a situation could hardly have arisen if Spenser had all along planned the poem with Arthur as its chief hero.

It would have been easy enough to make him the hero-in-chief. By all the rights of allegory and legend, the twelve exemplary knights belong in his court or train rather than in that of the Faery Queen. As virtues they are the parts of which Arthur is the sum, and as knights of romance Arthur is their natural lord. But the poet had begun by substituting the Faery Queen for Arthur in order to pay homage to a feminine sovereign, and he could not thereafter find a suitable place for Arthur in his poem.

Arthur was not his starting-point but "an afterthought," as Hurd observes. I believe that analysis of his place in the poem shows that he was a late addition to the plot which centered in the court of the Faery Queen and that he was added after the Order of Maidenhead, with its miscellaneous adventures modeled on Ariosto, had been reorganized into the more formal structure of twelve knights illustrative of the twelve virtues "according to Aristotle."

The plots of the first three books could have developed almost to their present form without any mention of Arthur. Let us see just what his part amounts to. In the first book he does not ap-

[2] Thomas Warton, *Observations on the Fairy Queen of Spenser* (London, 1762), I, 7.

[3] R. E. N. Dodge, "Spenser's Imitations from Ariosto," *PMLA*, XII (1897), 175; see also his edition of the poem, p. 133.

[4] *Edmund Spenser* (London, 1925), p. 175.

pear until Canto vii, stanza 29. He is there given a full-length portrait, and his entrance provides Una with an opportunity to review her misfortunes and those of Redcrosse. In the next canto, as the medium of "heavenly grace" (st. 1.3), he rescues Redcrosse and "slayes the Gyant, wounds the beast, and strips Duessa quight." In Canto ix Arthur tells the story of his upbringing and of his quest of the Faery Queen; he exchanges gifts with Redcrosse, they separate, and we hear no more of him. He has figured in 95 of the book's 621 stanzas.

In the second book Arthur plays a very similar part. He appears in Canto viii, stanza 17, saves Guyon from Pyrochles and Cymochles, and establishes a friendship with him. But instead of vanishing when he has done his good deed, he rides off with Guyon to the Castle of Alma, where they fight off a rabble and are entertained. In Canto x each knight selects a book from the store of Memory, and Arthur reads the chronicle of British kings, while Guyon reads that of "Elfin Emperours till time of Gloriane." In Canto xi Arthur defends the Castle of Alma, after Guyon has gone off to destroy Acrasia. The part concerned with Arthur comprises 182 of the 683 stanzas. Apparently the poet felt the need to enlarge the part of Arthur in order to make him the chief hero of the whole poem.

Yet in Book III he hardly found a place for him at all. Arthur makes only two brief appearances in the early cantos. He sets out, so we are told, from the Castle of Alma with Guyon, and they encounter Britomart, who unhorses Guyon. Arthur makes peace between them, and the three ride together until they are separated in pursuit of a fleeing damsel. We do not hear of him again until we reach Canto iv, stanza 45, where he is still in pursuit of the lady. He is overtaken by night, and the fervor of his denunciation of that goddess is attributed to his fear that the damsel may be "his Faery Queen." In Canto v, while searching for the lady, he comes upon her dwarf, who explains that she is Florimell and that she has fled from Faery Court. Arthur pledges his assistance in the search for her, and so he is left for the remainder of the book, engaged in a fruitless quest of Florimell.

This action is brief and inconclusive. It occupies only 57 stanzas. The ingenious suggestion has been made that the insignificance of Arthur's part in this book is due to the fact that, while magnificence (or rather magnanimity) included all of the other virtues, it did not include all in the same degree. The inference is that a touch of chastity was all that Spenser cared to assign to his hero. But this specious reasoning is an ineffectual attempt to account for an existing situation rather than an effort to discover the cause of that situation. Spenser certainly had no idea of minimizing the importance of the Queen's most celebrated virtue. Nor does the allegory control the plot of Book III, as it does in Books I and II, as we shall see when we come to examine these books.

In Books IV and V Spenser follows as exactly as possible the pattern of Arthur's part in Books I and II. In Book IV he appears in the eighth canto, coming to the rescue of the friends, Amyas and Placidas, and by the end of Canto ix his part in the book is completed. In Book V, as in Book II, he rescues the hero of the book and then goes on with him to visit a castle and to achieve a separate adventure, in Canto xi, illustrative of the virtue of the book.

In Book VI, as in Book III, Arthur appears in the early cantos. But there the parallel ends. He has a substantial part in Book VI, such as he does not have in Book III. Moreover, in Book VI for the first time, Spenser makes an effort to give Arthur's story some continuity. He is introduced with his squire, and we are told how they found each other after they had been separated at the beginning of Book III. This effort to make Arthur a real character in a continued plot corresponds to the new relation developed in Book VI between Arthur and the hero of the book. Arthur no longer rescues and co-operates with the hero, but instead he alternates with him, appearing in that part of the book from which Calidore is absent.

Arthur appears in Canto v, and, after the explanation of how he found his squire, he proceeds to the rescue of Serena. Then he punishes some discourteous knights, rescues his squire from the giant Disdain, and rides off to "a great adventure" (viii, 30), which is left for the next, and never forthcoming, book.

The new developments of his part in Book VI indicate that the poet was still struggling with the problem of making a place for Arthur. But even in Book VI he had hardly solved that problem in such a way as to make Arthur the predominant hero. The difficulty in which he had involved himself when he decided to represent the twelve virtues by twelve knights of Gloriana's court, and at the same time by Arthur, proved insurmountable.

If Arthur was an afterthought, he must have been a late addition to the plots of the first two books. In Book II an angel *in propria forma* is discovered guarding Guyon, but the angel departs inopportunely just when danger threatens, so that Arthur can come to the rescue. Obviously, Arthur and the guardian angel are doubling for each other in this passage, and Spenser is quite conscious of the similarity of function. Perhaps originally the angel awakened Guyon, and he defended himself. The appearance of this angel in Book II suggests that "heavenly grace" in Book I was an angel also, before Arthur was added to the poem. Spenser had precedent for divine intervention, both in his classical models and in Ariosto and Tasso, who introduce angels and devils as well as pagan divinities.

The Arthur of Book I performs the service, in the destruction of Duessa's beast and the redemption of the Christian man, which is performed by the Savior in the Revelation of John, from which the plot is largely borrowed.[5] But he also takes over the role of Sir Thopas and the name "Arthur." This is a most incongruous amalgamation. But if a supernatural being originally rescued Redcrosse, Arthur could be given a substantial part in the plan of the book by substituting him for that being. Once the rescuer of Redcrosse lost his supernatural character, he might be substituted also in the *Sir Thopas* plot in order to connect him suitably with the Faery Queen. By combining these three characters, the poet succeeded in creating for Arthur a substantial part in Book I, and the model was easy to follow in

[5] See chap. ix.

Book II, although it involved a weakening of the allegory. The angel should have been able to awaken or protect Guyon, and Guyon should have been able to defend himself, since he had already demonstrated his ability to defeat both Pyrochles and Cymochles. Once in the account of the fight Guyon's name is used in place of Arthur's.[6] It has been assumed that the poet forgot what he was doing, but it is possible that the passage was originally written about Guyon and that the poet failed to make the necessary change in name when he transferred the fight to Arthur. It has been remarked that Arthur's subsequent fight in defense of Alma belongs logically to Guyon and that the allegory duplicates that of Guyon's final exploit. Miss Spens suggests that the Castle-of-Alma allegory was the original ending of Book II. Certainly in the opening of Book III Guyon and Arthur appear coming from the castle, although in II, xii, Guyon had gone on the quest of Acrasia. It seems, therefore, that some late rearrangement has taken place in Guyon's story, such as the addition of Arthur might necessitate.

Another evidence of the late addition of Arthur to the plot is the lack of connection between Arthur's different appearances. Orlando appears very little in the early cantos of Ariosto, but his several appearances are strung together on a single thread of narrative. He is a character in an action which has a continuity of its own and which involves, sooner or later, most of the other characters in the poem. But Arthur has no such sustaining thread of continuity. In Books I, II, IV, and V his appearance is not once linked with the last episode in which he took part in the preceding book, and the link between Books II and III is inconsistent in several ways and obviously artificial.[7] Other characters, such as Britomart, Florimell, Amoret, and (with exceptions) Satyrane and Artegall have the continuity of their stories preserved from one book to another, but not so Arthur. He is not a character in a continued action, but a *deus ex machina*, until we come to Book VI. The reason for this is evident if we suppose that Arthur was a late addition to the poem who

[6] Canto viii, st. 48.8. The mistake was corrected in the 1609 edition.

[7] See my discussion of Book III in chap. xi below.

took over the parts of other characters as he could be fitted in. That would also explain his tendency to appear in the eighth canto.

Except for his part in the opening of the third book, Arthur presents throughout the same exalted character which the poet assigned to him in the letter to Ralegh, where he says: "So in the person of Prince Arthure I sette forth magnificence in particular, which vertue for that (according to Aristotle and the rest) it is the perfection of all the rest, and conteineth in it them all. . . . ." The reference to Aristotle has, however, misled many critics into assuming that, since Aristotle made magnanimity, and not magnificence, the master-virtue, Spenser accidentally used the wrong word and really meant magnanimity. But, according to the *Oxford English Dictionary*, in Spenser's day magnanimity was commonly looked upon as a subdivision of fortitude or courage, or as a synonym for fortitude.[8] Toward the close of the century "magnanimity" began to be used in the Aristotelian sense; but, since Spenser uses the word "magnificence" for Arthur's virtue, it is better to try to understand than silently to emend the passage. Magnificence was a kingly and inclusive virtue in Tudor times, as reference to the examples in the *Oxford English Dictionary* will show. It was associated with divine benevolence and with kingly greatness. It was used as a term of address to kings and was, therefore, a suitable virtue for Arthur.

Such a conception of the character of Arthur makes logical his substitution for the Savior in Book I. He is called "heavenly grace" and performs the part of divine benevolence. His substitution for the guardian angel in Book II is also in keeping with his character as magnificence (in the Elizabethan sense). The poet did not find a suitable place for such a character in Book III, and so he represents Arthur as simply a knight-errant

[8] H. S. V. Jones, "Magnanimity in Spenser's Legend of Holiness," *Studies in Philology*, XXIX (1932), 200–206, discusses Arthur as representing the medieval concept of magnanimity or fortitude. His discussion of this concept is very useful. Both Jacques Hurault, *Politicke, Moral, and Martial Discourses* (1595), pp. 286 ff., and Simon Harward, *Encheiridion Morale* (1596), substitute "magnanimity" for "fortitude," at the close of the century.

and mentions briefly his devotion to the Faery Queen. Here again he may be substituting Arthur for some other knight in an effort to get him into the book at all. His activity, the pursuit of Florimell, suggests that he has taken the place of a knight of the Order of Maidenhead.

The introduction of Arthur as a symbol of divine benevolence, kingliness in the highest degree, belongs to a stage in the development of the poem where the Faery Queen has become Gloriana. It is this exalted conception which the poet had in mind when he wrote the letter to Ralegh, in which he represents Arthur as the hero-in-chief of the whole poem. Yet the management of Arthur's part in the poem indicates clearly that he was a late addition to the plot, "a mere afterthought." Our next task, therefore, is to try to discover why Arthur was more attractive as the hero of Spenser's poem in 1589 than he had been in 1580.

VI
THE REPUTATION OF ARTHUR

> Where is King Arthur the venturer, with his Knights bold?
> or Sir Tristeram, that treasure of curtesye?
> or Sir Gawaine the good, with his helmett made of gold?
> or Sir Lancelott dulake, a Knight of Chiualrye?[1]

SOME critics, misled by the letter to Ralegh, have assumed that Spenser solved his problem of epic matter neatly and easily by employing the Arthurian legend as Vergil employed the Homeric matter and Ariosto the legendary wars of Charlemagne. Courthope says blithely:

> With the glorification of a patriot queen, Spenser was able, appropriately, to link all the legendary lore handed down to him by Geoffrey of Monmouth, together with the fables of the *Morte d'Arthur*, and with that local antiquarianism which, in the historical researches of men like Camden and Holinshed, had done much to kindle the English imagination.[2]

But the truth is that Spenser elected to honor his patriot Queen by substituting her for Arthur, giving to her the court and the order of knighthood which traditionally belonged to Arthur. When he finally decided to make a place for Arthur in the poem, he introduced him as Prince Arthur "before he was king," thereby antedating all but the boyhood of Arthur. It is no wonder that, as the late Professor Greenlaw observed, Spenser made very little use of Malory in the *Faerie Queene*.

Professor Maynadier, in his study of *The Arthur of the English Poets*, says:

> Arthur himself, as Spenser introduces him, is hardly recognizable as the older Arthur, nor do you see him much in the *Faerie Queene*, though from

[1] "The Fall of Princes," ll. 73–76, from *Bishop Percy's Folio Manuscript*, ed. J. W. Hales and F. J. Furnivall (London, 1868), III, 172. According to Percy's note, "This song should seem to have been wrote soon after the Death of Henry 8." Henry's death is commented upon in the last stanza.

[2] *Cambridge History of English Literature*, III, 268; see also E. Greenlaw, in *Variorum*, I, 345, and *Studies in Spenser's Historical Allegory* (Baltimore, 1932), pp. 1–58.

what the poet wrote to Raleigh, you would expect to see him often. . . . . Only the first quest . . . . is strongly reminiscent of any famous Arthurian quest.[3]

Actually, the Arthurian part of the first quest is the part contained in the letter to Ralegh and alluded to in only two stanzas (vii, 46–47) of the book itself. Otherwise, the legend of Redcrosse has quite other origins than the matter of Britain. Even the description of Arthur's person (Canto vii) has nothing of the legend about it except the dragon crest on his helmet. Not even his shield and his sword are the traditional ones.[4] The story of his dream of the Faery Queen is borrowed from Chaucer, and it is prefaced by an account of his upbringing, not by Merlin, but by a classical figure called old Timon. Except for these two brief passages in Canto vii, Book I has nothing in it which is traditional matter of Britain.

Book II has only the chronicle of British kings from Geoffrey's *Historia*, and it is not until we reach Book III that the matter of Britain is worked into the plot. Here it is part of the story, not of Arthur, but of the nonlegendary Britomart. She visits Merlin and is given an account of her descendants, in direct imitation of Ariosto's Bradamante, who also visits Merlin and learns of her descendants. There is no matter of Britain in the second instalment until we come to Book VI, where for the first time Malory is openly levied upon. Here Sir Tristram is

[3] Howard Maynadier, *The Arthur of the English Poets* (Boston: Houghton, Mifflin Co., 1907), p. 263.

[4] Maynadier (p. 266) suggests that the stone shaped like a woman's head in the center of Arthur's baldric may represent the virgin shield associated with Arthur, but I can see no connection. Spenser's Arthur carries a diamond shield which is imitated from that of the wizard in *O. F.*, II, 55 and 56, except that it is of diamond instead *di Piropo*, and it has added power like that of the Gorgon's head. Since the symbolism of the shield has been the subject of some discussion (see D. C. Allen, "Arthur's Diamond Shield in the *Faerie Queene*," *Journal of English and Germanic Philology*, XXXVI [1937], 234–43), it is worth noting that in G. Legh's *Accedens of Armory* (1562, 1568, 1576, etc.), fol. 29, the first shield is said to have been that of Minerva and is described as "a christalline shielde," the one she gave to Perseus, and also the one Ulysses took from Troy. In the Armida passage (*Gerusalemme Liberata*, xiv, 68, and xvi, 14 ff.), which Spenser knew so well, Rinaldo sees himself in a diamond shield, and the witch's spell is broken. The line of descent from Minerva and Perseus to Spenser's Arthur, with additions from Ariosto's and Tasso's adaptations, seems clear enough and provides the best clue to the significance of the shield.

introduced, the story of King Ryance and the mantle of beards is borrowed, and the Blatant Beast seems to echo Malory's Questing Beast.[5]

The situation can be summarized as follows: No clear and open borrowing from Malory appears in the poem earlier than Book VI. Geoffrey's *Historia* is drawn upon for a few lines in the account of Arthur in Book I and in the letter, and for the two cantos of British chronicle in II, x, and III, iii. The second part of this chronicle is a basic part of the story of Britomart and is used in imitation of a similar passage in Ariosto. Britomart was a late creation, as will be shown in the next chapter, and analysis of the part played by Arthur indicates that he was a late addition rather than an original plot idea in Books I and II.

It would appear, therefore, not only that Spenser did not begin with the idea of making Arthur the hero of the poem but that in the beginning he did not look upon either Malory or Geoffrey as source material for his poem. Chaucer, Ariosto, and the non-Arthurian romance of St. George were much more freely drawn upon.

We must, therefore, account both for Spenser's failure in 1578–80 to see the matter of Britain as the one inevitable basis for an English epic and for his attempt in 1589 to create the impression that Arthur was the chief hero of the whole poem. I believe that the solution of these two problems can be indicated by an examination of the reputation of Arthur before and during the decade (1579–89) when Spenser's plans were developing and his poem was growing.

There are two excellent studies of the reputation of Arthur

[5] Warton, in his remarks "Of Spenser's Imitations from Old Romances," introduces Malory with a great flourish and produces these examples from Book VI. Then he remarks that "further proofs of Spenser's copying this romance are perhaps superfluous" and ends weakly with a citation of Spenser's reference to Launcelot in the *View* (*Observations on the Fairy Queen* [London, 1762], I, 19–26). Besides the three borrowings in Book VI, Professor Maynadier (p. 271) thinks the name of the Castle Joyous in Book III may be from Malory. The list of borrowings has been extended by commentators who have begun with the assumption that the *F. Q.* is primarily a romance of Arthur and have adduced parallels in commonplace romance materials without regard to known sources (see, e.g., Marie Walther, *Malory's Einfluss auf Spenser's Faerie Queene* [Heidelberg diss.; Eisleben, 1898]).

which cover the sixteenth century,[6] but neither of them attempts a strictly chronological analysis which would indicate the materials available for a long poem, and so we must undertake that analysis here.

Medieval tradition recognized two distinct "matters" of Arthur—the historical and the fabulous. William of Malmesbury says: "It is of this Arthur that the Britons fondly tell so many fables, even to the present day; a man worthy to be celebrated, not by idle fictions, but by authentic history."[7]

The question whether Geoffrey belonged among the fablers or the authentic historians was always an open one. For the early Tudor period the two positions are illustrated by the English chronicle published by Caxton and by the new chronicles of England by Robert Fabyan. The latter says: "Of this Arthure is by Gaufryde recited a longe storye, & alowed by the English chronicle [i.e., Caxton], the whiche from other writers is greatly discordaunt. But yet all Authoures agreen that he was noble and vyctoryous in all hys deedes."[8] Fabyan goes on to say that he would like to report the noble deeds of Arthur for their moral, but that he is in doubt about them because of what he has read in Ralph Higden's *Polychronicon*, and so he will pass over. He mentions the twelve great battles against the Saxons and remarks that, according to Geoffrey, "he wrought wonders" in France but that the French and Roman chroniclers do not mention him; and so he leaves the whole story to the Welshmen, telling only of Mordred's treachery and Arthur's death in a brief way, making no mention of Guenevere or of the passing of Arthur to Avalon and his expected return.

Fabyan's history was abridged by John Rastell as *The Pas-*

[6] C. B. Millican, *Spenser and the Table Round* ("Harvard Studies in Comparative Literature," Vol. VIII [Cambridge, Mass., 1932]), has demonstrated the great popularity of Arthur throughout the Tudor period. R. H. Fletcher, *The Arthurian Material in the Chronicles* ("[Harvard] Studies and Notes in Philology and Literature," Vol. X [Boston, 1906]), surveys the sixteenth-century chronicles briefly in chap. xi.

[7] *William of Malmesbury's Chronicle*, trans. J. A. Giles ("Bohn's Antiquarian Library" [London, 1876]), p. 11.

[8] *The Chronicle of Fabian, Whiche He Nameth the Concordaunce of Histories, Newly Perused. And Continued from the Beginnyng of Kyng Henry the Seuenth, to Thende of Queene Mary* (1559), p. 92.

tyme of People (1529) in a critical spirit. He enlarged upon Fabyan's skepticism in respect to Arthur. It is not surprising, therefore, that Polydore Vergil discounted Geoffrey very heavily, following the lead of Higden, Fabyan, and Rastell. But his *Anglicae historiae libri xxvi* (Basel, 1534) appeared on the eve of the English Reformation, after the struggle with Rome was already joined. Polydore was an Italian and a Catholic, and his attack upon Geoffrey came at a time when the ancient empire of the Britains was being cited in support of Henry VIII's claim to independence from the Holy Roman Empire and the pope. A purely historical problem was thoroughly clouded by the emotions of national pride and religious prejudice. English vituperation of Polydore was as violent as though he had been quite alone in his skepticism.

However, Fabyan's position, and even his wording of it, was echoed by successive English chroniclers—Cooper, Grafton, and Stow—and by such distinguished scholars as Sir Thomas Elyot[9] and John Twyne.[10] The learned Thomas Cooper, in his continuation of Lanquet's *Epitome of Cronicles* (1549, 1559, 1560, and 1565), repeats Fabyan's statement about Arthur practically verbatim.[11] Grafton, who openly follows Cooper in many things, also quotes Fabyan on Arthur.[12] He dismisses Arthur's foreign conquests by saying that Arthur went to France, "where as sundrie Authors write, he wrought wonders." The 1570

[9] In the *Bibliotheca Eliotæ* (1538 ff.), under "Arthurus," "15 battles agaynst the Saxons" and the conquest of Scotland and Ireland are mentioned, but the other conquests are called "incredible fables." Elyot also rejected the story of the Trojan origin of the British, favoring a Welsh derivation of the name which he had learned from Richard Pace. The *Bibliotheca* was reprinted in 1545 and edited by Thomas Cooper in 1548, 1552, and 1559, and as Cooper's *Thesaurus* in 1565, 1573, 1578, 1584, and 1587.

[10] Twyne's learning is spoken of respectfully by Leland, Holinshed, and Camden. His *De rebus Albionicis, Britannicis atque Anglicis, commentariorum libri duo* was not published until 1590, but it reflects an enlightened, pre-Reformation attitude. He cites Vives and presents his material as a dialogue in which the speakers include the scholar, Nicholas Wotton, and two members of St. Augustine's monastery in Canterbury, John Dygon and Richard Fox, the last abbot. He calls Geoffrey *ille Homerus, ac mendaciorum pater* and attacks both the Trojan and the Arthurian legend.

[11] Ed. 1549, fol. 144^v. Same for the edition of 1559, ed. R. Crowley.

[12] *A Chronicle at Large* (1569), I, 105. See also his *Abridgement of the Chronicles of Englande* (1562, 1563, 1564, 1570, 1572).

Abridgement says that "he did meruelous thinges" (fol. 16^{v}). John Stow, who began publishing his *Summarie of Englyshe Chronicles* in 1565, repeats the formula established by Fabyan[13] and copies Grafton's skepticism about the French conquests. But he mentions the twelve battles against the Saxons and adds to the standard account mention of the Round Table and of the defeat of Lucius, the last very doubtfully. The 1573 edition repeats 1565, but by 1575 his dependence on Grafton has been reduced, and he quotes Malmesbury as to Arthur's worthiness "to haue aduauncement by true Histories" rather "than false Fables, being the onely proppe and vpholder of this his countrie."[14] And he adds Arthur's conquests in Scandinavia as far as Lapland, and in France.[15] In fact, it was Stow who reincorporated into the chronicles most of Geoffrey's romance. In the 1580 *Chronicles* (p. 15) he cites the *Historia* as "the receiued Brytish Historie," asserting that Geoffrey "translated out of the Brytishe tong." He gives Arthur the full count of conquests, "thirtie Kingdomes (such as they were in those dayes)."[16]

Meanwhile, in 1577 Holinshed's *Chronicles* appeared, prefaced by Harison's famous "Description of Britaine." Harison makes Arthur's "noble actes" include the subjugation of Scotland and the North "though manye vulgare fables haue rather steigned, then commended: yet al the scottish writers confesse, that he subdued great Britayne, and made it tributary to him."[17] Holinshed himself goes beyond Harison in his account of Arthur. He begins with the usual assertion that "of this Arthure many things are writen beyond credite," but he mentions the circumstances of Arthur's birth, his wife, and the British stories about his conquests, although he protects himself by discounting the latter. He also repeats Malmesbury's expression of regret that Arthur's real achievements are not recorded (pp. 131–37).

[13] Fols. 30^{v}–31. [14] Pp. 51–53.

[15] The Scandinavian conquests are from William Lambard (see below, n. 30).

[16] Pp. 85–86. The 1592 edition repeats 1580 except that it adds topographical details at several points.

[17] Fol. 42.

What had happened was that the defenders of Arthur, finding the ground swept from under them by enlightened historical criticism which pointed to the lack of corroboration of Geoffrey's *Historia* in Gildas and other contemporary sources, and which asserted that Geoffrey was inventing rather than translating as he pretended, set themselves to find other evidence. Nennius, who wrote before Geoffrey, mentioned the twelve great battles against the Saxons, and therefore that part of Arthur's story was looked upon as established. No one, not even Polydore, questioned that there had been a great king named Arthur. On the other hand, no one accepted Geoffrey's story that he had finally conquered Rome and been crowned emperor. Between these two extremes lay the battlefield over which historians, antiquarians, and Welsh patriots struggled. John Leland began the defense by gathering up all the local legends, traditions, and archeological remains he could find. He handled the foreign conquests doubtfully, however, and entirely discounted the conquest of Rome.[18] John Bale defended Geoffrey in 1548, citing Ponticus Verunnius as confirmation.[19] Sir John Price, another defender, stressed the importance of the Welsh records and attacked Polydore on the ground that he could not read them.[20] It was natural enough that the Welsh and the anti quarians should be the ones to rally to the defense of Geoffrey and of Arthur. But, while they presented evidence that there had been such a king as Arthur and that he had been very famous for various achievements and in various places, their search for local legends and relics did not produce a coherent story such as a poet might use for the plot of an epic. The great medieval fictions of Arthur's origin, of the doings of the knights of the Round Table, and of his passing were rejected by the historians as false fables. They were also distasteful to the Protestants because they contained elements of magic, witchcraft,

[18] *Assertio inclytissimi Arthurij regis Britanniae* (1544); see Richard Robinson's translation in the "E.E.T.S.: Original Series," No. 165 (London, 1925), pp. 42–44.

[19] In his *Illvstrivm maioris Britanniae scriptorvm*, fols. 84ᵛ–85.

[20] His *Historiæ Britannicae defensio* was written about 1553 but was not printed until 1573.

immorality, and "superstitious religion" (the latter in the monastic and Grail parts of the story).

A chronological examination of Arthur's reputation, both in serious history and in fiction, shows that he had a period of great popularity under the early Tudors, a middle period when remarkably little interest in him was shown, and a late Tudor period when he rose to great heights of popularity during the last two decades of Elizabeth's reign. This fluctuation of interest had both religious and political causes. The use which Henry VII made of the Welsh belief in the return of Arthur is well known and need not be reviewed here.[21] The Caxton publications of chronicles and of Malory belong in this period. The growth of Renaissance scholarship in England in the early years of Henry VIII and the antitraditionalism of the religious revolution, acting together, tended to discredit the sources of Arthur's story at a time when Tudor claims to the throne no longer needed buttressing. The antiquarians, Leland and Bale, were definitely reactionary in their defense of Arthur as well as in their anxiety over the destruction of the medieval libraries in England. They do not represent the main current of popular interests.

By mid-century Arthur's popularity, as it can be estimated from records of pageants, popular literature, and the chronicles, was at a low ebb. There was no effort made to celebrate the accession of Edward VI as the return of Arthur. He was Solomon and St. George but not King Arthur.[22] The advent of a female sovereign in Queen Mary presented a serious difficulty, and Mary was made a female worthy instead of a returned Arthur. Elizabeth presented the same problem to her courtiers, and they responded with the same solution. She was celebrated as Judith and Deborah and as one of the nine female worthies but not as the fulfilment of the Arthurian promise.[23] The sex

[21] See Lilian Winstanley, "The Arthurian Empire in the Elizabethan Poets," *Aberystwyth Studies*, IV (1922), 59–66; and Millican, chap. ii.

[22] An account of the coronation pageants is printed in J. Leland, *Collectanea*, ed. T. Hearne (London, 1770), IV, 310–33.

[23] See E. C. Wilson, *England's Eliza* ("Harvard Studies in English," Vol. XX [Cambridge, Mass., 1939]), chaps. i and ii. Roberta F. Brinkley, *Arthurian Legend in the Seventeenth Century* ("Johns Hopkins Monographs in Literary History," Vol. III

difficulty was a real one, and the political implications were no longer important. The Tudor claim to the English throne was no longer an issue, and the loss of Calais, the last bit of British empire on the Continent, made the vaunting tales of Arthur's conquests an empty mockery, particularly during the anxious early years of Elizabeth's reign. It must be remembered that there was little to suggest a return of English greatness in these years while they were passing. It was only after they were safely past that confidence in the caution, wisdom, and stability of the government threw its golden halo around the Queen.

Arthur had served a purpose in providing an appeal to the popular imagination in support of the Tudor house at its advent. Then the rising tide of scholarship had brought much of his history into question, and, aside from Welsh patriotism, there was no reason, political or otherwise, for insisting on the authenticity of the disputed Geoffrey until the antiquarians found a new use for the legend as support for the growing colonial and imperial ambitions which flourished in the latter half of Elizabeth's reign. It has already been pointed out that Arthur's conquests were used as a pretext for English claims of supremacy over the whole of the British Isles.[24] But these claims did not stop with Scotland, Ireland, and Wales. They were extended also to Iceland, Greenland, Norway, and most of Scandinavia. They were fostered alike by the Muscovy Company and by the voyagers to the Americas.[25]

[Baltimore, 1932]), p. 3, incautiously asserts that "the Arthurian ancestry of Elizabeth was given especial emphasis at the time of her coronation," but she cites no evidence, and I find none. Arthur did not figure in the coronation pageantry. See *The Passage of Our Most Dred Soueraigne Lady Quene Elyzabeth through the Citie of London to Westminster the Daye before Her Coronacion*, printed by Richard Tottel, January 23, 1558–59, reprinted in Holinshed's *Chronicles* (1587), III, 1172–80, and in John Nichols, *Progresses and Public Processions of Queen Elizabeth* (London, 1823), I, 38–60, and in *Tudor Tracts*, ed. A. F. Pollard (Westminster: Archibald Constable & Co., 1903), pp. 365–95; see also Il Schifanoya to the Castellan of Mantua, in the *Calendar of State Papers* [Venetian] *1558–80*, Vol. VII, ed. Rawdon Brown and G. C. Bentinck (London, 1890), pp. 11–19.

[24] Winstanley, pp. 61–66.

[25] E. K. Chambers, *Arthur of Britain* (London: Sidgwick & Jackson, 1927), chaps. iv and vii, pp. 231–32, points out the political use made of Arthur in the twelfth century and again at the end of the fifteenth. Arthur was a name to conjure with, not merely the hero of a romantic and impossible story.

It seems to have been this imperial ambition which was largely responsible for the recrudescence of enthusiasm for Arthur in the middle of Elizabeth's reign. The achievements of the voyagers fired the imaginations of Englishmen, and the learned antiquarian, John Dee, put forward the ancient conquests of Arthur as a basis for English claims to the newly discovered lands in North America and the Arctic.[26] His achievements as a mathematician made him a man of note to the voyagers, and his activities as an astrologer gave him access to the Queen. In 1577 he appealed to the reading public in favor of maritime expansion by publishing his *General and Rare Memorials Pertayning to the Perfect Arte of Navigation.*[27] This is largely an argument for "restoring . . . . the British Empire,"[28] which, we learn, includes "England, Ireland, and (by right) Scotland, and the Orknayes also." The same year Dee disclosed to the Queen her title to "Greenland, Estetiland, and Friseland." And the next year he prepared "Her Majesties Title Royall, to many forrain Countries, kingdomes, etc. . . . . for her Majesties use: and at her Majesties commandement." Part of this work he showed to such friends as Hakluyt and Mr. Daniel Rogers in 1578, but the Queen does not seem to have seen it until after Drake's return from his trip around the world in the autumn of 1580.[29]

Another antiquarian, William Lambard, had produced a document purporting to be from the laws of Edward the Confessor, and therefore independent of Geoffrey, which justified English claims to all of Scandinavia as far as the borders of Russia.[30]

[26] Millican (pp. 42–51) summarizes Dee's propagandizing activities. Dee's manuscript copy of Geoffrey of Monmouth, with his annotations, has been preserved in the College of Arms.

[27] The running title is "The Brytish Monarchie." Dee was interested in the chronicles in 1575 (see the *Lists of Manuscripts Formerly Owned by Dr. John Dee*, ed. M. R. James for the Bibliographical Society [Oxford, 1921], Nos. 52 and 69).

[28] Marginal note on p. 6.

[29] Millican, pp. 42–45.

[30] In *APXAIONOMIA* (1568) (see Millican, pp. 43–48, 76–77). The document was used by Dee in 1578 and translated by Hakluyt in his *Principall Nauigations* (1589), pp. 244–45.

This combination of imperial ambition and antiquarian enthusiasm furnished the motive for a rehabilitation of Geoffrey and of Arthur's story. But it was the return of Drake, in 1580, which more than any other single event stimulated the imaginations of Englishmen generally and fired them with a fresh enthusiasm for English maritime enterprise. As early as 1578 the Queen granted to Sir Humphrey Gilbert, one of Dee's friends, a patent to take possession of newly discovered lands, but it was Drake's return which did more than anything else to popularize this kind of adventuring.

What the first two decades of Elizabeth's reign gave to Englishmen was a sense of confidence in their own greatness and a feeling of considerable security and power, audible in the praises of the Queen, which are so much more fulsome and frequent in the last two decades of her reign than in the first two. It was only natural that the consciousness of present greatness should stimulate interest in past greatness also. Incited by self-confidence and imperial dreams, Englishmen of the 1580's produced a sudden abundance of publications inspired by Arthur's story.

In 1582 Richard Robinson presented the public with a translation of Leland's *Assertio*, and it is not without significance for Spenser that Robinson dedicated his work to Arthur, Lord Grey of Wilton, Sir Henry Sidney, and Thomas Smith, the leader of the Society of London Archers.[31] In 1584 David Powel made the most important single contribution to the rehabilitation of Geoffrey when he published Humphrey Llwyd's *Historie of Cambria*, a work which purports to be a translation of Caradoc of Llancarvan, a Welsh historian cited by Geoffrey as one of his authorities. Since Caradoc's account of Arthur was supposed to antedate Geoffrey, it was credited with great corroborative value. Powel followed it, the next year, with an edition of *Pontici Virunnii . . . . Britannicæ historiæ libri sex*, a work which was really a Latin prose condensation of Geoffrey,

[31] See Millican, pp. 54 ff. About the same time an unidentified "E.S." published *De rebus gestis Britanniae commentarioli tres*, which credits Arthur only with the twelve great battles against the Saxons. It is discussed by F. I. Carpenter, "Spenser Apocrypha," *The Manly Anniversary Studies in Language and Literature* (Chicago: University of Chicago Press, 1923), pp. 64–69.

but which was generally believed to be another independent authority.[32]

By 1586, when Camden published his *Britannia*, acceptance of much of Arthur's story had become the correct scholarly attitude. Camden is cautious and conservative rather than otherwise. He echoes William of Malmesbury's expression of regret that Arthur lived in an age

when ignorance (as it were) by fatall destinie bare such sway, that there was none to be found, by whose writings the renowne of Arthur might bee blazed, and commended to posteritie. A matter and argument doubtlesse, meet to have been handled by the skill and eloquence of some right learned man, who in celebrating the praises of so great a prince, might have wonne due commendation also for his owne wit. For, the most valiant Champian of the British Empire, seemeth even in this behalfe onely, most unfortunate, that hee never met with such a trumpetter, as might worthily have sounded out the praise of his valour.[33]

In 1588 Thomas Hughes made a Senecan tragedy out of Arthur's story,[34] and in 1589 Hakluyt included "Certaine Testimonies concerning King Arthur and His Conquests of the North Regions" in the second part of the *Principall Nauigations*, quoting from the 1587 edition of Geoffrey of Monmouth, the first edition to appear after Polydore's attack on his historicity.[35] For the time, the will to believe triumphed over the critical faculty, and the learned as well as the unlearned joined in the acceptance of Geoffrey's *Historia*. Professor Millican has discussed admirably the many publications mentioning Arthur in this period, and it is not necessary to describe them here.

[32] Powel's dedication to Sir Henry Sidney contains a defense of Arthur and of Geoffrey's *Historia*. As Lord President of Wales, Sidney was a natural patron of Welsh publications. But he seems to have been genuinely interested in British antiquities and to have prided himself on Welsh blood derived from his mother and involving a pedigree extending back to British antiquity. In this volume Powel also prints for the first time Giraldus Cambrensis' *Itinerarium Cambriae* and *Cambriae descriptio* with annotations and a dedication to Sir Philip Sidney.

[33] Philemon Holland's trans. (1637), p. 228. The original Latin will be found on p. 123 of the edition of 1587.

[34] *Certaine Deuises and Shewes Presented to Her Maiestie by the Gentlemen of Grayes-Inne at Her Highnesse Court in Greenewich, the Twenty Eighth Day of Februarie in the Thirtieth Yeare of Her Maiesties Most Happy Reigne* (1587/8). The play is usually referred to as the *Misfortunes of Arthur*.

[35] *Principall Nauigations*, pp. 243–44; and see Millican, p. 46 and *passim*.

What concerns us is the relation between the vicissitudes of Arthur's reputation and the growth of the *Faerie Queene*. When Drake returned from the Antipodes in the autumn of 1580, Spenser was already in attendance on Lord Grey in Ireland. By the time Powel's two publications appeared to rehabilitate Geoffrey as a historian, the *Faerie Queene* was well under way in some form.

As either fact or fiction, the story of Arthur was easily the best material for epic poetry available for an English poet. But while the struggle was going on over how much of it was fact and how much was fiction, anyone who attempted to make use of the Arthurian theme would find himself in immediate difficulty. Indeed, there is definite evidence that the subject was actually avoided during the years of controversy. It was a story well adapted to tragedy, as Thomas Hughes demonstrated in his *Misfortunes of Arthur*, published in 1588. Yet in 1578 Thomas Blenerhasset published the *Seconde Part of the Mirrour for Magistrates*, including the story of Uther but omitting that of Arthur. In one of his "Introductions" Blenerhasset apologizes for omitting Arthur and Cariticus by saying, "It is not much amisse, for of *Arthur* there be whole volumes."[36] Clearly, he felt that the subject was too much for him. The tragedy of Arthur was not added to the *Mirror* until 1610.[37] As late as 1586, William Warner was afraid of the Arthurian theme. He says:

> Yet blazing *Arthur* as haue some, I might be ouer-seene:
> He was Victorious, making one amongst the worthiest neene.
> But (with his pardon) if I vouch his world of Kingdomes wonne,
> I am no Poet, and for lacke of pardone were vndone.
> His Scottish, Irish, Almaine, French, and Saxon battelles got,
> Yeeld fame sufficient: these seeme true, the rest I credite not.[38]

As long as there was a dispute, the literary man was in a dilemma. If he made use of the fictional matter, he would offend

[36] Fol. 40.

[37] "The True Legend of Famous King Arthur, the Last of the Nine Worthies" is included in Robert Chester's *Loves Martyr* (1601), pp. 34–77; and Richard Niccols wrote "The Famous Life and Death of King Arthur" for his *Winter Nights Vision*, appended to his edition of *A Mirour for Magistrates* (1610), pp. 561–84.

[38] *Albions England* (1586), p. 80.

the historians by seeming to discredit Arthur as a historical figure, and he would offend the Puritans, who objected to fiction on principle. If, on the other hand, he tried to make a story out of the authenticated parts of Arthur's history, he would find his material not only impossibly circumscribed but also subject to constant change of status. The absence of an Arthurian tragedy from the *Mirror* and the general failure of poets and literary men to make use of Arthur, except in a vague, peripheral way in the royal entertainments of 1575 and 1578, can be accounted for by the controversial nature of his story during those years. And those were the years when Spenser was beginning to feel about for the subject of an epic poem. A decade later Hughes could handle the story of Arthur with considerable freedom,[39] and Spenser had decided to make Arthur the chief hero of his long poem. But ten years was as long, and as full of change, then as it is today, and we must not expect the letter to Ralegh, written in 1590, to represent the poet's plans as he conceived them in 1579. It was the state of Arthur's reputation during Spenser's college years, and the four years immediately following, which prevented the poet from recognizing him at once as the most suitable hero for an epic glorifying England.

Not only was Spenser hampered by the historical controversy but he was also influenced by the force of religious prejudice against the obviously fictional parts of Arthur's story. The early Protestants objected to fiction even when it had been sublimated into historical poetry. They "had rather haue good discipline deliuered plainly in way of precepts, or sermoned at large, as they vse," as Spenser remarks in his letter to Ralegh. The fictions of the *Morte d'Arthure* were particularly objectionable because they were full of "superstition." The Grail story dropped out of sight after 1521,[40] and Fabyan (followed by Cooper, Grafton, and the early Stow *Summary*) rejected the magical and supernatural elements in the stories of Arthur's

[39] Two lost plays, *The Life and Death of Arthur King of England* and *Uther Pendragon*, belong to the years 1597 and 1598, according to W. E. Mead's Introduction to Christopher Middleton's *The Famous Historie of Chinon of England* ("E.E.T.S.: Original Series," No. 165 [London, 1925]), p. xxxvii, n.

[40] Mead, *Chinon*, p. xlvi.

birth and passing and of the transportation of the Giant's Dance. Ascham was expressing a very common point of view when he said:

> In our forefathers tyme, whan Papistrie, as a standyng poole, couered and ouerflowed all England, fewe bookes were read in our tong, sauyng certaine bookes of Cheualrie, as they sayd, for pastime and pleasure, which, as some say, were made in Monasteries, by idle Monkes, or wanton Chanons: as one for example, *Morte Arthure:* the whole pleasure of which booke standeth in two speciall poyntes, in open mans slaughter, and bold bawdrye.[41]

Sir Philip Sidney's tutor, Nathaniel Baxter, in the dedication to his translation of Calvin's *Sermons* (1578), deplores the "reading of vile & blasphemous, or at lest of prophan & friuolous bokes, such as are that infamous legend of K. Arthur (which with shame inough I heare to be newly imprinted)."[42] He makes the basis of his objection clear by further reference to "the horrible actes of those whoremasters," Lancelot, Tristram, etc., and to "the vile and stincking story of the Sangreal." As late as 1589 Thomas Nash calls Arthur of the Round Table and such stories "the fantasticall dreames of those exiled Abbie-lubbers,"[43] and Sir John Harington, in asserting his belief in the historicity of Merlin and Arthur, makes it clear that he considered the magical and supernatural elements in the story a mere superstitious embroidery of the facts.[44]

The *Morte d'Arthure*, like most medieval literature, was Roman Catholic in spirit, at least in the eyes of the Protestants. Grafton, in the dedication of the 1570 edition of his *Abridgement of the Chronicles*, objects to the recent publication of books "bearing the name and Tytle of Collection of Stories, or Summaries of Histories . . . . which contayne fonde and vnmeete matter, as the memories of supersticious foundacions, fables and lyes foolishely stowed together." This may be another stab at

[41] *The Scholemaster* (1570), in *English Works* (Cambridge: University Press, 1904), pp. 230–31.

[42] *The Lectures or Daily Sermons, of the Reuerend Diuine, D. Iohn Caluine* (1578). See below, n. 46.

[43] *Anatomie of Absvrditie*, in *The Works of Thomas Nashe*, ed. R. B. McKerrow (London: A. H. Bullen, 1904), I, 11.

[44] *Orlando Fvrioso* (1607), pp. 22, 29–30.

his rival, Stow, but it applies much more aptly to the *Flores historiarum*, of which there were two issues in that year.[45] The publication of such works was suspected of encouraging the Catholics. It is not without significance, I think, that the only edition of the *Morte d'Arthure* between 1529 and 1578[46] was the one published in Mary's reign (1557).

There were purely political objections to the prophecies of Merlin, since these were too often applied to the delicate question of the succession. And there was objection to Malory and similar medieval fiction on the part of people who considered themselves too enlightened for belief in magic and fairy lore and who looked upon these books as relics of an age of ignorance

[45] Archbishop Parker was responsible for the publication of this work, the first edition of which appeared in 1567. The account of Arthur includes his defeat of the Romans and is interspersed with accounts of miracles. The whole work has a strong admixture of church history, with much celebration of bishops, martyrs, miracles, etc.

[46] The *Short-Title Catalogue of Books Printed in England*, ed. A. W. Pollard and G. R. Redgrave (London: Bernard Quaritch, Ltd., 1926), gives the date of this edition, printed by Thomas East, as 1585?, following H. Oskar Sommer, in his edition of *Le Morte Darthur by Syr Thomas Malory* (London, 1889–90), II, 8 n. Sommer deduces 1585 from a license for sixteen books, including the *Morte d'Arthure*, recorded in the Stationers' Register, March 12, 1581–82. He finds that one of these books was printed in 1586. But East had already printed at least five of them when the license was issued. Nathaniel Baxter described the *Arthure* as "newly imprinted" early in 1578 (see above, p. 75, for the quotation). Mr. William A. Jackson, of the Harvard College Library Treasure Room, has called my attention to Bernard Quaritch's *Catalogue of Books in English History and Literature*, No. 369 (London, 1922), Lot 648. Quaritch dates the East folio as 1578 on the evidence of the "state of the initials." Both Sommer and W. E. Mead (in his Introduction to *Chinon of England*, p. xxx) mention both a folio and a quarto edition as published by East in 1585. Mr. Jackson tells me that this error goes back to W. C. Hazlitt's *Hand-Book to the Popular, Poetical, and Dramatic Literature of Great Britain* (London, 1867), p. 14, where he distinguishes two folio editions on the basis of misinformation which he corrected in *Collections and Notes 1867–1876* (London, 1876), p. 13. His error was repeated, however, by Arundell Esdaile in *A List of English Tales and Prose Romances Printed before 1740* (London: For the Bibliographical Society, 1912), p. 97. Esdaile locates the second folio edition in the Cambridge University Library and asserts that in it East's name is spelled with a final *e*. But Mr. Jackson assures me that no such folio exists at Cambridge and that the pressmark cited for it by Esdaile is the old pressmark and not the modern one which Sayle gives for the East folio. Further confusion has arisen from the conversion of this ghost folio into a quarto. W. T. Lowndes, *Bibliographer's Manual*, ed. H. G. Bohn (London, 1875), I, 74, lists an undated East quarto, mentioned also by Sommer and by Mead. Sommer takes it for granted that there was a quarto edition, but the two copies of the East reprint which he locates—one the Bridgewater copy now at the Huntington Library and the other in the Huth collection—are both folios and of the same edition, that of 1578.

and superstition.[47] Evidence of Arthur's popularity, even among the vulgar, is very scanty during the middle third of the century, when the reformers were enjoying the first flush of victory and when the presses were chiefly turning out works of religious controversy.[48]

Not only the *Morte d'Arthur* but also *Arthur of Little Britain* had a revival in the 1580's.[49] Evidently, once the bars of critical skepticism were let down, the interest in Arthur overleaped the bounds of historicity entirely and extended into the field of romance. Arthur became a popular figure among all classes of readers as patriotism overrode religious and historical considerations alike.

The changing attitude of the times is reflected in Spenser's own publications. In the gloss to the "Aprill" eclogue (1579), "E. K." speaks with open scorn of "certain fine fablers and lowd lyers, such as were the Authors of King Arthure the great." This opinion does not purport to be Spenser's, but it reflects the attitude of an intimate friend who, presumably, had the same educational background as the poet. Yet in 1596 Spenser was ready to cite Arthur's conquest of Ireland as proof "by good recorde yett extant" of the English right of sovereignty.[50] The change in attitude toward Arthur and the reason for that change are both illustrated by these two quotations.

Apparently Sir Philip Sidney also changed his mind about the Welsh hero. In 1572 Humphrey Llwyd published a *Commentarioli Britannicae descriptionis fragmentum* (Cologne), which Thomas Twyne translated as *The Breuiary of Britayne* in 1573, and which Sidney and his friend Hubert Languet seem to have laughed at.[51] But in 1584 Sidney allowed Powel's edi-

[47] See Sidney Thomas, "Hobgoblin Runne Away with the Garland from Apollo," *Modern Language Notes*, LX (1940), 418–22.

[48] See Millican, pp. 194–95, n. 66; and Mead, *Chinon*, pp. xxv–xlvi, where there is a brief but useful survey of the evidence of Arthur's popularity in the sixteenth century.

[49] It was apparently printed in Mary's reign (1555?) and not again until 1582. *Huon of Bordeaux* was printed about 1534, and the next recorded edition was in 1601.

[50] *View of the Present State of Ireland*, ed. W. L. Renwick (London, 1934), p. 61.

[51] Millican, pp. 69–75; and W. A. Bradley (ed.), *The Correspondence of Philip Sidney and Hubert Languet* (Boston: Merrymount Press, 1912), pp. 35–40, 60–61.

tion of Llwyd's *Historie of Cambria* to be dedicated to him. The work was, in fact, prepared at the command of Sir Henry Sidney and was therefore especially under the patronage of the Sidneys.

It is probable that the condemnation of Malory was more general at Cambridge than elsewhere, since Ascham's influence was strongest there and since Cambridge was more concerned about the real, or historical, Arthur than was her sister-university, because she claimed Arthur as a founder.[52] Spenser was both a Cambridge man and a pupil of two disciples of Ascham, Richard Mulcaster and Gabriel Harvey. It does not seem at all strange, therefore, that as a youth with such a background Spenser did not, in 1578–80, see in Arthur the inevitable subject for the celebration of Queen Elizabeth.

Even his taste for antiquarian studies would be a bar to his use of Arthur as the subject of an epic poem. His laborious comparison of authors, which lies behind the chronicle of British kings in II, x, and III, iii, was not a method which *in extenso* would produce a heroic poem.[53] The scholar's conscience stood in the way of an imaginative creation based on Geoffrey, and the heat generated by the controversy formed an effectual wall of fire between Spenser and Malory.[54]

But by the 1580's, when Elizabethans were realizing the greatness of their age and were beginning to develop colonial ambitions, pride led them to look back also and to magnify whatever of greatness they could find in their past. The making of genealogies extended far beyond rational limits,

[52] W. L. Renwick, in his edition of *The Shepherd's Calendar* (London: Scholartis Press, 1930), p. 193, suggests the condemnation of Malory as a Cambridge tradition established by Ascham; Miss Lilian Winstanley, in her edition of Book I (Cambridge, 1915), pp. lxviii–lxix, expresses the same view.

[53] See his own account of his method, in the *View*, ed. W. L. Renwick (London, 1934), pp. 51–52; and Carrie A. Harper's *The Sources of the British Chronicle History in Spenser's Faerie Queene* ("Bryn Mawr College Monographs: Monograph Series," Vol. VII [Bryn Mawr, Pa., 1910]).

[54] Spenser seems not to have accepted the whole of Geoffrey even as late as 1596 (see Millican, pp. 92–93). It was the more enlightened opinion among the historians that the tale of Brutus, like that of Romulus and Remus, was fabulous; and this is the view which Spenser held.

and the Welsh genealogists proved too tempting a source of aggrandizement to be overlooked. As we shall see in the next chapter, the Order of the Round Table furnished not only fancy names for the Society of London Archers but also ancestors for some of the "new" nobility. Arthuriana were the rage of the moment, and by 1586 the village curate might recommend to the plowman that he "buy a booke of king Arthurs knightes, for the boy to read,"[55] and the Countess of Rutland's secretary paid five shillings for "K Arthure book" for his mistress and half that sum for "Mr. Camden's booke of the descripcion of England."[56]

Concerning Spenser's attitude toward Malory between 1580 and 1596, we know only this much: He did not make use of the name of a single one of Arthur's knights until he began Book VI. His borrowings of plot from Malory are so few and slight in the first three books (i.e., before 1590) that they could all have been added in the final polishing when these books were prepared for publication.[57]

We can hardly hope to fix an exact date for Spenser's conversion to the Arthurian theme, but I believe that we can postulate such a conversion as an explanation for the slight, schematic, and disconnected use made of Arthur in the poem, in contrast to the prominence given to him in the letter to Ralegh. Whatever the course of the poem may have been, it is clear that Spenser did not solve his problem of subject matter simply and immediately by recognizing the inevitability of the Arthurian theme. The history of the growth of Arthur's reputation seems to provide us with an explanation of this fact. But, whatever the cause, it is essential to any understanding of the structure of the poem to recognize that Arthur was a late and superficial addition and not a basic ingredient in the poet's plans.

[55] John Ferne, *The Blazon of Gentrie* (1586), II, 23.

[56] The purchase is dated May 7 (see *Historical Manuscripts Commission: The Manuscripts of His Grace the Duke of Rutland . . . . at Belvoir Castle*, IV [1905], 388).

[57] The very slight use made of Malory in Book I is commented upon by the editor of *Variorum*, I, 399.

VII
LEICESTER'S PLACE IN SPENSER'S PLANS

Or if thee please in bigger notes to sing,
Aduaunce the worthy whome shee loueth best,
That first the white beare to the stake did bring.
—"October," ll. 46–48

THE lines in which the poet discusses his epic ambitions in the "October" eclogue hardly leave room for question that he intended to include topical material in his long poem, as Vergil and Ariosto had done in theirs. He explains in the letter to Ralegh that the Faery Queen, Gloriana, and Belphoebe all represent Queen Elizabeth. But the identification of other characters is left to the reader's ingenuity. The earliest attempt to identify Prince Arthur was made by Dryden, who remarked: "But Prince Arthur, or his chief patron Sir Philip Sidney, whom he intended to make happy by the marriage of his Gloriana, dying before him, deprived the poet both of means and spirit to accomplish his design."[1] Upton was dissatisfied with this obviously mistaken suggestion,[2] and in his edition of the poem he argued that Arthur represented the Earl of Leicester. His position has come to be the accepted one, although there have been some dissenting voices. But if Arthur was not the chief hero of the early version of the poem, the whole problem of Leicester's place in Spenser's plans must be reconsidered.

If the Faery Queen was Spenser's starting-point, and the poem evolved from a compliment to the Queen's chastity to the final grandeur of Gloriana by several discernible steps, the lover

[1] *Essays of John Dryden*, ed. W. P. Ker (Oxford, 1900), II, 28.

[2] In his *Letter concerning a New Edition of Spenser's Faerie Queene* (London, 1751), pp. 7–8, he expresses the opinion that, although Arthur "traditionally" was supposed to represent Sidney, the rescue of Belge belongs rather to Leicester.

of the Queen must also have developed from the champion of chastity and enemy of lust, perhaps through an intermediate stage when he was a knight of Maidenhead, to the final conception of Arthur as the model of all virtues. But the two chief characters did not both develop at the same time. In fact, the love story did not develop at all beyond the initial situation. Spenser turned his attention to the court of the Faery Queen, created the Order of Maidenhead, and busied himself with the exploits of that order. Whoever took the place of Sir Thopas either became one of these knights or was neglected altogether. In the last chapter I explained why I do not believe that this person was called Arthur. Probably throughout a long middle period in the development of the poem the *Sir Thopas* plot dropped out of active use or out of the poem altogether. It seems to have been resurrected after much of the first instalment was written, when Spenser decided to add Arthur to his cast of characters.

However, it does not follow that, if Arthur was a late addition to the plot, the celebration of the Earl of Leicester had no part in the early version. Curiously enough, it has escaped the attention of students of the poem that two knights of the Order of Maidenhead were named as a compliment to the house of Dudley. Both of these knights figure in the first instalment of the poem. They are Arthegall, or Artegall (Spenser uses both spellings), and Guyon. They are named for the two most famous legendary earls of Warwick, and the earldom of Warwick was hereditary in the Dudley family, which in Spenser's day consisted of Ambrose, Earl of Warwick, Robert, Earl of Leicester, Mary, Lady Sidney, and the Countess of Huntington.

The Dudleys were descended from Margaret, eldest daughter and heir of Sir Richard Beauchamp, last and most famous of a line which had held the title to the earldom of Warwick since the Conquest.[3] The Beauchamp earls boasted descent from the ro-

[3] Margaret married John Talbot, Earl of Shrewsbury. Their daughter, Elizabeth, married Edward Grey, Baron and Viscount Lisle. Grey's daughter, Elizabeth, married Edmund Dudley, Henry VII's notorious tax-gatherer, who was the father of John Dudley, created Earl of Warwick in 1547. He was later Earl of Northumberland and lost his head for trying to put his daughter-in-law, Lady Jane Grey, on the throne. His

mance hero, Guy of Warwick, who was regarded as a historical personage until late in the eighteenth century.[4] The arms of the earldom of Warwick were supposed to have descended from him.

It is curious that no one has noticed that Guy's name was frequently lengthened to *Guyon* in the sixteenth-century version of his romance.[5] Spenser is merely using the longer form of the name of a very famous hero, who was closely associated with Warwick. He does not, so far as I can see, borrow any of the adventures of Guy for Guyon, but he very appropriately makes a palmer Guyon's companion. Palmers are not infrequent in the romances, but *Guy of Warwick* is a palmer romance par excellence.

When he had won Felice, Guy repented of his worldliness and spent the rest of his life (and a large part of the story) disguised as a palmer. In that disguise he visited the Holy Land, returned in time to defeat Colbrand, and lived and died at Guy's Cliff, just outside Warwick. Moreover, his faithful friend, Heraude of Arderne, on more than one occasion disguised himself as a palmer to help his friend. The garb of a palmer is, therefore, peculiarly appropriate for Guyon's mentor and alter ego.[6] And with the aid of this association, an Elizabethan reader, familiar with both forms of Guy's name as they appear in the

---

eldest surviving son, Ambrose, was restored to the earldom of Warwick by Queen Elizabeth (see Arthur Collins, *Letters and Memorials of State* [London, 1746], I, 10–16; and Sir Philip Sidney's defense of the Earl of Leicester, in A. Feuillerat's edition of *The Complete Works of Sir Philip Sidney* [Cambridge: University Press, 1923], III, 61–71).

[4] See "Guy of Warwick," *Dictionary of National Biography*. William Dugdale treats the romance as historic in *The Antiquities of Warwickshire* (2d ed., 1730), I, 374–76.

[5] The form *Gyowne* appears occasionally, as a rhyme word, in the fifteenth-century version of *The Romance of Guy of Warwick*, ed. J. Zupitza ("Early English Text Society: Extra Series," Nos. 25 and 26). The text printed by William Copland about 1560 spells the name *Guyon* in ll. 397, 1276, 1444, 1630, 1633, 1861, 1878, 1889, 1898, etc. (see the edition by Gustav Schleich in *Palaestra*, CXXXIX [1923]). The forms *Guyoun*, *Gyoun*, etc., occur also in the Auchinleck and Caius MSS, ed. Zupitza ("Early English Text Society: Extra Series," Nos. 42, 49, 59). *Variorum*, I, 389, records the far-fetched suggestion that the name *Guyon* was derived from *gyon*, a word which Caxton, in his *Life of St. George*, etymologizes as meaning "a wrestler." I. E. Rathborne suggests that *Guyon* is a French name intended "in some way" to celebrate "the Norman-French element in the ancestry of Elizabeth" (see *The Meaning of Spenser's Fairyland* [New York, 1937], pp. 179–81).

[6] See M. Y. Hughes, "Spenser's Palmer," *ELH*, II (1935), 151–64.

Copland text, would have had no difficulty in recognizing that Spenser had named his Knight of Temperance after the famous Warwick hero as a compliment to the house of Dudley.

If Guy was the most famous of the Saxon ancestors of the earls of Warwick and author of the Warwick arms, Arthegall was the most famous of the legendary British earls, a knight of the Round Table in the days of King Arthur.

Geoffrey of Monmouth very thoughtfully put into Arthur's court representatives of all the earldoms extant in his own day,[7] and he names Arthgall "quae Walguit (Warwick) appellatur." Thereafter, whatever historians might decide about the authenticity of Geoffrey's *Historia*, the genealogists found him too rich a mine to abandon. John Rous, the famous fifteenth-century Warwick antiquarian, constructed an elaborate *Roll* of the earls and benefactors of Warwick, which includes Arthegall. John Hardyng mentions "Arthegall therle of Warwycke [full] corageous,"[8] and Spenser may have taken one of his two spellings of the name from this source. An Elizabethan copy of the famous *Rous Roll* names "Artigallus, Arthall, or Artigalthus, Erle of the Citie of Caer gweire, now Warwick, a knyght of the round table, in Arthure's Dayes, a lord of the blode royall, wittie in all his Doynges."[9] A fourth spelling of the name, "Artigal," appears in the marginal gloss.

John Leland had access to a genealogy of the earls of Warwick which agreed substantially with Rous in its account of "Arthgal the first erle of Warwicke,"[10] although it differs from Rous in other respects. Richard Grafton mentions Arthgall in

[7] E. K. Chambers, *Arthur of Britain* (London, 1927), pp. 37–38, 47.

[8] *The Chronicle of Ihon Hardyng* (1543), fol. lxxi.

[9] John Rous made two of these rolls. One, now in the College of Arms, is in Latin and Lancastrian in tone; the other is English and Yorkist. The latter was printed by William Pickering in 1845 and edited and published by William Courthope in 1859 as *This Rol Was Laburd & Finishid by Master John Rows of Warrewik.* A rough-colored copy of the roll (Lansdowne MS 882), apparently made in the time of Elizabeth, is printed in T. Hearne's edition of the *Historia vitæ et regni Ricardi II* (Oxford, 1729). See p. 221 for the above quotation. It omits the saints and many of the English kings, whom Rous names as benefactors of Warwick, and devotes itself to the earls.

[10] See his *Antiquarii de rebus Britannicis collectanea*, ed. T. Hearne (London, 1770), IV, 125–28.

his *Chronicle*, giving the same details and in the same order as Leland. He says:

> In this tyme also I finde mencion made of a noble and valiant man called Arthgall, and he was the first Erle of Warwicke, and he was one of the knightes of the round Table of king Arthure, after whome folowed by succession Moruyde, and Merthrude. This Arthgal tooke a Beare for his beast because [of] the first sillable of his name which is *Arth* in the Britishe speche, and is in English a Beare.[11]

Arthegall's position as the first and Arthurian Earl of Warwick, and his connection with the origin of the Dudley badge, a bear with a ragged staff,[12] made him a most suitable vehicle of compliment to the Dudleys, and Spenser would have had to go no further than Grafton's *Chronicle* to find him.

The Arthegall-Warwick-Dudley connection has been missed because the champion of Irena in Book V has long been identified with Arthur, Lord Grey of Wilton, and uncritical commentators have made the simple equation: Arthegall is Lord Grey. But there is no reason to associate the lover of Britomart in Books III and IV with Lord Grey. Edmund Malone suggested that Arthegall is "a fictitious name, formed from the first syllable of Lord Grey's Christian name, and the French word *egal*,"[13] but the source of the name in British legend is incontestable.

John Upton attempted to make a rebus of Grey out of Spenser's description of Arthegall's crest and arms (III, ii, 25). The poet says that "his crest was couered with a couchant Hound," which Upton would have to be a *grey*hound. But Rous says

[11] *A Chronicle at Large and Meere History of the Affayres of England* (1569), I, 106. Grafton's immediate predecessors, Cooper and Fabyan, whom he cites elsewhere as authorities, do not mention Arthgall; but Grafton's motive for putting in this paragraph can be guessed. He dedicated the *Chronicle at Large* to Sir William Cecil, but the *Abridgement*, published the next year, is dedicated to Leicester.

[12] Rous ascribes the origin of the ragged staff to Gwayr, the immediate predecessor of Arthegall, "a noble prince of the blode Ryal of the brutayns ny cosyn to Kyng arthur," who slew a giant with such a club, or to one of his successors. He gives a shield decorated with this club to Gwayr and also to Arthegall and his two successors. M. A. Lower, in his *The Curiosities of Heraldry* (London, 1845), p. 164, attributes the same episode to Arthegall's son, Moruyde.

[13] *The Plays and Poems of William Shakespeare*, ed. James Boswell (London, 1821), II, 199.

that the first builder of Warwick was Guthelinus, "hole kyng of grete Brytayn in the time of King Alexander the Great," and beside his picture he puts a helmet surmounted by the crest of Wales; viz., upon a ducal coronet a cradle of fretwork in which is a greyhound in a couchant position. Spenser's couchant hound is not a rebus for Grey but a historic crest of the earldom of Warwick. The poet goes on to say that Arthegall's arms are very old and are inscribed "Achilles armes, which Arthegall did win." Here he is probably imitating Ariosto, who has Mandricardo wear Hector's armor (XIV, 43; XXIII, 78) and Ruggiero bear Hector's arms on his shield (XXVI, 99 ff.). The arms on Arthegall's shield seem to be symbolic and allusive rather than heraldic. Upton is certainly mistaken in identifying ermine with gris in an effort to make another rebus for Grey. Ermine and gris are two distinct furs, both in reality and in heraldry. Spenser says,

> And on his shield enueloped seuenfold
> He bore a crowned litle Ermilin,
> That deckt the azure field with her faire pouldred skin.

Ermine, as an animal, is very rare in English heraldry, but there was a legend that the arms of Brittany were ermine (the fur) because an ermine came and sat on Brutus' shield while he lay asleep one day when he was in that country.[14] Ermine was a symbol of purity, as azure was of nobility, and the crown, of royal blood. If we assume that the crown was gold, then the colors of Arthegall's shield were the same as those of the earldom of Warwick, which were "Chequy, Or and Azure, a chevron Ermine." Arthegall's ermine was "pouldred" because the animal was represented as sprinkled with black hairs in groups of three, just as the fur was pictured by the heralds.[15]

When in Book III he created Arthegall as the lover of Britomart, Spenser was paying a genealogical compliment to the

[14] See Lower, p. 55.

[15] See the "Ermine" portrait of Queen Elizabeth by Nicolas Hilliard, represented by a fine engraving in Henry Ellis' *Original Letters, Second Series* (London, 1827), Vol. III, Frontispiece. The portrait shows the animal on her left sleeve. It has a crown around its neck as a collar and is "pouldred." Probably the idea came from the brown tails which were commonly used to decorate the fur.

Dudleys, following exactly the model of Ariosto's romance of Ruggiero and Bradamante, which paid similar tribute to the ancient house of Este. The Artegall of Book V is made up of three different concepts, probably representing three different periods of composition. A determined effort has been made to see Lord Grey in each of the three parts, but the first part is made up of very stiff and formal allegories of justice, the second part is concerned with the romance of Britomart, and only the introductory stanzas in Canto i and the third part take up the rescue of Irena which has led to the association of Artegall with Lord Grey. In a recent article I have shown that in this passage Spenser was alluding to the rescue of Ireland undertaken by Sir John Norris in 1595 rather than to the earlier rescue (1580–82) by Lord Grey.[16] The contents of Book V will be discussed in due course. Here it is necessary only to notice that Book V was put together some years after Leicester's death, when the poet might, understandably enough, have dropped his effort to flatter the Earl.

When he created the romance of Arthegall and Britomart in the 1580's, Spenser worked into it not only the originator of the Dudley badge and allusions to the traditional Warwick arms, but also apparently a representation of the Dudley crest. The crest represented Agnes Hotot, who married a Dudley in 1395.[17] It commemorated her taking of her father's place in a trial by combat with one Ringsdale when her father was too ill to fight. She unhorsed her opponent, and then, when he was down, she loosened her helmet, letting down her hair and displaying her maidenly bosom. The crest showed a woman's head with hel-

[16] See "The Allegory of Sir Artegall in *F. Q.*, V, xi–xii," *Studies in Philology*, XXXVII (1940), 177–200; and see chap. xv below.

[17] See *The Visitations of Bedfordshire, 1566, 1582, and 1634*, made by William Harvey, Robert Cooke, and George Owen ("Publications of the Harleian Society," Vol. XIX [London, 1884]), p. 100; "H. S. G.," "The Dudleys and the Suttons," *Herald and Genealogist*, II (1865), 498. Dean Dudley says that the story is told by Martin of St. Ives, parson of Clapton, who wrote about 1390 (see *History of the Dudley Family* [Wakefield, Mass.: Dean Dudley, Publisher, 1886 ff.], p. 39 n.). This family tradition may have suggested the Amazonian attendants of Ambrose Dudley (also called Sutton) at his wedding in 1565 (see J. Leland, *Collectanea*, II, 666–69). It may also have had something to do with the Amazon episode in the story of Artegall in Book V.

met open and hair hanging down. It hardly seems a coincidence that Arthegall should be named in honor of the legendary creator of the Dudley badge and that Britomart should be a warrior maid who more than once presents an image of the Dudley crest by opening her helmet and letting her hair fall down (see III, ix, 20, and IV, vi, 19–20).

It is true that Britomart is a close imitation of Ariosto's Bradamante, who also on occasion opens her helmet and lets down her hair. But this parallel supports rather than refutes the allusion. Ariosto created the romance of Ruggiero and Bradamante as a genealogical compliment to his patrons, the brothers Ippolito and Alphonso d'Este. He traces the descent of the D'Estes from Ruggiero and Bradamante. Spenser is closely imitating Ariosto in his romance of Arthegall and Britomart; we should naturally expect Britomart, therefore, as well as Arthegall, to compliment in some way the Dudley family. The parallel has been obscured and largely missed because of the mistaken tradition which identifies Arthegall with Lord Grey of Wilton.

When it is recognized that Spenser was undertaking to do for the Dudleys what Ariosto had done for the D'Estes, the approximate date of creation of the romance of Britomart becomes determinable. The account of Britomart's descendants, which occurs early in her book (Canto iii), shows the use of material found in Powel's *Historie of Cambria*, published in 1584; and apparently the poet also consulted Camden, whose *Britannia* appeared early in 1586, and possibly Warner's *Albion*, which was not printed until late in 1586.[18] These datable borrowings indicate late 1585 or 1586 as the earliest probable date for the beginning of the story of Britomart. And if we glance at the fortunes of the Earl of Leicester, we can see why the poet was stirred to new effort in honor of the Dudleys at just that time. Leicester had been under something of a cloud since his

[18] Camden's work was licensed February 23, 1585/86. Warner's was licensed in November, 1586. Miss Carrie A. Harper finds an echo of Warner in Spenser only in Cordelia's reply to Lear and recognizes that this may be a coincidence (*The Sources of the British Chronicle History in Spenser's Faerie Queene* ["Bryn Mawr College Monographs," Vol. VII (Bryn Mawr, Pa., 1910)], p. 81 n.).

marriage in 1578. His prospect of marriage with the Queen was definitely gone, and his prestige was thereby somewhat impaired. But in the summer of 1585 the Queen decided to send an army to the aid of the Low Countries, and she appointed Leicester to the high command. His star seemed to be rising again, and Spenser, like others of the Earl's followers, was aroused to fresh hope and enthusiasm.

Once Arthegall has been identified as the legendary Arthurian Earl of Warwick, Spenser's insertion of his descendants into the line of British kings takes on new meaning. Merlin tells Britomart (III, iii, 26, 27):

> The man whom heauens haue ordaynd to bee
> The spouse of *Britomart*, is *Arthegall:*
> . . . .
> he is the sonne of *Gorlois*,
> And brother vnto *Cador* Cornish king,
> And for his warlike feates renowmed is.

According to legend, Uther Pendragon fell in love with the Lady Igrene, wife of Gorlois, and with the aid of Merlin he visited her, disguised as her husband. Afterward Gorlois was killed in battle, Uther married Igrene, and Arthur was born. The only son of Gorlois who is mentioned in the chronicles is Cador. In making Arthegall also the son of Gorlois and brother of Cador, Spenser is either inventing or following a tradition which I have not been able to trace. But it should be noted that John Rous says that Arthegall was "of the blode royall."

Spenser does not follow Geoffrey in his account of Arthur's immediate successors. Geoffrey says that Arthur left his crown to his nephew Constantius, son of Cador, from whom it was taken by Aurelius Conan, the *nephew* of Constantius. But Spenser follows a tradition reported by Stow[19] which makes Aurelius Conan also a nephew of Arthur and therefore a cousin of Constantius. Spenser says that the son of Britomart and Arthegall

> from the head
> Of his coosen *Constantius* without dread
> Shall take the crowne, that was his fathers right,
> And therewith crowne himselfe in th' others stead [st. 29].

[19] *A Summarie of the Chronicles of England* (1575), p. 54. This represents a correction of the 1565 *Summarie* (see fol. 32).

The unnamed son of Arthegall is here taking the place of Aurelius Conan. Spenser does not explain the claim of "right," but it may have had some justification in Warwick tradition,[20] or it may have been an invention of the poet's, in imitation of Ariosto, and in order to get the heir of his hero and heroine into the line of British kings. The earls of Warwick claimed descent from the ancient British kings but not necessarily descent of the ancient British kings from the earls of Warwick.

Professor Carrie A. Harper, in her study of the sources of the British chronicle history in the *Faerie Queene*,[21] comes to the conclusion that Spenser's chronicle was begun early, as an independent piece, which was revised later and converted into two cantos of the *Faerie Queene.* She finds that the poet derived the forms of the names which he used from some manuscript version of Geoffrey[22] and that his other chief sources were Holinshed (1577), Hardyng (1543), Stow (1580), and the *First Part of the Mirour for Magistrates* (1574). Of later works, Camden presents only two unique parallels, and four other books present one each. Obviously, the substance of the chronicle matter in II, x, and III, iii, could have been written by 1580. Miss Harper thinks that the poet would hardly labor so thoroughly over the details of a merely ornamental passage in the *Faerie Queene.* She calls attention to the fact that about 1580 Spenser was studying Holinshed in search of matter for his *Epithalamion Thamesis*, and she expresses the opinion that the early version of the chronicle was written at about the same time.

In view of the place given to Arthegall in Spenser's chronicle, I believe the most significant fact is that in 1580 Spenser had completed a *Stemmata Dudleiana.* The title definitely indicates a genealogical poem. He says of it in his letter to Harvey:

Of my *Stemmata Dudleiana*, and especially of sundry Apostrophes therein, addressed you knowe to whome, muste more aduisement be had, than so

[20] Rathborne (pp. 228 ff.) suggests that Spenser made these changes in order to clear Elizabeth's ancestry of the taint of usurpation.

[21] See n. 18.

[22] Nearly two hundred manuscripts of Geoffrey are still preserved (see the list in Acton Griscom's edition of *The Historia regum Britanniæ of Geoffrey of Monmouth* [London: Longmans, Green & Co., 1929], Appendix I).

lightly to sende them abroade: howbeit, trust me (though I doe neuer very well,) yet in my owne fancie, I neuer dyd better.[23]

An effort has been made to identify this piece with the *Ruines of Time*, and some of the old matter from the apostrophes may have found its way into the later composition. Spenser was apparently a very thrifty poet. But the *Ruines* are not a *stemmata*, and Gabriel Harvey says that the *Stemmata* was in Latin.[24] What is important for this study is not the problematical relation of the *Stemmata* to the *Ruines* but the fact that Spenser prepared a *Stemmata Dudleiana*.

His interest in Arthegall and Guyon came, unmistakably, out of a knowledge of the Dudley genealogy, and it is quite possible that his early studies in the British chronicle were the product of this interest. The Dudleys traced their descent not only from the ancient earls of Warwick but also from the line of ancient British kings. The genealogy is given in David Powel's edition of Humphrey Llwyd's *Historie of Cambria* (1584).[25] Powel dedicated the work to Sir Philip Sidney and published it at the direction of Sir Henry Sidney. Lady Sidney was Leicester's sister. Powel traces the Dudley blood back to Cadwallader, the last of the British kings, and so, of course, to the whole line of kings. He says that he used a "Brytish booke" which had been corrected by Robert Glover, the famous Somerset herald. Some of Glover's genealogies were published by his nephew, Thomas Milles,[26] and these do not go back of Roderick the Great, Prince of Wales, who descended from Cadwallader. But Glover was interested in the earlier and legendary earls of Warwick. He made a complete transcript of the histories and genealogies in the *Rous Roll*, and he also made notes on four other pedigrees

[23] *Oxford Spenser*, p. 612.

[24] *Ibid.*, p. 620.

[25] See p. 397.

[26] *Catalogue of Honor* (1610). According to this work, the Powys lands descended from Roderick to a certain Hawys who married an Englishman, the first Lord Powys, from whom "the Greys of the North" descended (see pp. 290 ff.). The Dudleys descended from these Greys, as well as from the lords of Malpas, who also claimed descent from Roderick the Great. Ambrose Dudley put twenty-one coats-of-arms on his Garter plate in 1561, including those of Warwick, Beauchamp, Talbot, Grey of Ruthin, Lisle, Sutton, Malpas, etc. (see the *Herald and Genealogist*, V [1870], 118–19 n.).

of the earls of Warwick.[27] The manuscript which contains this collection is dated 1572. At that time Leicester's marriage with the Queen was still talked of.

In 1580, when Spenser had just finished his *Stemmata Dudleiana*, Robert Cooke, Clarencieux King at Arms, completed a pedigree for the Earl of Leicester. It is described as a beautiful, large folio volume.[28] At Leicester House, Spenser would have access to the necessary genealogical materials, probably even to some copy of the *Rous Roll.*

A *Stemmata Dudleiana* worthy of the name, and of the poet, could hardly have begun any later than with Brutus. The British chronicle as it appears in the *Faerie Queene* breaks into two parts. The genealogy from the son of Britomart and Arthegall to Cadwallader appears in III, iii, and the earlier section, from Brutus to Uther, appears in II, x, where it seems to be rather artificially grafted into an already overlong book. It is represented as a book which Arthur reads. But Arthur does not learn of his ancestry from it, as we might expect, since it breaks off abruptly with Uther, and he does not know that he is Uther's son. It has been suggested that the chronicle was put into Book II because the Elizabethans believed that history taught morality. But that point could have been made without putting a long and elaborate section of history into the poem to prove it. Several critics have agreed with Miss Harper that the section of chronicle in II, x, was probably put there because the poet had found a use for the second section of his chronicle material in the story of Britomart and wanted to preserve the chronological order of the whole.

Both sections, as they finally appear, are represented as celebrating the great ancestry of Queen Elizabeth. She also descended from Brutus, via the succession of British kings to

[27] MS Ashmole 839 (see W. H. Black, *Descriptive .... Catalogue of the Manuscripts Bequeathed .... by Elias Ashmole* [Oxford, 1845]).

[28] It is preserved among the manuscripts of the Marquis of Bath at Longleat, Wiltshire (see G. Gatfield, *Guide to Printed Books and Manuscripts Relating to English and Foreign Heraldry and Genealogy* [London, 1892], p. 355). I have not seen this manuscript. *The Pedigree of Sir Philip Sidney by R. Cook, Clarenceux*, copied by A. Nesbitt and privately printed in 1869, does not go back of the Conquest.

Cadwallader. But there the two lines separated, except that both the Tudors and the Dudleys claimed descent from Roderick the Great. Perhaps it is only a coincidence, but Spenser's account of the Queen's lineage ends with Cadwallader, except for some scattered references to famous queens and the stanza on Roderick the Great.

The situation can be summarized as follows. In 1580 Spenser wrote that he had completed a *Stemmata Dudleiana* which he realized it would not be wise to publish at that time.[29] About 1585–86, when Leicester was appointed to command in the Low Countries, he began a romance of Arthegall and Britomart patterned on the genealogical tribute which Ariosto had created for his patron. If Spenser had a genealogical study of the Dudleys on hand, he would certainly make use of it, and we are not surprised to find Arthegall and Britomart worked into the line of British kings. The publication of Powel's book in 1584 showed that genealogical celebration of the Dudleys was not dangerous. Their claim to noble blood had been attacked in the scurrilous pamphlet called *Leicester's Commonwealth*, and Sir Philip Sidney wrote a defense of his uncle which may have helped to turn Spenser's thoughts in that direction again.

But Leicester died suddenly late in 1588; and when the first three books of the *Faerie Queene* appeared in 1589/90, the British chronicle was fitted with apostrophes to the Queen, and a fairy genealogy had been added which compensated to some extent for the fragmentary state of the account of the Queen's ancestry, but hardly for the intrusion into it of the first Earl of Warwick.

Guyon and Arthegall were named for famous earls of Warwick, and a compliment to the Dudley family was clearly intended. But I do not believe that either Arthegall or Guyon "represents" either the Earl of Warwick or the Earl of Leices-

[29] Pedigrees setting forth claims to royal blood, however remote, were always dangerous in the Tudor period. Leicester was already under a cloud for having married the Queen's second cousin. His sister was married to the Earl of Huntington, one of the chief Protestant claimants to the succession. We know that in 1580 Leicester was interested in his ancestry, perhaps because he hoped for an heir, but he would certainly object to the publication of a genealogy of the Dudleys because it would be certain to arouse jealousy and resentment.

ter. There seem to be some topical *allusions* which, like the selection of the names, served to flatter the Dudleys, but I trust that no one will try to see Lettice Knollys in Acrasia, or Anne Russell in Britomart, albeit Anne was fond of the somewhat masculine sport of hawking.

The motto of the Garter is put into the mouth of Arthegall (IV, vi, 6.1), and both Leicester and Warwick were Garter knights. Both Arthegall and Guyon are knights of Maidenhead, an order which imitates that of the Garter. Moreover, Guyon is especially devoted to the Faery Queen. He carries her picture on his shield—a fact which is mentioned no less than five times in his book. Eulogies of the Queen are put into his mouth in three places (II, ii, 40–42; ix, 4–6; x, 70–76). Allusion to Leicester's long devotion to the Queen may very well be intended. In II, vii, 50, when Guyon refuses the hand of "faire Philotime" (love of honor), he does so in terms which do not seem to have been inspired by the allegory, or the narrative, but which might be interpreted as an allusion to Leicester's marriage. Guyon says:

> But I, that am fraile flesh and earthly wight,
> Vnworthy match for such immortall mate
> My selfe well wote, and mine vnequall fate;
> And were I not, yet is my trouth yplight,
> And loue auowd to other Lady late,
> That to remoue the same I haue no might.

The description of Philotime's court has been compared with the account of court life in *Mother Hubberds Tale*, lines 877 ff., where Elizabethan court life is clearly indicated. Moreover, Guyon's plea of a previous bond might be compared with the well-known reference to "his late chayne" in *Mother Hubberds Tale*, lines 619–30.

It is possible that Spenser saw in Leicester the special champion of temperance, though in the political rather than in a private moral sense. But it does not follow that the illustrations of temperance in Book II represent Leicester's activities in any direct and topical way. Perhaps some further allusions can be found in the affairs of Arthegall; but, since Spenser is openly emulating Ariosto here, it would be wise to study the annotations of the *Orlando Furioso* and observe the way in which Ariosto was supposed to have handled his topical matter as a clue to the way in which Spenser was probably handling his. A few topical allusions are quite a different matter from a continued topical allegory.

I believe, however, that Guyon was a knight of Maidenhead, especially devoted to the Faery Queen, before he became the embodiment of temperance. It seems possible that in him we have the first substitute for Sir Thopas. The quest of Acrasia could have been planned as an illustration of chastity before it became the culminating episode of the Book of Temperance. The canto which describes the theft of Guyon's horse (II, iii) is written in what I believe was the tone of Spenser's early Ariosto imitation. The story of the recovery of the horse is suddenly produced in Book V (iii, 29–36), but the end is so far removed from the beginning that it looks more like an old fragment thriftily utilized at a convenient spot than like an effort to pick up a thread unobtrusively dropped many cantos earlier. If it had been Spenser's purpose to reintroduce his early heroes into later books, he could easily have given Guyon a part in the tournament which precedes the recovery of the horse. But, instead, Guyon appears suddenly without introduction or excuse, is on the scene for just eight stanzas, and then is not mentioned again.

In two places Guyon's name appears in stories about other heroes. Once, in the fight with Pyrochles and Cymochles, he is named instead of Arthur, and once early in Book III he is named where Redcrosse is indicated. In both cases the author made a mistake, but it is an open question whether the mistake was a failure to make necessary changes in names when he transferred stories from Guyon to other characters or whether he lost track of his own story as he wrote it.

Beyond these possible indications that Guyon once figured more largely in the adventures of the knights of Maidenhead we cannot go at present. But it is certainly not improbable that

Spenser's desire to celebrate Leicester as well as the Queen resulted in the introduction of Guyon and Arthegall into the early version of the *Faerie Queene*.

On the other hand, I do not believe it is at all probable that he ever intended Prince Arthur as a compliment to Leicester. This identification, though of long standing,[30] seems to me to be entirely vitiated by its failure to take into account the evidence of Arthur's place in the development of the poem, the chronology of the events which Spenser is supposed to be suggesting, and, above all, the significance of King Arthur in Tudor politics.

I have pointed out that the part of the lover of the Faery Queen failed to grow and that Arthur, as a historical or legendary hero, has so slight and disjointed a part that he was probably added late in the development of the first three books, possibly after Leicester's death, when the poet was converting his British chronicle material into tribute to the Queen. I have indicated how he may have supplanted two or three other figures.

Whether or not the late addition of Arthur to the poem be accepted, the contention that Spenser was trying to promote a marriage between the Queen and Leicester implies a doubt of the poet's sanity or moral decency. Leicester was regularly and legally married to the Countess of Essex in 1578, and the first we hear of the *Faerie Queene* is in 1580. Leicester's marriage put a definite end to all hope that he might marry the Queen.[31] Thereafter, while Leicester's wife lived, no sane man could have advocated such a thing.

[30] See above, p. 80.

[31] Camden says that the Earl of Sussex was glad that "by this Marriage he [Leicester] was now put beside all Hope of marrying with the Queen" (see *The History of .... Elizabeth* [4th ed.; London, 1688], p. 233, under the year 1579). E. K. Chambers thinks that Leicester had practically abandoned hope by 1567 (*Sir Henry Lee* [Oxford, 1936], p. 33). Sir Sidney Lee makes the date 1572 ("Robert Dudley," *Dictionary of National Biography*). The entertainment at Kenilworth in 1575 has been interpreted as an effort in that direction (J. W. Cunliffe, "Gascoigne and Shakspere," *Modern Language Review*, IV [1908–9], 231–33, and C. R. Baskervill, "The Genesis of Spenser's Queen of Faerie," *Modern Philology*, XVIII [1920–21], 49–54). As late as the autumn of 1578 Gabriel Harvey expresses the hope that Leicester may become a royal spouse (*Gratulationes Valdinenses*, p. 5).

But the most serious objection to the theory that Arthur was intended at any time to represent Leicester is an ideological one. Any courtier might be represented by an Elizabethan poet as the lover of the Queen, but to have called such a lover Arthur would have been to make prophetic implications about the succession amounting literally to high treason. Arthur was the great king who was to come again to rule England and create a new golden age. Only the king or his heir could therefore properly or safely be represented as Arthur. Henry VII had cultivated the Arthurian legend because it strengthened his claim to the throne. If Elizabeth had been a man, she would have been celebrated as the returned Arthur. But no person of lesser rank could be properly, or even safely, so represented. It is indicative of the significance attached to the name that the pretender who claimed to be the son of Elizabeth and Leicester, and who was in the pay of Spain, called himself Arthur.[32]

Camden says that in his youth he "heard some oftentimes say" that Leicester planned to "obtrude upon the English some Bastard-son of his for the Queen's *natural* Issue";[33] but no friend of Leicester's would suggest such an ambition in the Earl. The question of the succession was a delicate and dangerous one throughout the reign, and the Queen was extremely sensitive about it.[34] She would have been outraged if any poet had dared to celebrate one of her courtiers as King Arthur.

[32] See "B. C.'s" letter from Madrid, May 28, 1588, printed in Henry Ellis, *Original Letters, Second Series*, III, 135–36.

[33] *History*, p. 167, under 1571.

[34] In 1571 a statute made the writing of books about the succession a crime (see Camden, pp. 166–67). Lord Henry Howard was in serious trouble in 1581 over a book of prophecies which concerned the succession (see *Calendar of State Papers, Domestic, 1581–90*, ed. R. Lemon [London, 1865], pp. 1 ff.; and Howard's *Defensative against the Poyson of Supposed Prophecies* [1583], reprinted in 1620, pp. 116^{v} and 120–21^{v}). A. E. Parsons, "The Trojan Legend in England," *Modern Language Review*, XXIV (1929), 253–64, 394–408, sketches some of the problems involved; and see Kerby Neill, "The *Faerie Queene* and the Mary Stuart Controversy," *ELH*, II (1935), 192–214, for one phase of the subject. The Earl of Essex was so frightened that he pretended to be sick in 1594 when Doleman's book which discussed the succession was dedicated to him (see G. B. Harrison, *The Life and Death of Robert Devereux Earl of Essex* [New York: Henry Holt & Co., 1937], pp. 88–90; and *Historical Manuscripts Commission Report on the Manuscripts .... at Penshurst Place* [London, 1934], II, 182–84).

The entertainment at Kenilworth in 1575 has been cited as evidence that Leicester was associated with Arthur, but the Arthurian association is rather with Kenilworth than with Leicester. The Round Table was revived there in the thirteenth century,[35] and the fiction upon which the Elizabethan entertainment was based was that "the Castle of *Kenelworth* should seeme stil to be kept by *Arthurs* heires and their servants."[36] The late Professor Baskervill argued that Leicester overshot his mark in glorifying himself,[37] but the entertainment by no means goes so far as to suggest that Leicester is the returned Arthur. It merely suggests that Leicester possessed Welsh royal blood.

A similar argument is put forward in regard to the pageants welcoming the Earl to the Low Countries in 1586. In one of these was represented, "as if it had beene in a cloud or skie, Arthure of Britaine, whom they compared to the earle."[38] Again, actual identification is avoided, but the adulation of Leicester in these pageants was offensive to the government, and the account of them which was prepared for the second edition of Holinshed's *Chronicles* (1587) was censured by the Privy Council and excised. Also expurgated was "A Discourse of the Earles of Leicester by Succession."[39] After Leicester's death in 1588 there was no longer any objection to the matter of the pageants, and Stow published most of it in his *Annales* in 1592. But, if Spenser knew of these pageants before 1592, he prob-

[35] The Arthurian associations of Kenilworth are noticed by Warton, *Observations on the Fairy Queen* (London, 1762), I, 28 n.; see also Mary E. Giffin, "Cadwalader, Arthur, and Brutus in the Wigmore Manuscript," *Speculum*, XVI (1941), 109–20.

[36] C. B. Millican, *Spenser and the Table Round* (Cambridge, Mass., 1932), p. 105, from Gascoigne's account, which gives more of the Arthurian background than Laneham's *Letter* does.

[37] *Op. cit.*, p. 51.

[38] I. L. Schulze, "Spenser's Belge Episode and the Pageants for Leicester in the Low Countries, 1585–86," *Studies in Philology*, XXVIII (1931), 235–40. Mr. Schulze does not mention the expurgation of the account of the pageants from the 1587 Holinshed.

[39] The unexpurgated text was printed by Henry Ellis in his edition of the *Chronicles* (1808), IV, 630–52. Most of the surviving copies of the 1587 edition show the expurgations, however.

ably knew also of the expurgation, and he would hardly attempt to please the Queen by flouting her council and echoing the objectionable matter.

Arthur's rescue of Belge in Book V has been cited repeatedly as evidence that Arthur "represents" Leicester. But again chronology is against it. It is true that contemporary reports of Leicester's achievements in the Low Countries bear some resemblance to Spenser's account of the rescue of Belge,[40] although Leicester's real accomplishments were negligible. If Spenser had written the Belge episode before Leicester's death, he might have taken an optimistic view of Leicester's achievements; but, even so, I do not believe that he would have deliberately added fuel to the Queen's anger over Leicester's acceptance of too much sovereignty from the Dutch states by representing him as Prince Arthur.

But there is no reason to suppose that the Belge episode was written before 1593 or 1594 at the earliest. It appears in a section of Book V which I have shown was the last part of the second instalment to be completed.[41] It is a true picture of the rescue of Holland, with English aid, in the years from 1591 to 1595. From 1585 until about 1591 Dutch fortunes declined steadily, but the tide of war turned in 1591, and by 1595 most of the cities had been freed from Spanish control. Since there is no reason to suppose that the passage was written before 1590, there is no reason to interpret it as inaccurate adulation of Leicester, who died in 1588, instead of as a true picture of the Dutch situation in 1593 or 1594.

I think that it is very doubtful whether Spenser would have ventured to represent Belge as rescued by Arthur if Leicester had lived. As it was, no single English commander could be looked upon as the savior of the Netherlands, and so it was quite safe to assign that exploit to Arthur. There was no living individual in Spenser's day who could be safely and appropriately celebrated as King Arthur. But he could serve as an appro-

[40] See Viola B. Hulbert's "The Belge Episode in the *Faerie Queene*," *Studies in Philology*, XXXVI (1939), 124–46.

[41] See above, n. 16.

priate symbol of English greatness, or of the English nation, and I believe that it was so that Spenser intended to represent him.

He must have known of the Queen's own suggestion that her proper mate was England. When her first parliament asked her to select a husband, she replied:

> I have already joyned my self in Marriage to an Husband, namely, the Kingdom of *England*. And behold (said she, which I marvell ye have forgotten,) the Pledge of this my Wedlock and Marriage with my Kingdom. (And therewith she drew the Ring from her Finger, and shewed it, wherewith at her Coronation she had in set form of words solemnly given her self in Marriage to her Kingdom.)[42]

This dramatic episode was well known to the annalists of the day. There was a popular ballad called "A Song between the Queen's Majesty and England" (1558/59) which represents England as the true lover of the Queen.[43] It is as the symbol of the greatness of England that Arthur is the true lover of the Queen, the rescuer of Belge, and the representative of that magnificence, akin to divine benevolence, which is the highest attribute of kings.

Guyon and Arthegall are recognizable tributes to Leicester, at least in the choice of names. They sufficiently account for John Florio's statement (printed in 1591, before Book V was published) that Leicester was "thrice-fortunate in hauing such a herauld of his vertues as Spenser. Curteous Lord, Curteous Spenser, I knowe not which hath purchast more fame, either he in deseruing so well of so famous a scholler, or so famous a scholler in being so thankfull without hope of requitall to so famous a Lord."[44]

[42] Camden, *History*, p. 27. J. Nichols, *Progresses and Public Processions of Queen Elizabeth* (London, 1823), I, 63–65, gives a different text. Rathborne (p. 248) concludes that this was the conception behind Spenser's Arthur.

[43] Reprinted in J. W. Hebel and H. H. Hudson, *Poetry of the English Renaissance, 1509–1660* (New York: F. S. Crofts & Co., 1932), pp. 408–10; see also E. C. Wilson, *England's Eliza* ("Harvard Studies in English," Vol. XX [Cambridge, Mass., 1939]), pp. 4–6, 217–18.

[44] *Second Frutes* (1591), "Epistle Dedicatory," sig. A3^{v}. Florio may refer to matter in the *Complaints*, published very early in 1591.

Spenser could celebrate his patron and the Queen's favorite by introducing into his cast of characters two of the most famous legendary earls of Warwick, but Arthur was too great a name for the greatest subject in the land. Henry VII had used the legend of Arthur to bolster his claim to the throne, and he had named his heir Arthur. We are not justified in suspecting Spenser of having so little judgment as to undertake to celebrate as Arthur a courtier who had no legitimate prospect either of marrying the Queen or of succeeding her.

VIII
THE PROCESS OF COMPOSITION

> There by th' vncertaine glims of starry night,
> And by the twinkling of their sacred fire,
> He mote perceiue a litle dawning sight
> Of all, which there was doing in that quire.
>
> —VI, viii, 48.1–4

ONCE we recognize the improbability that Spenser began with Book I, Canto i, and wrote straight through, and once we begin to look at the six existing books, or even at the first three books, of the poem as the product of an evolutionary process which began, not with Redcrosse and Una "pricking on the plaine," but with the idea of celebrating Elizabeth under the guise of the Faery Queen, we begin to see in the structural difficulties and narrative inconsistencies, in the uneven style and the divergence of the poem from the announced plan, evidences of a wavering course in the planning and composition of the poem. This wavering extends not only to the choice of a basic plot but also to the selection of epic models.

In the beginning, according to the "October" eclogue, Spenser wanted to be the English Vergil, and, according to Gabriel Harvey, he undertook to "emulate" Ariosto. When the romances of Florimell and of Britomart and Arthegall were added to the poem, his emulation amounted to rather close imitation of the *Orlando Furioso*. But in the structure of Books I and II the influence of Vergil is predominant.[1] These books have as the basis of their structure the illustration of holiness and temperance and seem to represent a period when Spenser's guiding idea was not the emulation of Ariosto, or even primarily the

[1] See Merritt Y. Hughes, *Virgil and Spenser* ("University of California Publications in English," Vol. II [Berkeley, 1929]), pp. 317 ff.

celebration of the Faery Queen, but rather the creation of a sustained, continued allegory in illustration of virtue.

In the end the poet attempted, not entirely successfully, to combine these two general themes and models in his poem. But analysis of the contents of the several books seems to indicate that he worked at the poem fitfully as one idea or another aroused him to fresh effort or as time permitted. As our knowledge of his life in Ireland is gradually extended, it becomes apparent that between 1580 and 1589 the poet saw periods of active service in government business, broken probably by periods of relative inactivity. As secretary to Lord Grey (1580–82) he must have been very busy attending on the general during an active military campaign. But between Lord Grey's departure in 1582 and Spenser's appointment as clerk of the council of Munster in 1584 there may have been a period of relative quiet. The assumption of the clerkship, which made him virtually the secretary of Sir John Norris, probably proved distracting for a year, but after the departure of Norris (lord president of Munster) in the summer of 1585, affairs in Munster seem to have drifted along rather sluggishly, if we can judge from the slow progress made in the arrangements for the plantation of English settlers there.

These periods of leisure correspond very closely with the development of the *Faerie Queene* as I have indicated it in the preceding chapters. When Spenser went to Ireland in 1580, he took with him, along with several works now lost, a composition called the *Faerie Queene* and written in emulation of Ariosto. I have indicated some reasons for thinking that this piece borrowed the plot of Chaucer's *Sir Thopas* and was in a much lighter and more Ariosto-like vein than the present poem of that name.

Some time later, and if we can trust the report of Lodowick Bryskett it was after Lord Grey left Ireland (i.e., in 1582–84), Spenser was busy illustrating the moral virtues. The romance of Britomart represents still another direction taken by the poem—a direction which, as I pointed out in the last chapter, was probably closely related to Norris' departure from Ireland in 1585, at the time of the appointment of Leicester to command in the Low Countries.

This tentative reconstruction of the general progress of the poem gives us two periods of Ariosto imitation, separated by a period of concentration on the moral virtues. We can hardly discover whether or not the poet reorganized his general plan each time he reached out in a new direction for material, but we can see that in its final form the poem combined three groups of materials: the Faery Queen with her Order of Maidenhead busy in the pursuit of Florimell, the formal illustration of the moral virtues, and the romance of Britomart. And to this combination has been added Prince Arthur in his dual role as illustration of virtue and lover of the Faery Queen—an addition which must have necessitated considerable revision of some parts of the existing material.

We have good evidence of Spenser's facility and patience in revising his work. We have his revisions of his early translations from Du Bellay and Marot. Something of the care with which he polished the *Shepheardes Calender* is indicated by the addition of the sestina to "August," as a finishing touch, after the gloss had been completed. This last-minute addition also illustrates his accretive method of working.

Lodowick Bryskett represents him as recommending that the translation of Giraldi's dialogues might "happily fare the better by some mending it may receiue in the perusing, as all writings else may do by the often examination of the same."[2] And we need not doubt that he practiced what he preached. According to his own account, the *Lay of the Bregog and the Mulla* was first created as an independent piece. Then it was imbedded in *Colin Clouts Come Home Againe*, and, finally, *Colin Clout* was revised with additions shortly before its publication. Several considerations have led modern critics to believe that *Mother Hubberds Tale* and the *Ruines of Time* include early material, revised and added to for a later purpose. Professor W. L. Renwick comments in his edition of the *Complaints* on "Spenser's

[2] *A Discovrse of Civill Life* (1606), Introd., p. 28.

habit of working in patches."[3] We know that several old pieces were worked over for use in the *Faerie Queene*. I have suggested that the British chronicle history was revised from the old *Stemmata Dudleiana*. The *Epithalamion Thamesis* mentioned in 1580[4] surely furnished the germ for the elaborate description of the marriage of the Thames and the Medway in Book IV. But since Spenser made use of Camden and the second edition of Holinshed for his final version, the revision could not have been made before 1587 at the earliest.[5]

In "E.K.'s" gloss to "March" we hear of a translation "into Englishe Rymes" of Politian's Latin version of the first idyl of Moschus. Yet, when we meet the final form of this piece in Book III of the *Faerie Queene* (vi, 11–25), we find it metamorphosed so as to fit it into its place in the elaborate introduction to the account of the Garden of Adonis. It has also taken on echoes of the prologue and epilogue of Tasso's *Aminta*, which might conceivably indicate an intermediate stage in the history of the passage.[6]

We know that Spenser was brought up in a school of composition which laid great stress on polishing. Gabriel Harvey urged him to "bestow one seuennights pollishing and trimming" upon one of the lost works,[7] and Spenser's reference to the *Dreames* seems to indicate that he worked over that piece with great care.

Something of the method of composition advocated by critics

[3] London: Scholartis Press, 1928, p. 227. See especially his brilliant analysis of the *Ruines of Time* in this volume, pp. 189–90, and in *Edmund Spenser* (London, 1925), pp. 60–61. See also the discussions of Spenser's composition in Carrie A. Harper, *The Sources of the British Chronicle History in Spenser's Faerie Queene* ("Bryn Mawr College Monographs," Vol. VII [Bryn Mawr, Pa., 1910]), and in Helen E. Sandison, "Spenser's 'Lost' Works and Their Probable Relation to His *Faerie Queene*," *PMLA*, XXV (1910), 134–51.

[4] *Three Proper, and Wittie, Familiar Letters* (1580), in the *Oxford Spenser*, pp. 612 and 627.

[5] Harper, pp. 10–17; C. G. Osgood, "Spenser's English Rivers," in *Transactions of the Connecticut Academy of Arts and Sciences*, XXIII (1920), 65–108.

[6] J. D. Bruce, "Spenser's *Faerie Queene*, Book III, Canto vi, St. 11 ff., and Moschus' Idyl, *Love the Runaway*," *MLN*, XXVII (1912), 183–85. The *Aminta* was not printed until 1581.

[7] *Three Letters*, in the *Oxford Spenser*, p. 620.

and composition teachers of the day, and evidently practiced by Spenser, can be observed by comparing the two versions of Sir Philip Sidney's *Arcadia*.[8] The *Arcadia* was thought of by its author and his contemporaries as a heroic poem, comparable to the *Faerie Queene*. It has a complex plot, and we can see how Sidney elaborated in revision, enriching the language, elaborating the narrative, adding descriptive details, inserting episodes, and at the same time working to bring the whole into conformity with Renaissance critical theories of the epic.

The existence of these two versions of the *Arcadia* compensates to some extent for our lack of manuscript variants of the *Faerie Queene*. It enables us to see an Elizabethan poet in the very act of grappling with the enigmas of technique and structure which confronted Spenser. We can gain considerable insight into Spenser's probable aims and methods by examining Sidney's, although Spenser's plot is so much less closely knit than Sidney's that it allowed its author much greater freedom for rearrangement.

We know that Spenser revised his shorter pieces, sometimes more than once. From the revision of shorter pieces to the rearrangement of longer ones is a short step, and one which there is no reasonable doubt that he took. Sometimes, as in Book I, the revision has been done so thoroughly and carefully that little evidence of the earlier stages in the development of the book can be detected, but the case is different in the much more hastily constructed Book III, and throughout Books II–VI there are narrative inconsistencies and difficulties of plot and allegory which can be accounted for on the basis of rearrangement and changes of plan.

Once, at the end of Book V, where the unmistakably formative influence of the topical allegory fixes the date of composition, we seem to catch a glimpse of the actual process of creation

[8] See S. L. Wolff, *The Greek Romances in Elizabethan Prose Fiction* (New York: Columbia University Press, 1912), pp. 345 ff.; R. W. Zandvoort, *Sidney's Arcadia: A Comparison between the Two Versions* (Amsterdam: N.V. Swets & Zeitlinger, 1929); and K. O. Myrick, *Sir Philip Sidney as a Literary Craftsman* ("Harvard Studies in English," Vol. XIV [Cambridge, Mass., 1935]). M. S. Goldman has a very useful chapter on Sidney's aims and intentions in his *Sir Philip Sidney and the Arcadia* ("Illinois Studies in Language and Literature," Vol. XVII [Urbana, 1934]), pp. 144–67.

by which an old passage was reinterpreted and augmented and then added to again and once again, as idea led to further idea, until the elaborate whole was completed and cemented neatly into its place (see chap. xv). The study of Spenser's use of enjambment, the results of which I have summarized in Appendix II, suggests that he sometimes created a series of adventures around a single set of characters, as in the case of Braggadochio or of Florimell, and then broke up and intermingled these series in imitation of Ariosto.

But to a remarkable extent Spenser seems to have worked in rather small pieces, even in his long poem. His method of composition may have been partly dictated by his busy life[9] and partly by his failure to find a single epic action, a basic narrative, to give clear outline and general structure to his poem. But the most important factor in this situation was the poet's own peculiar bent. He was a creator of mosaics, a worker in stained glass, not an architect. His imagination was pictorial, not dramatic. He saw the world as a series of vignettes which had meaning and relationship in the realm of ideas rather than in the realm of action. He was interested, not in the analysis of individual characters and emotions and their shaping of events, but in the principles of good and evil as these are symbolized at various moments in human affairs. Redcrosse in the Cave of Despair is a generalized picture of a human state of mind. Hamlet, questioning whether to be or not to be, is a character under emotional stress which leads to action. The dramatist is interested in the character in action; Spenser is interested in the state of mind. He creates a speaking picture of it, and his poem is a succession of these speaking pictures.

But the relation between one picture and another is not one of cause and effect but largely one of juxtaposition. His is the art of the medieval stained-glass window, with its formal ordering of delicate, beautifully colored pictures arranged to tell a story. Spenser created lovely bits and fitted them together

[9] Professor Renwick remarks that Spenser was "the only first-rate poet who ever spent all his maturity in such pressure of affairs" (see his edition of the *Complaints*, p. 225).

with great skill, but the general structure, the connecting frame of lead and iron, is hardly strong enough to support the weight of colored glass put into it. And, like the worker in stained glass, Spenser's conception of structure is schematic, not organic, as appears from the plans of such works as the *Shepheardes Calender*, the *Teares of the Muses*, and the *Fowre Hymnes*, as well as the *Faerie Queene*. He worked by putting together small pieces, with an eye for harmony and symmetry, making a large composition out of many small ones.

It is a mistake to treat the longest work of such a poet as a seriatim composition, completely planned from the beginning. It leads to an undue emphasis on the general structure of the poem at the expense of an appreciation of the poet's methods and achievements. We ought rather to approach the work with a recognition that it had a history of development, that it did not spring full-armed from the poet's brow, complete in its complicated plot and its narrative inconsistencies.

It seems clear that Spenser did not have the whole complex plot described in the letter to Ralegh in mind when he began this poem. He probably began with one element of the final plan, and his choice of a title suggests that it was an element involving the Faery Queen. However, when Books I–III were printed in 1590, the Faery Queen had disappeared into the wings, and Redcrosse, Guyon, and Britomart, in turn, take the center of the stage. In effect, the Faery Queen plot is the frame, into which these three books have been more or less fitted, and then the first part of the frame has been removed. It is as if Chaucer had reserved the Prologue of his *Canterbury Tales* for the end and had written a letter explaining that he had done so. We have left only the individual tales which contain allusions to the missing frame.

And so, having learned what we can about the place of the Faery Queen and of Arthur in the general development of the poem, it is time to turn to the individual books to see what we can discover about the process which produced each of them and the relation of each to the others.

IX
THE CREATION OF BOOK I

> As bright as doth the morning starre appeare
> Out of the East, with flaming lockes bedight,
> To tell that dawning day is drawing neare,
> And to the world does bring long wished light;
> So faire and fresh that Lady shewd her selfe in sight.
>
> —I, xii, 21.5–9

MORE than any other in the whole poem, the first book is a complete and satisfactory whole. It has a beginning in the separation of Redcrosse from Una; a middle, including a climax and a reversal, in the struggle with Orgoglio; and an end in the final victory of Redcrosse and his betrothal to Una. The postponement of the wedding is an obviously artificial device for incorporating the narrative into a larger frame, but the book remains a complete structural unit which has been fitted into Spenser's larger plans rather than evolved out of them.

In order to discover how this book was created, we must first consider the materials used. These have been identified as a combination of the medieval *Libeaus Desconus* and the St. George legend.[1] But the borrowing from *Libeaus*, which is used to fit the adventure of Redcrosse into the larger frame of Faery Court, is confined entirely to the scene described in the letter to Ralegh and to two stanzas of recapitulation in the text (vii, 46–47). We do not know just how far the elaboration of the St. George legend had gone in the version which Spenser was using, but there is reason to believe that it had already been combined with some medieval *enfance* story, such as Spenser sketches in x, 60–66, and that it had assimilated the dragon fight from *Sir*

[1] See *Variorum*, I, 379–95.

Bevis, echoed in Canto xi.[2] It had also been given religious significance through the identification of the dragon with the devil. But even with these elaborations the St. George material is confined to a few stanzas in Cantos i, vii, and x and to the conclusion (Cantos xi–xii). The whole course of the wanderings of Redcrosse and Una, which make up the substance of the book, is derived from other sources.

Of these, by far the most important, both structurally and allegorically, is the New Testament Revelation of John.[3] The borrowing of many details from the Revelation has been noticed, but the full extent and significance of the relationship between the two works has not been explored. Spenser's chief characters —Una, Redcrosse, Arthur, Duessa, the dragon, and the seven-headed beast—all owe significant debts to characters in the Revelation (chaps. 12 ff.). Una derives much both in narrative and in allegory from the beautiful woman in the Revelation who is attacked by a dragon and driven into the wilderness. This woman was commonly identified as the spouse of Christ, celebrated also in the Canticles, who was understood to represent the church militant on earth. Spenser says that Una has been driven from her home by a dragon when she sets out in search of a champion. She takes refuge in the wilderness on two occasions, and there are echoes of the Canticles in the description of her betrothal. Duessa and her seven-headed steed (Cantos vii–viii) have long been recognized as derived from the whore of Babylon and the seven-headed beast in the Revelation. The hero of John's vision is Christ, who descends from heaven on a white horse and slays the seven-headed beast, as Arthur slays Duessa's beast. Christ also finally slays the dragon

[2] Warton, *Observations on the Fairy Queen* (London, 1762), quoted in *Variorum*, I, 395–96; and Rosemond Tuve, "The Red Crosse Knight and Mediaeval Demon Stories," *PMLA*, XLIV (1929), 706–14. G. H. Gerould, *Saints' Legends* ("Types of English Literature" Vol. V [Boston: Houghton Mifflin Co., 1916]), p. 319, points out that the St. George story in Richard Johnson's *The Most Famous History of the Seauen Champions of Christendome* (1596) is a fusion of the traditional saint's legend with the romance of *Sir Bevis*, and he thinks it unlikely that the fusion was original with Johnson.

[3] The pervasiveness of the Revelation is partially indicated in the notes collected in the *Variorum*. It was recognized by Warton and defended by Wilson (see *Variorum*, I, 368–72).

and is united with his bride, as Redcrosse slays his dragon and is united with Una. In fact, not only the climax but the whole narrative structure of Book I is a combination of the St. George legend with the second part of the Revelation.

The identification of St. George with Christ, the dragon-slayer of the Apocalypse, was probably not original with Spenser. St. George was the champion of Christianity as early as Lydgate's poem. As patron saint of England and of the Order of the Garter, he retained his popularity through the Reformation. Probably the Roman church's removal of St. George from its calendar because he was a purely mythical figure helped his popularity in England. It removed from him the odium of "superstitious worship" and left him a national hero and symbol. The learned John Selden explains the situation very neatly when he says: "Your more neat judgements, finding no such matter in true antiquity, rather make it symbolicall then truely proper. So that some account him an allegory of our Saviour Christ; and our admired *Spencer* hath made him an embleme of Religion." He also quotes Chaucer's line about St. George, "For Christs cause is his, well knowen yee."[4] If Spenser did not find St. George already identified with the dragon-slayer of the Revelation, he was certainly familiar with interpretations which pointed in that direction, and his combination of the two associated and similar stories is exactly the kind of thing which has been pointed out as characteristic of his handling of several classical myths and allusions.

But the significance of this combination cannot be grasped until we understand the significance and importance attached to the Revelation in Spenser's day. The identification of the pope with the Antichrist of the Revelation was suggested by Wyclif.[5] But the early Protestants distrusted the book because Catholic theologians used it to support their doctrines of purgatory and the Mass. Luther attacked the authority of the whole book, and Erasmus expressed the opinion that the author

[4] See his notes on Song IV of *Poly-Olbion by Michael Drayton Being the Fourth Volume of His Works*, ed. J. William Hebel (Oxford: Shakespeare Head Press, 1933), p. 85.

[5] See his *Tractatus de ecclesia*, ed. J. Loserth (London: For the Wyclif Society, 1886), V, 356–57.

was not the beloved disciple. But Oecolampadius defended the authority of the Revelation, and John Bale, while he was in exile in Germany in 1540–48, wrote *The Image of Bothe Churches after the Moste Wonderfull and Heauenly Reuelacion of Sainct John the Euangelist*. The book went through at least four editions in as many years (1548–51). It is a running commentary on the Revelation and represents the book, and especially the second half of it, as a prophecy of the Protestant Reformation. This interpretation seems to have been a great comfort to the Marian exiles, and in 1557 their great friend, the Zurich theologian, Henry Bullinger, published *In Apocalypsim conciones centum*, which elaborated upon Bale's interpretation. It was printed in London both in Latin and in English in 1561. The Geneva Bible (1560) adopted a similar interpretation.[6]

Early in the seventies there was a fresh crop of studies of the Revelation. Bale's *Image* was again reprinted about 1570. In 1573 William Fulke, the great Cambridge Hebraist (later [1578] master of Spenser's college, and a retainer of Leicester's), published some Latin *Praelectiones* on the Revelation, which were translated in the same year by George Gyffard, also of Cambridge, who dedicated his work to Ambrose Dudley, Earl of Warwick, Leicester's brother.[7] A second English edition of Bullinger's *Sermons upon the Apocalips* also appeared in 1573, and in 1574 Arthur Golding published a translation of Augustine Marlorate's *Catholike Exposition vpon the Reuelation of Sainct Iohn*. Fulke, Gyffard, and Golding were all Cambridge men,[8] and the publication of three books on the Revelation in two years argues a considerable interest in the subject during Spenser's residence there.

But our poet was already familiar with the Protestant inter-

[6] The marginal gloss on chap. 17 says: "The beast signifieth ye ancient Rome: ye woman that sitteth thereon, the newe Rome which is the Papistrie" (see fol. 120). So also in the English edition of 1576.

[7] *Praelections vpon the Sacred and Holy Reuelation of S. John* (citations of Fulke refer to this translation). In 1596 Gyffard published a volume of *Sermons* which he dedicated to the Earl of Essex, urging him to join the army mounted on white horses which fights against Antichrist (see Revelation).

[8] Fulke was the storm center of much of the trouble over Cartwright. He enjoyed Leicester's patronage and was made master of Pembroke Hall on May 10, 1578. Gyffard was M.A. of Christ's College in 1573. Golding belonged to an older generation.

pretation of the Apocalypse through his verse translations for Jan van der Noot's *Theatre for Worldlings* (1569).[9] The *Theatre* contains sixteen vision poems by Petrarch and Du Bellay and four sonnets by Van der Noot himself. The four Van der Noot sonnets versify the passage in the Revelation which the Protestants regarded as emblematic of their movement. These describe (1) the seven-headed beast, (2) the woman who rides it, (3) the avenger who descends from heaven on a white horse and slays the beast, and (4) the coming of the New Jerusalem as the bride of Christ. Van der Noot's commentary devotes only twenty leaves to the sixteen "Epigrams" and "Sonets" of Petrarch and Du Bellay, and the remaining eighty-six leaves to the interpretation of his four apocalyptical sonnets. The seven-headed beast is, as we should expect, a symbol of the congregation of the wicked as represented by the Church of Rome (fols. 20ᵛ–32). The woman who sits upon the beast is also a symbol of the things the Protestants hated in the old church (fols. 43ᵛ–50ᵛ). The avenger is Christ (fol. 64), and his white horse represents the Protestant ministers (fol. 63ᵛ).

Van der Noot's exposition in general follows Bullinger and the accepted Protestant interpretation as set forth by Fulke and Marlorate. Spenser has simply nationalized the allegory, making the avenger Prince Arthur, whom he calls "heavenly grace." Duessa wears the triple crown of the papacy, and the drama of the destruction of Antichrist (the beast) is made the climax and turning-point in the story of Redcrosse. The final triumph of Redcrosse over the dragon takes its narrative from the St. George story, but its allegory is based on the Revelation, and the betrothal of Redcrosse and Una agrees with the conclusion of the Revelation. Van der Noot says of the coming of the New Jerusalem,

> The holy Citie of the Lorde, from hye
> Descendeth garnisht as a loued spouse [ll. 3–4].

[9] W. J. B. Pienaar discusses Spenser's connection with the *Theatre* translations in "Edmund Spenser and Jonker Jan van der Noot," *English Studies*, VIII (1926), 33–44, 67–76. He also describes the relation of Van der Noot's *Visions* to Spenser's treatment of the same passage in the Revelation in *F. Q.*, I, viii. See also Louis S. Friedland's Introduction to the *Theatre* (New York: Scholars' Facsimiles & Reprints, 1939).

Una displays a great brightness when she is unveiled, like the woman in the Revelation (12:1).

Upton, who usually notices the borrowings of descriptive detail from the Revelation in Book I, is mistaken, I believe, in looking among Roman marriage customs for the ceremonies described by Spenser in Canto xii. He recognizes that the music (st. 39) is from the Revelation. But the laying-on of hands (st. 37:1–3), the lighting of a "housling fire" (i.e., a consecrated or communion fire) which is sprinkled with holy water and from which an ever burning lamp is lighted, and, finally, the sprinkling of the posts with wine, symbolic of the blood of the Passover—all these rites were, I believe, intended to suggest the symbolism of Christian consecration rather than a pagan wedding.

The Revelation, like Book I, ends with the slaying of the old dragon and the marriage of Christ with his church. The river of life and the tree of life, which figure in the battle waged by Redcrosse, appear also in the Revelation and may have got into the St. George legend from that source. The part played by Christ in the Revelation has been divided between Arthur and Redcrosse, Arthur functioning as "heavenly grace" and Redcrosse performing the human mission of the Savior.

Redcrosse is described as wearing the armor of the Christian man prescribed in Ephesians. Gyffard, in the dedicatory epistle to his *Praelections* (1573) addressed to Ambrose Dudley, says:

> The lyfe of man (right Honorable) is sayd of the holy man Iob to be a continuall warfare on earth: wherby it is evident, that so long as we remayne in the tabernacle of this fleshe, we are euen in the middest of this difficulte and daungerouse fighte, compassed in on euerye syde with huge Armies of feyrce and cruell enemies, ... As the holy Apost[l]e S Paule witnesseth Ephes. 6 . . . . Being therefore so weake and feble of our selues . . . . and encounter[ing] . . . . that old serpent . . . . the holy ghost warneth all those that wilbe the true souldiours of Christ, to put on all the armour of God: to haue there loynes gyrded about with veritie, etc.[10]

Duessa, like the whore of Babylon, is richly dressed (Rev. 17:4), yet her body is crooked and deformed (Fulke, fols. 111–111^v). Her golden cup in both cases is filled with "stinking lies

[10] Cf. Ephesians and Spenser's letter to Ralegh.

and filthie monstrouse errours," and, in both cases, comparison is invited with the cup of Circe.[11] Fulke is paraphrasing the gloss of the Geneva Bible on 17:1, when he says of the temptation of mankind:

> Worthely is the Church or Romishe religion whose whole authority dependeth vppon that city of seuen hilles, compared to a famouse and noble harlot, which enticed the mindes of men to her filthy loue with whorishe deceipts, and false coloures as it were with harlotlyke enticementes [fol. 110].

We are reminded of Duessa's dalliance with Redcrosse and of her relations with the "Sans" brothers and Orgoglio. Arthur wounds one of the heads of the beast. One of the heads of the beast in Rev. 13:3 has a wound which Bale says represents the losses of authority and power recently suffered by the Roman church.

It is these associations of Book I with the Revelation which give depth and significance to Spenser's allegory, and it is the drama of the Apocalypse, interpreted as prophesy of the Reformation and combined with the legend of St. George, which serves as the plot of Book I.

In view of this relationship, the history of Spenser's interest in the Revelation becomes doubly significant. As a schoolboy he made translations for Van der Noot's *Theatre* (1569), and while he was at Cambridge (1573–74) three important books on the Apocalypse were printed. In 1579–80, when he was finishing the *Shepheardes Calender*, he wrote to Gabriel Harvey:

> I take best my *Dreames* shoulde come forth alone, being growen by meanes of the Glosse, (running continually in maner of a Paraphrase) full as great as my *Calendar*. Therin be some things excellently, and many things wittily discoursed of *E. K.* and the Pictures so singularly set forth, and purtrayed, as if *Michael Angelo* were there, he could (I think) nor amende the best, nor reprehende the worst.[12]

The gloss to the *Shepheardes Calender* does not "run continually in maner of a Paraphrase," but that in Van der Noot's *Theatre* does. The *Theatre* also, like Spenser's *Dreames*, has its poetical visions illustrated by pictures.

[11] Bullinger, *Sermons upon the Apocalips* (1561), p. 511.

[12] *Oxford Spenser*, p. 612.

To Spenser's letter Harvey replied:

> *Extra iocum*, I like your *Dreames* passingly well: and the rather, bicause they sauour of that singular extraordinarie veine and inuention, whiche I euer fancied moste, and in a manner admired onelye in *Lucian*, *Petrarche*, *Aretine*, *Pasquill*, and all the most delicate, and fine conceited Grecians and Italians: (for the Romanes to speake of, are but verye Ciphars in this kinde:) whose cheifest endeuour, and drifte was, to haue nothing vulgare, but in some respecte or other, and especially in *liuely Hyperbolicall Amplifications*, rare, queint, and odde in euery pointe, and as a man woulde saye, a degree or two at the leaste, aboue the reache, and compasse of a common Schollers capacitie. In whiche respecte notwithstanding, as well for the singularitie of the manner, as the Diuinitie of the matter, I hearde once a Diuine, preferre *Saint Iohns Reuelation* before al the veriest *Mætaphysicall Visions*, and iollyest conceited *Dreames* or *Extasies*, that euer were deuised by one or other, howe admirable, or superexcellent soeuer they seemed otherwise to the worlde. And truely I am so confirmed in this opinion, that when I bethinke me of the verie notablest, and moste wonderful Propheticall, or Poetical Vision, that euer I read, or hearde, me seemeth the proportion is so vnequall, that there hardly appeareth anye semblaunce of Comparison: no more in a manner (specially for Poets) than doth betweene the incomprehensible Wisdome of God, and the sensible Wit of Man. But what needeth this digression betweene you and me? I dare saye you wyll holde your selfe reasonably wel satisfied, if youre *Dreames* be but as well esteemed of in Englande, as *Petrarches Visions* be in Italy: whiche I assure you, is the very worst I wish you.[13]

Harvey does not make it clear whether or not Spenser's *Dreames* follow the model which he most admired; but we can at least be sure that the poet had the Revelation presented to him as a model for this type of writing not only in 1569 but again in 1580; and we need not be surprised when the beast of the Apocalypse turns up again in his work after the passage of another decade.

Once we recognize the importance of the Revelation in the structure of Book I, we can begin to understand how the poet planned the book. The basis of the narrative and of the allegory alike are produced by an amalgamation of the saint's legend and the Revelation, in which the hero is a combination of St. George and Christ, and the heroine is both the lady rescued by St. George and the bride of Christ of the Revelation and of the Song of Solomon ("*Canticum canticorum* translated" is among Spenser's lost works).

Spenser's model for narrative technique is Vergil. Like Vergil, he represents the wanderings of a national hero who moves

[13] *Ibid.*, p. 628.

through a series of adventures to a climactic achievement. In each story the narrative is divided into twelve parts, and in each the adventures of the hero are varied, especially in the first half of the book, by the adventures of a heroine. There are many specific debts to Vergil in subject matter as well as in form, as Professor Hughes has pointed out,[14] especially in the descent into hell.

The book is also indebted to Ariosto for story material, which has been curiously and cleverly interwoven with the matter out of the Revelation. The preliminary dragon fight in Canto i preserves details from the attack of the dragon on the lady in the Revelation. Error emits a Nile-like effluvium (i, 20–21) like the flood which the dragon sends after the beautiful woman (Rev. 12:15). This flood is elsewhere (16:13) described in the Revelation as containing "vncleane spirits like frogges," and the Geneva gloss says that these are "the Popes ambassadours." Spenser's dragon emits books and papers and also frogs and toads.

The device for separating Redcrosse and Una is, on the other hand, of romance origin. Both Ariosto and Tasso contributed matter for it. Ariosto and Vergil supply the scene of dalliance between Duessa and Redcrosse. But the flight of Una into the wilderness derives basically from the Revelation. The House of Pride is structurally as well as allegorically the antithesis of the House of Holiness, and both are created out of materials from other sources; but Ariosto and Tasso contributed to the events which occur at the House of Pride. The encounter with Orgoglio and Duessa, which brings Redcrosse to the dungeon, prepares the way for the rescue by Arthur, which comes out of the Revelation. But the subsequent stripping of Duessa is directly imitated from the *Orlando*. When he has told his story, Arthur gives Redcrosse "few drops of liquor pure," which suggest the water of baptism and fit the character of Arthur as Savior, which is borrowed from the Apocalypse.[15] Redcrosse has

[14] Merritt Y. Hughes, *Virgil and Spenser* ("University of California Publications in English," Vol. II [Berkeley, 1929]), pp. 368–77; and *Variorum*, "Commentary" on ii, 7.4, 24; iii, 31, 34, 36, etc.

[15] F. M. Padelford argues that this precious fluid (I, ix, 19) is the wine of the Protestant communion. But the wine is symbolic of Christ's blood as shed for man, whereas

still to visit the Cave of Despair, be disciplined in the House of Holiness, and see the vision of the New Jerusalem before he is ready to fight the dragon, release Una's parents, and receive Una as his betrothed. The dragon fight comes from the St. George story, but the significance of the whole allegory is determined by contemporary interpretations of the Revelation.

There can be no question that the guiding influence in the creation of Book I was the moral and religious allegory, but the extent to which this allegory refers topically to the events of the Reformation is an open question. The interpretation of Spenser's allegories must remain to a considerable extent a matter of the individual reader's conception of the creative process. We are here concerned, not with what can be made of the poem, but with what the poet had chiefly in mind as he planned and wrote. We know that Tasso created his poem first and allegorized it afterward. We know that allegorical interpretation is capable of almost unlimited flexibility and elasticity. Spenser invited his readers to look for "darke conceits," and he perhaps knew that they would find some which had never occurred to him. But we must distinguish between those passages which were born allegorical, those which achieve allegory by virtue of a happy coincidence, and those which have allegory thrust upon them. We are concerned here only with such significances and implications as clearly guided the poet's pen and influenced the process of creation.

In the present instance the general "moral" allegory of Christian experience clearly dominates the structure of the book. The reminiscences of the Apocalypse indicate that Spenser was thinking also of the English Reformation as predicted in the Revelation. If he had in mind specific historical events, that allegory has been subordinated to the moral and narrative re-

---

Arthur is the symbol of "heavenly grace" represented by the water of baptism. Professor Padelford is clearly mistaken about the book which Redcrosse gives Arthur in return. He would have it to be the Book of Common Prayer, but Spenser says that it is "his Saueours testament." The English Bible is a suitable gift from the religious man to Heavenly Grace as represented by Arthur. In Rev. 10:8–10 an angel presents a little book which the church is commanded to receive. Fulke (p. 66) identifies the book with the Gospel. For Padelford's argument see *Variorum*, I, 472.

quirements of the plot, and therefore it makes its appearance in the foreground only occasionally by way of allusion rather than as continued topical allegory. As soon as we try to fit the history of the Reformation in England into the story of Redcrosse, we encounter difficulties and begin to compromise with the chronology of events and the plain meaning of the text. Thereafter, what ingenuity and sophistry can accomplish is not the concern of the present study. England, like Redcrosse (and Mankind), encountered Error and lost Truth, became involved with Rome (under the usual Protestant symbol of the whore of Babylon), and was rescued by Divine Grace. But there the parallel ends. The Cave of Despair and the House of Holiness belong to the moral development of Everyman, and the attempt to equate them with phases of the Reformation results in distortion of both history and the poem. Spenser would hardly describe the accession of Elizabeth as a period of despair in contradiction of the chroniclers, who represented it as a time of great relief and rejoicing. And surely he would not create the very monastic House of Holiness as a symbol of the Elizabethan compromise. An attempt has been made to find historical counterparts even for the three "Sans" brothers, but they are obviously the antitheses of the three Christian virtues. Sansfoy is the opposite of faith, Sansjoy of hope, and Sansloy of charity, or love, the law of God.

If we agree with Greenlaw that the "historical allusions do not constitute the 'continued allegory,' "[16] we are free to see allusions where they seem plainly intended, without attempting to fit the whole narrative into the Procrustean bed of history. We can see in the books and papers vomited by Error (i, 20–23) allusion to the fulminations of Rome against the Protestants, and in Kirkrapine the greedy clerics destroyed by the dissolution of the monasteries, without being obliged to accept the false charge against Una in Canto ii as an allusion to the fate of Anne Boleyn or to equate Arthur with Leicester or Orgoglio with Philip of Spain.

[16] Edwin A. Greenlaw, *Studies in Spenser's Historical Allegory* (Baltimore, 1932), p. 67.

The "continued allegory, or darke conceit," of Book I is the struggle of the religious man with sin. Spenser indicates the widest possible interpretation of this moral allegory. The parents of Una are Adam and Eve,[17] because, according to many biblical commentators from Philo Judaeus onward, all truth was revealed in the Garden of Eden before the Fall. Una (Truth) is therefore their daughter. Redcrosse is not merely England but every Christian who seeks salvation. Some of his adventures have reference to the contemporary religious struggle, but I believe that the Protestant interpretation of the Revelation should be our guide in the study of the primary meaning and structural plan of the book and not any theory that Spenser was trying to write a *roman à clef*.

What the poet has done is to lace together apocalyptical and moral allegories with a thread of narrative spun out of various sources, but chiefly out of Ariosto. From the point of view of the poet's purpose, the allegories are primary and the narrative is secondary. The structural design of the book is one of balanced elements, as in the two dragon fights (Cantos i and xi), the two educational institutions (the houses of Pride and Holiness), the two forms of pride (Lucifera and Orgoglio), and even Una's two sojourns with ignorance. It is a schematic rather than an organic plot, made by poising one set piece of allegory against another rather than by narrative complication.

The process which produced it was one of elaboration and accretion, such as may be observed to a lesser extent in the two versions of the *Arcadia*. There is every evidence that it was polished with the greatest care. It has by far the highest percentage of compound words of any book in the poem, and the frequent use of compounds is characteristic of the poet's most elaborate compositions.[18] Book I has many fewer rhymes of preterites in *-d* or *-ed* than any other book, and this phenomenon seems to be the product of Spenser's extreme care about

[17] See xii, 26, and II, i, 1, for direct mention of Eden, and I, vii, 43, for indirect reference. The brazen tower (xi, 3, and letter) is a common symbol of the world, where mankind (Adam and Eve) is shut up by Satan (the dragon), when expelled from Eden (i, 5).

[18] See below, Appendix III.

rhymes.[19] Book I also has a substantially lower enjambment ratio than the other books,[20] especially in the episodes of the conquest of Error, Una's encounter with the lion and with Ignorance and Blind Devotion, the procession of the seven deadly sins, the rescue of Una by the satyrs, and most of the second half of the book, beginning with the encounter between Redcrosse and Orgoglio. These are the parts of the story most directly indebted to St. George and the Revelation, and it is possible that they were the earliest parts to be written and that the story was expanded by additions chiefly to the first six cantos.

There is a richness and elaboration in the development of various ornamental passages, such as the famous tree list, the cave of sleep, the visit to hell, the procession of the seven deadly sins, etc., which suggests that the book has undergone much revision and polishing. There is also a richness and variety in the use of various sources, including the Bible, the classics, and earlier English literature, as well as Ariosto and Tasso, which suggests the mending it received in the perusing "as all writings else may do by the often examination of the same."

There is much less borrowing from, and imitation of, Ariosto in this book than in any other of the six. Only in Canto vi is there an imitation of Ariosto's technique, and there also occurs the most extensive borrowing of incident from the *Orlando*. Elsewhere the echoes and reminiscences of Ariosto are thoroughly adapted to Spenser's theme, and often, as in the introduction of Archimage, an initial borrowing from Ariosto seems to have been overlaid by one from Tasso.[21] Before he finished this book he had read both the *Rinaldo* and the *Gerusalemme Liberata*.

[19] See below, chap. xii.

[20] See below, Appendixes I and II.

[21] Details in the description of Archimage may have come from the *Rinaldo*. A detail or two of the bleeding tree from the *Gerusalemme Liberata* seems to be superimposed on an episode out of Ariosto. A simile in Canto iii, 31, and the joust in Canto v are strongly suggestive of the *G. L.* Perhaps the account of Arthur's helmet (vii, 31) is from Tasso, although both poets follow Vergil. The general situation in Cantos ix–x of a Cave of Despair followed by a Hill of Hope has been thought to suggest the *Rinaldo*, although it is a natural sequence. Canto xi, 21, has been traced to the *G. L.* (see H. H. Blanchard, "Imitations from Tasso in the *Faerie Queene*," *Studies in Philology*, XXII [1925], 198–204).

Book I must have been begun early in the period (1580–90) in which the first three books were written, because the structure and plot of Book II are closely modeled on it. But it may have been begun as an independent piece. Its relation to the apocalyptical sonnets translated for the *Theatre* suggests that it may have developed out of that work, or out of the lost *Dreames*, if that was modeled on St. John, as Harvey's remarks suggest. Or the St. George story may have come out of the lost *Legends*, and the borrowings from the Canticles in the description of Una suggest that the lost translation of *Canticum canticorum* played a part in the creation of the legend of Redcrosse. But the absence of any considerable passage involving the Faery Queen and the relative unimportance of Ariosto as a model and source of material seem to indicate that this book was not originally begun as an imitation of Ariosto intended to celebrate Elizabeth under the guise of the Faery Queen. It represents a different and more serious undertaking, intended to make of its author an English Vergil.

But if Book I was begun early, it was not completed until very late in the 1580–90 period. Some lines in xi, 7, have been understood to refer to the defeat of the Spanish Armada in 1588. Spenser invokes his muse:

> Faire Goddesse lay that furious fit aside,
> Till I of warres and bloudy *Mars* do sing,
> And Briton fields with Sarazin bloud bedyde,
> Twixt that great faery Queene and Paynim king,
> That with their horrour heauen and earth did ring.

But the most conclusive evidence that Spenser reviewed Book I near the end of the 1580–90 period consists in the full, if superficial, agreement between the plan outlined in the letter to Ralegh and the story told in Book I. I have already indicated how I think that Arthur was added to the plot. He plays the part of the Savior of Mankind as it is described in the Revelation, he introduces the only matter of Britain in this book, and he links the story of Redcrosse with that of the Faery Queen by adopting the part of Sir Thopas in Chaucer's *Tale* and by having Una tell him the beginning of her adventure as that is told in the letter.

All this is accomplished in Cantos vii, viii, and the opening of ix. Both the person of Arthur and the *Sir Thopas* story could have been added to a plot in which "heavenly grace" originally had a divine representative without disturbing the bases of the story. References to the Faery Queen as Gloriana occur in this book only in the opening of the first canto and in connection with the account of Arthur (Canto vii), and the adoption of the name "Gloriana" seems to have been a late addition to the plan of the frame plot.

Book I must have been in existence in some form before Spenser decided to illustrate the twelve moral virtues "according to Aristotle and the rest,"[22] for he would hardly have begun the illustration of Aristotle with so un-Aristotelian a virtue as holiness. The main plot of the book is as independent of Aristotle as it is of the Faery Queen.

In fact, the relation of the basic plot of Book I to the three unifying elements in Spenser's final plan—the Faery Queen, Arthur, and the Aristotelian virtues—strongly suggests that the allegory of triumphant Protestantism which the poet evolved out of the legend of St. George and the Revelation of John was neither the historical beginning of the *Faerie Queene* nor a product of the plan described in the letter. On the contrary, it was superficially but adequately adapted to that plan, as if the plan were a late development, superimposed upon already existing materials. It would seem that, when he prepared the manuscript of the first instalment for publication, Spenser polished Book I with minute and loving care; but he did not find time to make final corrections in Book II until he reviewed it for the second edition, and Book III was assembled in great haste, as we shall see.

Whether Book I developed out of an independent poem or whether it was originally written as the quest of a knight of Fairy Court, in either case there must have been a beginning of a poem called the *Faerie Queene* which Harvey saw in 1580. Book I is not that beginning. The preliminary developments of the frame plot have been removed, leaving "the beginning of

[22] For further discussion see below, chap. xvii.

the whole worke . . . . abrupte and as depending vpon other antecedents." This abrupt beginning with a secondary story was, in all probability, the result of rearrangement of material and changes of plan such as would result from a decision to illustrate each virtue in a separate book and to add Arthur to the story as the hero-in-chief.

This rearrangement of his materials left Spenser with the abrupt beginning which he tries to smooth out in the letter and with a body of early writing about the Faery Queen and various other characters which was probably largely concerned with chastity and which he drew upon for later books. The result of his labors is a book which perfectly conforms to the final plan as outlined in the letter to Ralegh; but the legend of Redcrosse had its origin in quite different ideas and was incorporated into the 1589 plan by superficial changes and additions, not evolved out of it.

X
THE EVOLUTION OF BOOK II

> She is the mighty Queene of *Faerie*,
> Whose faire retrait I in my shield do beare;
> She is the flowre of grace and chastitie,
> Throughout the world renowmed far and neare,
> My liefe, my liege, my Soueraigne, my deare.
>
> —II, ix, 4.1–5

THE most obvious fact about the structure of Book II is its close imitation of Book I.[1] Not only is there the same framework of knightly quest but there are two castles, of Medina and Alma, corresponding in position and significance to the houses of Pride and Holiness in the first book. And in the same position between them, and serving the same purpose as Orgoglio's castle in Book I, is the Cave of Mamon in Book II. Arthur comes to the rescue of the hero at the same point (Canto viii) in each book, and the struggle of Redcrosse with the three "Sans" brothers is paralleled by Guyon's struggle with the brothers Pyrochles and Cymochles. The Palmer serves as a substitute for Una, albeit an inadequate one, since he has no independent adventures, and Guyon takes the leading role in every episode except those in Cantos iii and xi. Acrasia is the antagonist, in place of Duessa, but she has a much smaller part. She is mentioned in the first canto when Guyon finds the dying Amavia and the babe with the bloody hands, but there are only two passing references to her in the body of the book, and she does not appear until we reach Canto xii.

Structurally the quest of Acrasia takes the place in Book II which is supplied in Book I by the legend of St. George. But

[1] See Ernest A. Strathmann, "The Structure of Book II of the *Faerie Queene*," abstracted in *Variorum*, II, 467–71; and H. S. V. Jones, *Spenser Handbook* (New York: F. S. Crofts & Co., 1930), pp. 172–74.

the poet filled in his quest framework with a simple, episodic, allegorical exposition of the moral virtue of temperance in place of the closely associated and richly significant matter of the Revelation which he used in Book I.

Again, as in the study of Book I, our chief resource in this attempt to discover Spenser's method of composition is the analysis of his handling of his materials. The basic narrative, the quest of Acrasia, has been traced to the famous allegory of Alcina and Logistilla in the early cantos of the *Orlando Furioso:*[2]

> Ruggiero is carried by the hippogriff to an island of Alcina, where he encounters Astolpho metamorphosed into a tree. The tree warns him of the wiles of the enchantress Alcina, to whom Astolpho has fallen victim. Ruggiero sets out to avoid Alcina's city and to go the steep and thorny path to her virtuous sister Logistilla's kingdom. But on his way he encounters a rabble of beast-headed men with whom he battles. He is rescued by two ladies who invite him to overcome the hag Avarice, and having done so he enters the city and becomes Alcina's favorite lover. Meanwhile, Bradamante, his betrothed, sends the witch Melissa to him with a magic ring which reveals the ugliness beneath Alcina's seeming beauty. Ruggiero flees from the palace of pleasure, and after a difficult journey he reaches Logistilla's city and is taught to guide the hippogriff.

Ariosto's allegory is based on such classical antecedents as the fable of Prodicus on the choice of Hercules, the Table of Cebes, and the Pythagorean explanation of the letter *Y*. The long, hard way to Logistilla's kingdom and the easy way to Alcina's naturally suggest both biblical and classical allegories of the roads to virtue and vice.[3] Guyon's encounter with Amavia, in Canto i, serves the same purpose as Ruggiero's encounter

[2] See S. J. McMurphy, *Spenser's Use of Ariosto for Allegory* ("University of Washington Publications in Language and Literature," Vol. II [Seattle, 1924]), pp. 24–30. C. W. Lemmi finds a very interesting parallel to Guyon's adventures in Trissino's *L'Italia Liberata dai Gotti*, but, in view of Spenser's familiarity with the work of Ariosto and Tasso, this parallel is not sufficiently strong to establish Spenser's acquaintance with Trissino ("The Influence of Trissino on the *Faerie Queene*," *Philological Quarterly*, VII [1928], 220–23).

[3] Miss McMurphy concludes (pp. 15 ff.) that Spenser used Fornari's commentary (1549) on Ariosto, which supplied notes for the 1584 edition of the *Orlando* used by Harington. She is mistaken in her assertion that Thomaso Porcacchi's "nuoue Allegorie & Annotationi" did not appear until 1612. The first edition was in 1568 (see Giuseppe Agnelli and Giuseppe Ravegnani, *Annali delle edizioni Ariostee* [Bologna: Nicola Zanichelli, 1933]). Porcacchi's edition was frequently reprinted and certainly could have been known to Spenser.

with Astolpho,[4] and the realms of Alma and Acrasia are recognizable substitutes for those of Alcina and Logistilla, although Spenser has reversed their positions and has substituted Tasso's garden of Armida for Ariosto's city of Alcina.

If we can assume that the borrowing of allegory from Ariosto was Spenser's starting-point in the construction of Book II, we are in a position to understand, in a general way, how the book was put together. It falls naturally into three main parts: a rather miscellaneous beginning (i–iii), a central section illustrating temperance through Guyon's struggles with Pyrochles and Cymochles (iv–viii), and a closing section made up of the allegories of the Castle of Alma and the quest of Acrasia. Of these three sections, the central one is the best constructed and most coherent. It seems clearly to have been planned and written on the model of Book I, and therefore written after Book I had taken on substantially its final form. But the first and last sections, which include the quest of Acrasia, consist of much more miscellaneous materials and seem to belong to several different periods of composition.

Book II opens with the machinations of Duessa and Archimage as these characters are carried over from the end of Book I. The poet accounts fully for the escape of Archimage from the prison to which he was consigned by Redcrosse and for the attack of Duessa and Archimage on Guyon. The elaborate use made of Duessa and Archimage and the close relationship between this passage and the end of Book I indicate that the last canto of Book I was substantially complete before this link between Books I and II was written.

There is, however, something suspiciously artificial about the link. It gives a large part to Duessa, who is never mentioned again in Book II but is supplanted by Acrasia. It also gives prominence to Archimage, who makes only three brief appearances in the book, leaving his story in a fragmentary state. These fragments may be either vestiges of an earlier story or a

[4] This is Miss McMurphy's interpretation. Spenser had used the episode of the speaking tree in I, ii, 28 ff., where Fradubio warns Redcrosse of the enchantress Duessa. The stripping of Duessa in Book I is also borrowed from Ruggiero's experience with Alcina.

halfhearted attempt to work Archimage into a narrative which had been created without him. Probably they are partly both, for Archimage appears in Canto iii, which I have given reasons for thinking was an early creation originally belonging to the early *Faerie Queene* plot, and he appears also in this link with Book I which must have been written after Book I was substantially finished. Perhaps Spenser created Archimage as a counterpart of one of Ariosto's magicians and then, much later, thought of carrying Archimage and Duessa along as the enemies of each knight in turn. But he did not succeed in creating substantial parts for them in Book II.

Having introduced Guyon and linked him with Redcrosse, Spenser sets him on his quest. For this purpose the episode of the death of Amavia is employed. This episode was clearly written before Spenser decided to make all twelve quests originate at the court of the Faery Queen, since it is from the dying Amavia that Guyon first hears of the wicked Acrasia, and from her he takes the babe with the bloody hands. Canto ii, on the other hand, tells the alternative story (sts. 42–45), described in the letter to Ralegh, of the Palmer's complaint in Faery Court as the origin of Guyon's quest. Canto ii also contains the only reference in the whole poem to the annual feast. Clearly, Canto i was written before, and Canto ii after, Spenser added the annual banquet to the frame plot. Canto ii also describes Guyon's visit to Medina and so gives an Aristotelian flavor to the account of temperance. But the quest of Acrasia was begun as an imitation of Ariosto rather than as an illustration of Aristotle's idea of temperance.

Probably Canto iii was revised when Canto ii was written in order to enlarge the praises of the Faery Queen, to add the name "Belphoebe" as a compliment to Ralegh, and possibly to create a part for Archimage in Book II, although the early Ariosto imitation which seems to have supplied the story of the theft of Guyon's horse may well have included an enchanter, since Ariosto has several of them.

The central cantos (iv–viii) describe Guyon's struggles with Furor and Occasion and with Pyrochles and Cymochles, in imitation of the encounters of Redcrosse with Sansfoy, Sansloy, and Sansjoy and in illustration of temperance. These form a group of coherent and well-knit allegories which betray very little about their antecedents and the process of their creation. But the situation in the last five cantos is quite a different one. Here we have the formal, uneven, and largely uninspired[5] account of the Castle of Alma balanced against the highly poetic description of the Bower of Bliss.

Since the basis of Spenser's allegory was clearly Ariosto, I believe we can trace with some degree of probability the creative process by which these cantos came into existence. The most striking features of Spenser's allegory are the reversal in the positions of the two realms and the contrast in style between the descriptions of the Castle of Alma and the Bower of Bliss. This contrast is so striking as to make it extremely unlikely that the two allegories were written at nearly the same time. One is a formal medieval allegory, worked out with all the over-literalness which is the worst blemish of the type. The other is a close imitation of Tasso, done in the best Renaissance manner. That the same poet wrote both is surprising enough; but it is quite improbable that they were planned and written as companion pieces.

One critic has suggested that the Castle of Alma was an early piece worked over for its present use. Analysis of the contents of the passage seems to support this conjecture. It begins with a wooden description of the body (ix, 21–32), which is purely formal and does not mention Guyon and Arthur. The next section, on the affections, is more imaginative and less formal, and it introduces Arthur and Guyon into the action. The whole tone of the passage contrasts with what has gone before and appears, both in manner and in content, to have been written after Spenser had adopted the final plan for Book II. The account of the mind which comes next (sts. 45–52) returns to the formal and impersonal method of description which distin-

[5] This is the opinion of E. Dowden, H. J. C. Grierson, Lowell, Cory, De Sélincourt, and Dodge, among others (see *Variorum*, I, 365, 367; II, 197, 198, 286–88; and the *Cambridge Spenser*, pp. 133–34).

guished the account of the body. This situation supports the conjecture that the account of the body and the mind was an old piece, worked over to fit its present place in the poem by the insertion of the passage on the affections which mentions Arthur and Guyon and by some changes in the introduction and the conclusion.

If the allegory of Alma and Acrasia belonged originally to the early Ariosto imitation, the reversal in the position of the two realms was probably made when the poet decided to turn his allegory into a quest of Guyon paralleling in structure the legend of Redcrosse. The Castle of Alma fills the same moral and structural place in Book II which the House of Holiness fills in Book I. But the book retains some traces of the development of Spenser's ideas about Acrasia and of the reversal of the position of the two realms.

Spenser was, of course, conscious of the derivation of Ariosto's and Tasso's island enchantresses from Circe, and in his accounts of Acrasia there are traces of both Alcina and Circe as well as of Armida. Circe used drugs to transform her discarded lovers, Alcina (Ariosto) used magic to turn them into trees and monsters, and Armida (Tasso) chained her victims in an enchanted fortress. Amavia's account of the enchantress in Canto i, which was probably written before the adaptation of Tasso supplanted that of Ariosto in Canto xii, is imitative of Circe:

> Her blisse is all in pleasure and delight,
> Wherewith she makes her louers drunken mad,
> And then with words and weedes of wondrous might,
> On them she workes her will to vses bad [st. 52].

But when, in Canto v, Acrasia is mentioned again, Spenser's imagination has been fired by Tasso:

> The vile *Acrasia*, that with vaine delightes,
> And idle pleasures in her *Bowre* of *Blisse*,
> Does charme her louers, and the feeble sprightes
> Can call out of the bodies of fraile wightes:
> Whom then she does transforme to monstrous hewes,
> And horribly misshapes with vgly sightes,
> Captiu'd eternally in yron mewes,
> And darksom dens, where *Titan* his face neuer shewes [v, 27].

In the final account of the Bower of Bliss the "darksom dens" have vanished. The unfortunate lovers, reminiscent of Ariosto and Homer, attack Guyon in broad daylight in the guise of beasts. In Tasso, also, beasts attack the hero, but these are not transformed lovers but magic animals created by the witch. Both Ariosto and Tasso certainly contributed to the creation of the Bower of Bliss. The question is whether Spenser created the whole allegory of Amavia, Acrasia, and Alma in imitation of Ariosto before he substituted the Tasso imitation for the city of Alcina in Ariosto[6] and whether the reversal of the position of the two realms was part of the original design or the result of the revision.

It has been observed[7] that Book III opens with the situation as it would have been at the end of Book II if Arthur and Guyon had defended the Castle of Alma together, since Book III opens with both Arthur and Guyon coming from the Castle of Alma after she has cured them of their wounds. But meanwhile, in II, xii, Guyon had gone off on a long journey to the Bower of Bliss. The situation suggests that II, xii, was added, or put in its present place, after the opening of Book III was written. It has been argued that the combat with the vices in Canto xi originally belonged to Guyon and served as the final exploit of the book, comparable to the dragon fight in Book I.[8] Such a theory is plausible, and an examination of the canto reveals that some hasty workmanship has combined a rather crude beginning (sts. 1–19)[9] with a very fine account of the duel between Arthur and Maleger (sts. 20–49).

[6] The *Gerusalemme Liberata* was first printed in a surreptitious edition in 1580 and in an authorized edition in 1581. There is no indication of when the book reached Spenser.

[7] See Janet Spens, *Spenser's Faerie Queene* (London, 1934), chap. i; J. H. Walter, " 'The Faerie Queene': Alterations and Structure," *Modern Language Review*, XXXVI (1941), 38–39.

[8] See above, n. 7.

[9] Stanzas 6–15 descend to the level of the worst parts of the Castle of Alma. Stanza 6 mentions twelve bands of assailants, divided into seven and five, the five attacking the five senses. But there the allegory breaks off. In st. 15 "two brethren giants" who defend the castle are mentioned, but they take no part in the action. Obviously they are not Arthur and Timias, or Arthur and Guyon, as Kitchin suggests, since none of these three is ever described as a giant.

There is also a curious duplication of beast-headed rabbles such as might result from a reversal of the positions of the two realms of Alcina and Logistilla. Such a rabble attacks Ruggiero before the gates of the city of Alcina, and Spenser describes a similar attack on Guyon and Arthur before the gates of the Castle of Alma.[10] Another such mob attacks the castle in Canto xi and is driven off by Arthur,[11] and finally Guyon encounters just such a mob before the Bower of Bliss.[12] If the passage began as an imitation of Ariosto's allegory, and the position of the two countries was reversed when the Tasso imitation supplanted the Alcina part of the borrowing from Ariosto, then the duplication of these allegorical mobs would be a natural result. The first mob would be transferred along with the rest of the Bower of Bliss, and a new mob (this time of Irish kerns) would have to be created to greet Guyon's entry into the first of the castles, which now became that of Alma.[13]

A process of evolution which might produce this book out of the early *Faerie Queene* plot can be reconstructed. If Guyon was a character in the early attempt to emulate Ariosto, as I suggested in chapter vii, his part in the allegory of Alma and Acrasia could easily have grown out of that early Ariosto imitation. Spenser, in the course of borrowing from Ariosto's narra-

[10] These are described in much the same terms as are used of the wild Irish kerns in the *View* (see M. M. Gray, "The Influence of Spenser's Irish Experiences on *The Faerie Queene*," *Review of English Studies*, VI [1930], 414–16).

[11] These are sometimes described as Ariosto's transformed lovers and sometimes as the monstrous vices of medieval allegory. Miss Spens (pp. 17, 22–23) notes this inconsistency. It may have been the result of Spenser's having adopted such an interpretation of Ariosto as that of Harington, who says that Ariosto's beast-headed men represent the seven deadly sins (see *Orlando Furioso*, p. 47). M. Y. Hughes has pointed out to me that the beasts encountered by Arthur and those encountered by Guyon have the same allegorical significance.

[12] R. E. N. Dodge, "Spenser's Imitations from Ariosto—Addenda," *PMLA*, XXXV (1920), 91–92, noted that the beastly defenders of the Bower of Bliss are not Tasso's (*G. L.*, XIV, 73, and XV, 51–52) but Ariosto's (*O. F.*, VI, 26 ff.), since they are transformed lovers who are later freed from the enchantment (*O. F.*, VIII, 14 ff.).

[13] The reference to the "fennes of Allan" in this passage (ix, 16) indicates that it was written after Spenser acquired New Abbey in County Kildare, where he resided occasionally between 1582 and 1584 (see J. C. Smith [ed.], *Spenser's Faerie Queene* [Oxford, 1909], I, xii, n. 2; and Raymond Jenkins, "Spenser and the Clerkship in Munster," *PMLA*, XLVII [1932], 110).

tive, would naturally be attracted by the allegorical passage, especially if Guyon was inspired by Sir Thopas and began as the champion of chastity. There may also have been an early pageant or vision of the castle of the body which was used as an equivalent for Ruggiero's visit to the realm of Logistilla.

If Spenser had on hand some part of a poem involving Guyon when he undertook to create a book on temperance as a companion piece for his book on religious virtue, he could have made the Book of Guyon by using the allegory of Alcina and Logistilla as his basic plot and by filling in, in the central section, with Guyon's struggles against Pyrochles and Cymochles, and Furor and Occasion, in imitation of the struggles of Redcrosse against the three "Sans" brothers.

Perhaps a later revision replaced Guyon by Arthur in the final combat with Cymochles and Pyrochles and gave him a part in the visit to the Castle of Alma, including the fight with Maleger which concludes it. If so, the poet must, either earlier or at the same time, have reversed the position of the two realms so as to leave the quest of Acrasia for Guyon's final exploit. Finally, when Spenser decided to use Britomart's story in Book III, he inserted the first section of his British chronicle into Canto x.

Evidence of the early creation of Guyon consists of his connection with the studies for the *Stemmata Dudleiana*, his special devotion to the Faery Queen, the use of his name instead of Arthur's in the fight with Pyrochles and Cymochles[14] and instead of that of Redcrosse in Book III, and, finally, in two minor stories told of him in Book II.

These stories involve two plots which have clearly been submerged or subordinated to later structural plans. The first of these is the theft of Guyon's horse by Braggadochio. The recovery of the horse and the punishment of the thief are de-

[14] Modern editors emend "Sir Guyon" to "Prince Arthur." Other mistakes of the kind occur at IV, iv, 2.4, where Scudamour is named for Blandamour, and VI, vi, 17.7, where Calidore is named instead of Calepine. These two mistakes might be the result of the poet's momentary confusion of two names of similar sound or of the printer's misreading of a difficult manuscript. But in the passage in III, ii, 4.1, where Guyon is named instead of Redcrosse, no emendation is possible because the two names have different metrical values (see *Oxford Spenser*, "Critical Appendix").

layed until the third canto of Book V, causing an obvious dislocation of the narrative.[15] The other submerged plot which is set going in this canto is the theft of Arthur's sword by Archimage in order to promote an attack on Guyon. The sword is mentioned in Canto vi (47.6), and at the climax of the book (viii, 19–49) Pyrochles begs the sword of Archimage to use against its master. But how Arthur lost it and Archimage gained possession of it, we are never told. The point of this story is that the sword cannot be used against its rightful owner. When Arthur becomes the antagonist of Pyrochles and Cymochles, the sword has to be his. But it must originally have been Guyon's if Guyon originally did the fighting.

Not only are both these episodes borrowed from Ariosto, but they are imitated from passages touched with Ariosto's peculiar humor, and, if the tale of the Squire of Dames represents the tone of Spenser's beginning, these two bits of narrative correspond in tone with that beginning.

I have already indicated the method by which Arthur could have been introduced into Book II. Certainly the moral allegory breaks down with the advent of Arthur in this book. It has been objected that Guyon's swoon, when he emerges from the Cave of Mamon, is without moral justification.[16] Also, his guardian angel should have been able to awaken Guyon when danger threatened. We feel some disappointment, moreover, when the two enemies whom Guyon has shown his ability to overcome are in the end dispatched by Arthur while Guyon sleeps.

The whole course of the book, after the appearance of Arthur, presents a double resolution. Canto x has a double chronicle (of British kings and elfin emperors), and Cantos xi and xii present two grand exploits, either of which would satisfactorily close the book. One is achieved by Arthur, the other by Guyon. The two together weigh down the close and present a much less artistic and satisfactory outcome than that of Book I.

[15] See above, chaps. iv and vii.

[16] J. S. Harrison, *Platonism in English Poetry of the Sixteenth and Seventeenth Centuries* (New York: Columbia University Press, 1903), pp. 62–63.

Evidently Spenser saw that the part he had given to Arthur in Book I was too small if he was to be made the chief hero of the whole poem. But when he undertook to extend Arthur's part, he involved himself in almost continuous allegorical difficulty. The defense of the Castle of Alma is Guyon's duty; yet he is made to slip away ignominiously, leaving Arthur to defend it. Arthur is simply doubling for Guyon in an adventure which, in turn, duplicates the allegory of the destruction of the Bower of Bliss. The two allegories represent two different ideas for the final battle in the illustration of temperance.

There are some lines in the account of Arthur's fight with Maleger, mentioning Arthur's quest as the pursuit of glory, which suggest that this passage was written after the final plan had matured. Spenser says (xi, 31.6–9):

> The whiles the Prince prickt with reprochful shame,
> As one awakt out of long slombring shade,
> Reuiuing thought of glorie and of fame,
> Vnited all his powres to purge himselfe from blame.

This may be an early foreshadowing of the final conception of the Faery Queen as the idea of pure glory, but in another part of this passage (st. 21) the arrows of the Indians are alluded to, and we know that during Ralegh's visit to Kilcolman in 1589 America shared with poetry in the conversation and left a mark on the proems which Spenser provided at the last minute. In ix, 4, there is mention of Elizabeth's "puissaunce in warre" which could hardly have been written before 1586, or justly before 1588. The Queen was praised for her peace policy until she entered openly into the Netherlands wars late in 1585. Spenser combines the two themes:

> Far reach her mercies, and her prayses farre,
> As well in state of peace, as puissaunce in warre.

These evidences of late polishing of the last third of Book II are slight in themselves, but they support the structural evidence and have a certain cumulative value.

The reasons for thinking that the British chronicle was a late addition to this book include considerations of its origin, its relation to the continuation used in the story of Britomart (III,

iii), and its function in Book II. The first two of these reasons have already been sufficiently discussed. As for the third, it has been argued that a knowledge of genealogy was a part of the preparation of Arthur and Guyon for their final conquests of vice.[17] But neither Guyon nor Arthur is conscious of any personal connection with what he is reading. Arthur remains ignorant of his relation to Uther, and Guyon has no connection with the fairy genealogy of Elizabeth.[18] The reading of history was, of course, considered valuable moral training, but Spenser could have represented his knights as reading history without inserting a whole canto of it into an already overlong book.[19] The long chronicle breaks up the unity and continuity of the four culminating cantos. It is presented as flattery of the Queen, but its function is duplicated by the fairy genealogy, which takes up much less space and is much more grandly inclusive in its scope.

The fairy genealogy contrasts sharply in style with the British chronicle, corresponding in this respect with the Proem of Book II, which alludes to Gloriana's "great auncestry," said to be presented "in couert vele." There is nothing covert about the British chronicle, so that the fairy genealogy must here be meant. It seems probable that this fanciful sketch of the Queen's descent from Adam and Eve was, like the Proem, one of the finishing touches added to the final version of the first instalment, after the British chronicle had been put in. But the chronicle is not really connected with the story of Arthur, in spite of the fact that he is represented as reading it. It came into Book II via the romance of Britomart and Arthegall.

Guyon's praises of the Faery Queen in Canto ii probably also belong to the last revision, since they include a description of the annual banquet (the only mention of it in the entire poem) and an account of the inception of Guyon's quest which agrees

[17] W. S. Webb, "Vergil in Spenser's Epic Theory," *ELH*, IV (1937), 62–84.

[18] I. E. Rathborne, *The Meaning of Spenser's Fairyland* (New York, 1937), pp. 65 ff., interprets this genealogy as meaning that the Queen is descended from all the great kings of the earth.

[19] Book II is 62 stanzas, or over an average canto, longer than Book I, which is the second longest book in the poem.

with what is said of it in the letter to Ralegh but not with the events described in Canto i.

This analysis of the legend of Guyon gives us at least three periods of composition. There was an early set of Ariosto-like adventures probably including the imitation of Ariosto's allegory of Alcina and Logistilla. Perhaps about 1582–84 Spenser decided to convert his material into more formal allegories of the moral virtues, and the legend of Guyon was created along lines which paralleled the structure of the Book of Redcrosse. This revision probably included the creation of the central section. But at a later date, probably after the publication of Camden's *Britannia* in 1586, and almost certainly after the appearance of Powel's *Historie of Cambria* in 1584, one and perhaps two revisions added to the book the British chronicle and the part of Arthur. Some touches, such as much of the flattery of Elizabeth, the fairy genealogy, and the praises of the Faery Queen in Canto ii, as well as the Proem, seem to have been added just before publication.

The relation of the structure of Book II to that of Book I—its mechanical conformity and correspondence in the position and character of the episodes, its schematic organization out of heterogeneous materials, and its treatment of Arthur—furnishes evidence not only that Book II was patterned on Book I but also that it was put together out of materials partly written in imitation of Book I and partly created with other plans in mind. The castles of Medina and Alma teach no lesson. They fail to function as valuable training for the hero in the way that the houses of Pride and Holiness train Redcrosse.[20] The allegory of Book II has suffered from the poet's preoccupation with larger structural problems.

Especially in the first and last sections, Book II is made up of heterogeneous materials. The last third contrasts with the successful close of Book I, in spite of its great canto on the Bower

[20] R. E. N. Dodge, in "Spenser's Imitations from Ariosto," *PMLA*, XII (1897), 191–92, comments that the plot of Book II is merely "a string of unprogressive episodes" in which the Braggadochio-Belphoebe episode, the chronicle of British kings, and Arthur's combat with Maleger "mar the narrative unity, if they do not absolutely destroy it." Jones (p. 173) notes the lack of effect of plot on character in Book II.

of Bliss. Where in Book I Redcrosse is prepared in the House of Holiness for his final conflict, fights the dragon, and is united to Una, we have in Book II the visit to the Castle of Alma, the British chronicle, Arthur's fight with Maleger, and Guyon's destruction of the Bower of Bliss. These four, grand, imposing pieces are not sufficiently related to one another and to the quest. They betray only too clearly that the book has been assembled according to the pattern of Book I (with additions to the part of Arthur) rather than planned and written from the first with that pattern in mind.

XI

THE EMULATION OF ARIOSTO: BOOK III

Euen the famous *Britomart* it was,
Whom straunge aduenture did from *Britaine* fet,
To seeke her louer (loue farre sought alas,)
Whose image she had seene in *Venus* looking glas.
—III, i, 8.6–9

IN THE conduct of both the narrative and the allegory Books III and IV and the Florimell and Britomart sections of Book V differ strikingly from Books I and II. Where in the first two books the allegory is primary and the narrative is controlled by it, in Books III and IV, where Spenser borrows heavily and continuously from Ariosto, the allegory, as in Ariosto, is occasional and ornamental. It is incidental to the narrative rather than the guiding principle of its composition.[1]

The thread of narrative upon which the episodes of Book III are hung is the pursuit of Florimell. After the opening, in which, as in Book II, there is an encounter between the retiring and the oncoming knight, Guyon, Britomart, Arthur, and Timias are separated from one another in the pursuit of Florimell. Guyon drops out of sight, and the poet takes up in turn the adventures of Britomart, Arthur, and Timias. Canto vi describes the birth and place of upbringing of Amoret, and then the story turns back immediately to the pursuit of Florimell and the adventures of her pursuers. Britomart's story frames that of Florimell at the beginning (i–iii) and end (ix–xii), and the Timias-Belphoebe and Garden of Adonis material is inserted in the middle (v–vi); but the pursuit of Florimell is the thread of narrative upon which the episodes of this book are strung.

[1] R. E. N. Dodge, "Spenser's Imitations from Ariosto," *PMLA*, XII (1897), 190–95, contrasts Book III with Books I and II in plot, conduct of the narrative, and allegorical method.

Because of its structural importance we must begin by examining this story. It has not been observed how completely Spenser's Florimell is modeled on Ariosto's Angelica. The two sets of narratives present a close and continuous parallel both of incident and of narrative method.

The *Orlando Furioso* begins with the flight of Angelica from Charlemagne's camp. She encounters three of her lovers in succession. The first, Rinaldo, she hates and fears, and she flees from him. The second, Ferrau, fights with Rinaldo until the two discover that Angelica has fled. Then they set out after her. In the opening of Book III, Florimell, who has fled from the Faery Court, appears on the scene pursued by a forester. Spenser echoes verbally the encounter between Ferrau and Rinaldo in the encounter between Guyon and Britomart, which opens Book III. In both cases the knights set out in pursuit of the damsel and are separated by a fork in the road. Meanwhile, Angelica crawls under a bush to rest in hiding and overhears a third lover, Sacripant, lamenting his loss of her. She comes out, and he promptly attempts to rape her but is prevented by the arrival of Rinaldo, who fights with him while Angelica runs away again and takes refuge with a hermit.

As I pointed out in chapter iv, Belphoebe's encounter with Braggadochio in Book II parallels Angelica's story at this point, except that the positions of the knight and the lady are reversed. There is also an echo of this episode in Book I where Una's protector, Satyrane, encounters Sansloy, and she runs away while the two are fighting (Canto vi).

Ariosto breaks up the next series of Angelica's adventures by interpolating other matters, but the sequence is as follows: The hermit, in turn, becomes enamored of Angelica, but she escapes him easily. So he sends a demon after her to possess her horse. The horse carries her to the seashore and swims with her to an island where the hermit is waiting. He promptly attacks her, but fortunately he is old and impotent, and so he falls asleep and she is carried off by a band of Ebudans to be used as food for a monster sent against them by Proteus. Spenser's Florimell (III, vii and viii) takes refuge, not with a hermit, but with a witch whose son furnishes the motive for a further flight. The witch sends a magic beast to devour the horse instead of a spirit to possess it. Both heroines reach the seashore, but Spenser substitutes a lewd fisherman in a boat for Ariosto's swimming horse and island attack.[2] The whole story of the Ebudans is dropped by Spenser in favor of the wooing and imprisonment of Florimell by Proteus himself.[3] Angelica is rescued from the monster by Ruggiero, who tries in his turn to attack her, but she vanishes. During her subsequent wanderings she finds and heals the wounded squire, Medoro, and the discovery of their love idyl drives Orlando mad. Instead of the rescue by Ruggiero and the love affair with Medoro, Spenser tells of Florimell's rescue by Marinell and of their love and marriage. But he has imitated Ariosto's story of Angelica and Medoro in the story of Timias and Belphoebe in Book III, so that in the affairs of Florimell and Belphoebe we have imitations of practically every episode in Ariosto's story of Angelica.

The completeness with which Spenser has imitated the whole story of Angelica suggests that, like several of his contemporaries, he first put together and retold a story which Ariosto had wilfully broken up,[4] and then himself quarried his early narrative for material to incorporate in other stories as his plans developed. Such a process would parallel his treatment of the

[2] E. Koeppel points out that the fisherman episode has a parallel in Antoninus Liberalis' *Metamorphoses*, Fab. 40, in the story of Britomartis. He argues that Spenser's episode is a combination of Ariosto and Antoninus (see *Variorum*, III, 332–34). H. M. Belden, "Two Spenser Notes," *MLN*, XLIV (1929), 526–28, argues for the *Helen* of Euripides as the source of the Proteus story, but Ariosto is clearly the basis of the whole Florimell narrative, whatever other material may have been used as embroidery.

[3] The last parallel was observed by Koeppel (see *Variorum*, III, 333).

[4] John Stewart of Baldynneis translated the Orlando-Angelica part of Ariosto about 1580. His translation illustrates a tendency, recognized by Harington, on the part of Ariosto's readers (see S. J. McMurphy, *Spenser's Use of Ariosto for Allegory* ["University of Washington Publications in Language and Literature," Vol. II (Seattle, 1924)], p. 22). Harington equipped his translation of the *Orlando* with directions for putting the various stories together. He says in his "Advertisement to the Reader": "Further, where diuers stories in this worke seeme in many places abruptly broken off, I haue set directions in the margent, where to find the continuance of euery such storie, though I would not wish any to reade them in that order at the first reading, but . . . . he may the second time not vnconueniently vse it" (see 2d ed. [1607], sig. A1).

second idyl of Moschus, which he first translated and then adapted to its place in the narrative of Book III.

Spenser's main changes in the story of Angelica, as he finally tells it, are the reduction of the magical and extravagant parts and the elevation of the heroine's character from that of a coquette and source of vice in others to that of a chaste lady in distress who is the object of chivalrous solicitude. In this he may have been influenced by the allegorizers who interpreted Angelica as the honor that men seek after, and the pursuit of Florimell may have been the germ of the idea which finally gave us Gloriana.

The less admirable traits in Angelica's character are transferred to the false Florimell, as Miss McMurphy has observed. She is created by a witch, just as false Angelicas are created by the magician Atlantes to lure her lovers into his magic castle. Spenser has reduced the number of phantom ladies to one false Florimell, giving her the coquetry and essentially cold selfishness of Angelica and providing her with a separate story, borrowed largely from that of Ariosto's Doralice, the mistress of Mandricardo, who in turn furnishes part of the character of Braggadochio, one of the false Florimell's lovers. The snowy Florimell has been traced to various sources,[5] but I believe that the false Angelicas are the most probable original because of the relation of the real Florimell to the real Angelica.

The continuity of Spenser's imitation of the story of Angelica is not immediately apparent and has escaped notice because both Ariosto and Spenser have broken it up by the interpolation of other stories.[6] Ariosto interwove the story of Bradamante with that of Angelica in the opening cantos of the *Orlando*, and Spenser combines the story of Britomart with that of Florimell in the opening of Book III. But Britomart's story is

[5] See *Variorum*, III, 268. Gough suggests the *Helen* of Euripides (see his edition of Book V [Oxford, 1918], pp. 193–94, 197). Belden ("Two Spenser Notes") argues for this source. There were also false Gueneveres.

[6] H. C. Notcutt, "The *Faerie Queene* and Its Critics," *Essays and Studies by Members of the English Association*, XII (1926), 79–83, reviews the story of Florimell in its temporal order. He points out that it is incorporated in Books III, IV, and V, as parts of the story fit the moral pattern of these books.

modeled on Bradamante's much less consistently than Florimell's follows Angelica's.[7]

Both poets begin with the sudden appearance of this heroine who immediately unhorses a knight, much to the latter's chagrin. When Bradamante next appears, Ariosto tells very briefly who she is and whom she is in love with, recapitulating the story told by Boiardo. Spenser at this point shows no evidence of acquaintance with Boiardo but substitutes a story of Britomart's Welsh origin and borrows from Vergil's *Ciris* her name and much of the story of how she came to fall in love.[8] He also attempts to connect Britomart with Florimell by adding her to the party scattered in pursuit of the fleeing damsel and by making her overthrow Florimell's lover, details not found in Ariosto.

Bradamante's next adventure is her encounter with a disconsolate lover who tells her that his sweetheart is being held prisoner by a magician. Spenser has transferred this situation to the end of Book III and used it to introduce Britomart's rescue of Amoret. Besides these changes, he has interpolated, between Britomart's first appearance and the story of her life, an account of her visit to the house of Malecasta, a narrative created by borrowing a later experience of Bradamante's at Tristram's tower (Canto xxxii), and combining it with Bradamante's encounter with Flordespine (Canto xxv).[9] Both poets, by the time they reach Canto iii, are ready to give an account of the heroine's descendants as revealed to her by Merlin. When he has finished this canto, Spenser has nothing further to add to Britomart's story in this book, except her attack on Marinell,

[7] Dodge has described the Britomart-Bradamante parallels fairly thoroughly, but he did not observe the extent and continuity of the Angelica-Florimell relationship.

[8] Warton points out the borrowing (*Observations* [1807], I, 117), Belden ("Two Spenser Notes," pp. 528–31) emphasizes the debt to the *Ciris*, and M. Y. Hughes (*Virgil and Spenser* ["University of California Publications in English," Vol. II (Berkeley, 1929)], pp. 348–54) discusses the parallel fully.

[9] Dodge (p. 187) has noted the parallel between Tristram's tower and Malbecco's castle (III, ix), but he does not record the closer parallel between Britomart's defeat of the champions of Malecasta and Bradamante's defeat of the defenders of Tristram's tower. Spenser used still other features of this episode in IV, i, 9–16. H. H. Blanchard has shown that the Malecasta episode is also indebted to Tasso's *Rinaldo* (see *Variorum*, III, 288–90).

which is not indebted to Ariosto, her small part in the seduction of Hellenore, and her rescue of Amoret.

If Spenser had decided when he began to write Book III that he was going to make a book "of Britomartis a Lady knight, in whome I picture Chastity," it does not seem probable that he would have given her no more part in the book than enough to get her story going (part of Cantos i–iv) and the culminating episode (xi–xii). But if he had on hand a fairly complete story of Florimell, modeled on that of Angelica, and the beginning of a story of Britomart and her love for Arthegall (that story is not completed even in Book V), he could have made the present book by (1) substituting Britomart for one of Angelica-Florimell's lovers in the opening episode, (2) introducing an exemplum of chastity (the Malecasta episode) near the beginning, and (3) removing the Scudamour-Amoret episode, which in Ariosto introduces the visit to Merlin, to the end of the book where it could serve to introduce the final illustration of chastity, the rescue of Amoret.

The chief difficulty with this rearrangement seems to have been that it broke up the story of Florimell and made some rewriting in it necessary and that it gave the concluding cantos to Britomart instead of completing the adventures of Florimell. If Spenser had made Britomart's grand exploit the rescue of Florimell from Proteus, or from Busyrane, the moral would have been the same, and the organization of the book would have been much improved. He did not do so, probably because Florimell's rescue was already written in some form, and all he could do was to increase the importance of Amoret by introducing the story of her birth and upbringing into Cantos v and vi, where he was inserting the new story of Timias and Belphoebe and making use of the allegory of the Garden of Adonis. But this insertion further broke up the tale of Florimell and left him with important sections of her story left over to be worked into later books.

His difficulty was not that he could not invent exploits for Britomart which illustrated chastity but that he had conceived her story as a love story, modeled on Ariosto's tribute to the house of Este. He could not adapt this beginning to his Book of Chastity without more re-writing than he had time for. He succeeded in creating for her a grand final exploit, the rescue of Amoret, but he did so at the expense of the story of Florimell. Indeed he was clearly embarrassed throughout the book by the need to give prominence to the theme of chastity.

Spenser's apologists have devised an interpretation of chastity to fit the contents of the book. But Spenser's own conception of that virtue was thoroughly conventional, as is indicated by what he says of it directly in the letter to Ralegh and in this book and by his motive for including a book of chastity in the first instalment. He wished to flatter the Queen by praising a virtue on which she prided herself. He could hardly have hoped to please her if he had given that virtue the interpretation which his critics have credited to him.[10] He has much to say of chastity, by which he evidently means virginity, in the Timias-Belphoebe episode, which he seems to have written when he was giving the book its final form. But Spenser shows himself to have been uneasily aware that much of the book had been written with other ends in view than the illustration of chastity. His uneasiness appears in the letter to Ralegh, where he describes the final episode—Britomart's rescue of Amoret—as if that were the main plot of the book, brushing aside the adventures of the first ten cantos as "many other aduentures . . . . intermedled, but rather as Accidents, then intendments." So far as he is concerned, the rescue of Amoret is Britomart's chief exploit in defense of chastity, and even that exploit was perhaps not originally written about Britomart, as we shall see.

It is a hastily concocted book, made very largely out of materials written with other plans in view than the illustration of chastity by a knightly quest. The degree of haste is indicated by the many loose ends and narrative inconsistencies, which are much more frequent in this book than in any other of the six.

It cannot be argued that Spenser was sacrificing his narrative to his allegorical purpose in Book III, since that book has fewer genuine moral allegories than any other in the poem, and there

[10] See *Variorum*, III, 312–29.

are no clearly intended historical or topical allegories, so far as I can see, except the Timias-Belphoebe passage. Therefore, we cannot blame the allegory for the failures in narrative sequence and consistency.

On the other hand, it must be noticed that these narrative difficulties occur almost entirely in the first and last sections, where Spenser's departures from the order of Ariosto might lead us to think that there had been some rearrangement of material. In the very first episode Guyon and Arthur appear together, coming from the Castle of Alma, although Guyon, after his visit to Alma, had gone off on a long journey to the Bower of Bliss. It has already been suggested that this inconsistency is the result of replanning and that the defense of Alma's castle was once the crowning achievement in Book II.[11] In that case, the opening of Book III is an older piece of writing than the Tasso imitation at the close of Book II.

There are several further difficulties. Guyon is on horseback, although he had lost his horse in II, iii, and had gone on foot throughout Book II. The encounter between Guyon and Britomart has been objected to as lacking in allegorical significance.[12] The episode repeats the device used to link Books I and II, but no attempt is made to provide motivation for Guyon's attack on Britomart, such as was provided for the encounter at the opening of Book II. We are a little surprised to learn that the stern destroyer of the Bower of Bliss is the "gentlest knight that euer armour bore." Furthermore, this is Britomart's first tilt; yet she sustains the encounter like a veteran, and not a word is said of her inexperience. The story plunges *in medias res* with so little regard for narrative consistency that we suspect it of being lifted *ex mediis rebus* and used to introduce Book III because it parallels the introductory episode in Book II.

The second episode does not follow perfectly from the first, since in the first Guyon has his Palmer, but Arthur's Squire is

[11] Miss Spens comes to this conclusion in *Spenser's Faerie Queene* (London, 1934), p. 18, and J. H. Walter concurs (" 'The Faerie Queene': Alterations and Structure," *Modern Language Review*, XXXVI [1941], 37–58).

[12] Miss Spens, pp. 18–19.

not mentioned, while in the second (i, 14–18) the Squire appears, but the Palmer is suddenly missing. Moreover, the behavior of Arthur and Guyon is not in character. The two set off in pursuit of Florimell, leaving the really dangerous pursuit of the forester to Timias.[13] And the motive assigned to them is not in keeping with either temperance or chastity:

> The Prince and *Guyon* equally byliue
> Her selfe pursewd, in hope to win thereby
> Most goodly meede, the fairest Dame aliue [st. 18].

Obviously these lines belong to an earlier imitation of the pursuit of Angelica rather than to the Book of Chastity. Britomart is also out of character in this passage. She

> Would not so lightly follow beauties chace,
> Ne reckt of Ladies Loue. . . . .

So she goes her own way, showing a callous indifference to lust at her first encounter with it.[14] These first two episodes serve to set going the adventures of Britomart and Florimell, but it is improbable that they were written in their present order or with a book of chastity in mind.

The third episode is Britomart's adventure at the house of Malecasta, and the canto heading furnishes evidence that the canto was revised after the heading was written. We are told: "Duessaes traines and Malecastaes champions are defaced." But Duessa is not mentioned in the text, and the defeat of the retainers of Malecasta forms only the introductory part of Britomart's adventure at Castle Joyous. Apparently, after the canto heading was written, "Duessaes traines" were taken out and the Malecasta episode was extended in order to make it serve as an exemplum of the titular virtue. The elaborate banquet scene and the Tasso-like lines which describe Malecasta's intrusion into Britomart's bed may represent the elaborations.

[13] Miss Spens, p. 19.

[14] If this is an early episode, converted by the change of names to its present use, the last line might have read, "But after the foule foster *Palladine* did striue." That quest belonged to the defender of chastity, but *Timias* is a perfect metrical substitute for *Palladine*. This is the first time that Arthur's Squire is given a name, although he appears in Books I and II with his master.

Redcrosse was probably introduced into this canto when Duessa was excised from it. He obviously was brought in, in an effort to tie the first three books more firmly together. But the presence of Redcrosse in this passage has little allegorical significance, and the mention of Guyon instead of Redcrosse at the beginning of the next canto suggests that some rearrangement of parts has been imperfectly made.

Cantos ii and iii are taken up with Britomart's account of herself and her love for Arthegall. The transitions in this section are well managed, except that the closing stanza of Canto iii, which brings us back to Britomart and Redcrosse again, entirely ignores the contents of Canto i. We are told that Britomart and her nurse set out to seek Arthegall:

> Ne rested they, till that to Faery lond
> They came, as *Merlin* them directed late:
> There meeting with this *Redcrosse* knight, she fond
> Of diuerse things discourses to dilate,
> But most of *Arthegall* and his estate [iii, 62.1–5].

It might be argued that the omission of all reference to the events described in Canto i is a deliberate avoidance of repetition. But there are other reasons for believing that the contents of the first canto were hastily arranged out of pieces of narrative selected, rather than written, for that purpose. The disappearance of Britomart's nurse, Glaucè, from the events in Book III is another instance of inconsistency. She reappears in the 1596 ending of Book III and takes a part in the action of Book IV. All these narrative discrepancies point to hasty rearrangement of the material, especially in Canto i.

The final exploit of Britomart in the first half of the book, the overthrow of Marinell, shows a confusion in the time sequence, since in Canto i, Britomart encounters the fleeing Florimell on the day *before* she overthrew Marinell, yet the wound which she gave Marinell is later mentioned as the cause of Florimell's flight from Faery Court. Probably the whole passage, including Britomart's overthrow of Marinell, the sea nymph's rescue of her son, and Arthur's apostrophe to Night (the only part he has in this book except for his brief appearance in Canto i) were added when the book was being hastily arranged in its present form.

The linking passage (iv, 44.6–47.5) in which Spenser recalls the situation of Guyon, Arthur, Timias, and Britomart when they separated in the pursuit of Florimell is very Ariosto-like. But it includes the amazing statement about Britomart:

> Yet did false *Archimage* her still pursew,
> To bring to passe his mischieuous intent,
> Now that he had her singled from the crew
> Of courteous knights, the Prince, and Faery gent.....

This is the last mention of Archimage in the entire poem and the only mention of him in Book III. Evidently, when Spenser wrote the lines, either he had some lost story of Britomart in mind or he intended some story which he never told. The first seems the more probable, because the mention of "Duessaes traines" in the heading of Canto i indicates that some story about Duessa, who worked with Archimage, has been omitted. Probably Archimage's machinations against Britomart were lost at the same time.

After this bad joint, the narrative moves on smoothly enough through the whole central part of the book, involving Arthur's futile pursuit of Florimell, the Timias-Belphoebe story, Venus' search for Cupid, the birth of Belphoebe and Amoret, and the description of the Garden of Adonis. These two cantos (v and vi) are highly ornamental, and they show how skilfully the poet could put together unrelated matters when he took the time and pains.

At least the Timias-Belphoebe story was apparently written or adapted after Ralegh had undertaken to sponsor the poem at court. The love idyl has been satisfactorily identified as a compliment to Ralegh in his relations with the Queen. Spenser pointed his allusion, so that it could not be missed, by referring in the Proem of the book to Ralegh's *Cynthia* and stating that Belphoebe was named out of compliment to the *Cynthia* and by introducing tobacco into the story. There are two further bits of confirmatory evidence which have not been noted. Spenser, in his representation of Ralegh as the humble squire who is afraid to tell of his love, echoes the role in which Ralegh represents himself in his poem "To Queen Elizabeth."[15] The allusion would hardly be missed by Ralegh's friends. Ralegh himself seems to acknowledge his identification with Timias, since, in "The 11th: And Laste Booke of the Ocean to Scinthia," written apparently in 1592, he employs Spenser's name, "Belphoebe," for the Queen instead of his own "Cynthia."

The whole section (Cantos v–vi) beginning with the idyl of Timias and Belphoebe is so well integrated and so superficially related to the rest of the book that it may have been created as a unit and set into its place after Ralegh visited Kilcolman in the summer of 1589.[16] The Timias-Belphoebe story is followed by the adaptation of Moschus' idyl, which is made to introduce the allegory of the Garden of Adonis. The excuse given for the elaborate description of the garden is that Amoret was brought up there. But Amoret is not mentioned again for four cantos, and her upbringing by Venus is described in quite different terms in IV, x. The caprice which made her a twin of Belphoebe is never explained or even hinted at again.

In the second half of the book Spenser turned back to the story of Florimell for material and perhaps at that time elaborated it by adding the story of the false Florimell. Her story is coherent and consistent, except where the poet has annexed to it the tale of the Squire of Dames. He goes on to tell the story of Hellenore and then concludes with Britomart's rescue of Amoret.

All these three concluding stories show narrative inconsistencies. I have already discussed in chapter i the many bad joints and evidences of early composition in the tale of the Squire of Dames. The story of Hellenore also shows evidence of patching. It is conceived in the humor of Ariosto and appears

[15] Agnes M. C. Latham, *The Poems of Sir Walter Ralegh* (London: Constable & Co., 1929), pp. 104–5. Miss Latham (pp. 187–90) says that the poem occurs in many manuscripts of the period. J. W. Hebel and H. H. Hudson, *Poetry of the English Renaissance 1509–1660* (New York, 1932), pp. 132–33 and 938–39, express the opinion that most of Ralegh's poetry was written between 1579 and 1586.

[16] Raymond Jenkins, "Spenser: The Uncertain Years, 1584–1589," *PMLA*, LIII (1938), 356 n., suggests that Spenser was Ralegh's neighbor at Youghal in 1588. But they could hardly both have been there at the same time in that year.

to be an early piece worked over to fit it into Book III by making a place for Britomart in it so that she will not appear abruptly in Canto xi.

The tale of Hellenore combines ideas from several sources. The situation of a jealous old man with a young wife may have come from Chaucer.[17] But the complete degradation of the wife and the husband's search for her seem to have been suggested by Lucian's dialogue, *The Runaways*, where a husband is represented as searching for his wife, who has run away with three slaves.[18] She is being held in common by the slaves (like Hellenore among the satyrs), and one of them (like Paridell), as the husband says, "went off with my wife because I took him in." The parallel is suggestive of Spenser's admiration for Lucian as recorded by Gabriel Harvey about 1579.

Throughout the story of Malbecco, Spenser's tone contrasts strongly with the moral gravity of the first two books. It is flippant and unsympathetic, in the manner of Ariosto or Lucian. And two motifs from Ariosto are introduced. The forced hospitality at the beginning is borrowed from Bradamante's experience at Tristram's tower and Malbecco's visit to his wife disguised as a goat imitates Norandine's visit to his wife in similar disguise. Both of these stories show Spenser's relish for the more savage elements in Ariosto's humor.

But if the story was created early, when Spenser was trying to continue Chaucer's *Sir Thopas* in Ariosto's vein, the presence of Britomart and the superb metamorphosis of Malbecco into a symbol of jealousy seem to belong to a later revision and polishing. Besides these two additions, Miss Harper has suggested that the account of Paridell's ancestry was originally a part of the chronicle material used in II, x, and III, iii. There does not seem to be much point in giving an exalted Trojan ancestry to

[17] Ariosto has several stories of jealous husbands and unfaithful wives, but none which centers on the wife's complete debauchery and the husband's pursuit of her. Neither do any of them have the May and December motif.

[18] Lucian, *Works* (Loeb ed.), V (1936), 54–99. I. E. Rathborne quotes Professor J. B. Fletcher as suggesting Lucian's *Vera historia* as the source of this episode, but I believe that *The Runaway's* is the story meant (see *The Meaning of Spenser's Fairyland* [New York, 1937], p. 149 n.).

so base a knight. If any topical allusion is intended, it has not yet been satisfactorily explained; but the passage may originally have belonged to the early concept of the knights of Maidenhead.

The Squire of Dames has been carried along in the introductory episode of the evil custom of the castle and the forced entry, but after the party has gained entrance he is not mentioned again. Perhaps he did not figure in the old version of the seduction of Hellenore, and so he vanishes at the point where the poet ceased to re-write.

The final exploit, Britomart's rescue of Amoret, presents one further problem. It includes the Masque of Cupid, which has been identified as an old piece,[19] and it refers to Britomart as "he" several times (xii, 34.4, 42.2, 4, 5). These mistakes occur close together, as if the poet had grown inattentive for a moment either in the process of composition or, as seems more likely, in the process of revision of stanzas which did not otherwise require re-writing. The passage may have been worked up for a masculine representative of chastity (possibly Sir Thopas or Guyon or Scudamour) before the poet decided to make Britomart the heroine of Book III. In considering the whole passage, it should be borne in mind that, while the introductory situation (Canto xi) is borrowed from Bradamante's experience at the Castle of Atlantes, the masque and the events which happen in the castle are not borrowed from Ariosto and do not belong to the Britomart-Bradamante imitation.

Recently it has been suggested that Spenser borrowed certain elements of this episode from Ortuñez de Calahorra's *Mirrour of Princely Deedes and Knighthood* (1578 ff.).[20] In the *Mirrour* Rosicleer, who, like Scudamour, is a knight of Cupid and has a similar shield, arrives at a cave guarded by an enchanted

[19] A. B. Grosart, *The Complete Works . . . . of Edmund Spenser* (Privately printed, 1882–84), I, 99, thinks that the *Court of Cupid* mentioned in "E. K.'s" letter prefixed to the *Shepheardes Calender* is "certainly" the same as the Masque of Cupid. For other suggestions see *Variorum*, III, 299–301.

[20] Dorothy F. Atkinson, "Busirane's Castle and Artidon's Cave," *Modern Language Quarterly*, I (1940), 185–92.

fire.[21] He enters and releases a lady who, like Amoret, has been imprisoned by a magician-lover. In both stories the detail of an exposed and bloody heart figures, but in the *Mirrour* the heart is the magician's, while in Spenser it is Amoret's.

If Spenser was writing with the *Mirrour* episode in mind, it seems very probable that Scudamour was at first the rescuer of Amoret and that, when the episode was revised to serve as the final exploit of Britomart in defense of chastity, the story of Bradamante furnished an initial situation which suggested the Rosicleer story and that Spenser combined the two so as to make Britomart the heroine of the rescue, reducing Scudamour's role to one patterned on that of the treacherous knight in Ariosto who lured Bradamante into a trap by his story of an imprisoned lady.[22]

Whatever the history behind any single episode, it is evident that Book III was arranged rather than written as a book of Britomart. Spenser's decision to include in his first instalment a book "of Britomartis a Lady knight, in whome I picture Chastity," would have been easy enough of fulfilment if he had made up his mind while the book was still to write. But the evidences of hasty rearrangement in Book III seem to indicate that he had on hand the beginning of a love story of Arthegall and Britomart and a series of adventures involving the pursuit of Florimell by the knights of Maidenhead. Out of these he made the present book, in great haste, perhaps as late as the

[21] E. Koeppel, "Die englischen Tasso-Übersetzungen des 16. Jahrhunderts," *Anglia*, XI (1889), 355–56, points out the wall of flame in both the *Rinaldo*, V, 58–61, and the *G. L.*, XIII, 35–36.

[22] Perhaps Scudamour's rescue was later fused with the account of his entry into the Temple of Venus in IV, x. In *The Second Part of the Myrror* (1583), p. 281, there is a knight, Claridiano, who falls in love with "a pastora," or shepherdess, and disguises himself in shepherd's apparel. She has a brother, Corydon. The new shepherd calls himself Filipensio, which might suggest Philip Sidney but more probably was intended for Philip Howard, since the translation is dedicated to Lord Thomas Howard. Menalcas sings. But the resemblances to *F. Q.*, Book VI, are very general. The pastoral tone of this part of the *Mirrour* perhaps reflects the literary fashion set by the *Arcadia*, since it was not published until 1583. The original *Mirrour* has as its leading lady the princess Briana, and Crudor's lady, in *F. Q.*, Book VI, is named Briana. On fols. 69–70 Rosicleer rescues a babe from a bear, as does Calepine in *F. Q.*, Book VI. On the whole, it seems probable that Spenser read this romance, probably rather late in the development of his long poem.

summer of 1589. Ralegh visited him in the early summer, he arrived in London in November, and the *Faerie Queene* was entered in the Stationers' Register on the first of December, 1589.

If Book III was so far from completion that one and perhaps two cantos, involving the Timias-Belphoebe episode, could still be written after Ralegh made his offer of sponsorship, it is small wonder that Book III shows every evidence of hasty workmanship in contrast to Books I and II. In fact, it seems possible that the Book of Chastity was put together after the patronage of Ralegh and the court presentation came in sight. Under these circumstances the poet would be anxious to insert as much flattery of the Queen as possible into the first instalment, and a book on chastity seemed required. Britomart was the poet's choice for the heroine of the book, but her story was a love story originally created in honor of the Dudleys. However, Leicester died suddenly in the late autumn of 1588, and in that year also Queen Elizabeth put on armor and played the warrior maid at the camp at Tilbury. Therefore, when it became expedient to transform the Britomart material into a compliment to the Queen, a reference to her "great auncestry" and some compliments to chastity were all that had to be supplied. From the story of Britomart the introduction and the genealogy could be used, and the Malecasta and Amoret episodes were given prominence as illustrations of the titular virtue. Florimell's story was used as filler. Arthur had a place made for him, albeit a very small one, and some odd bits which had a bearing on chastity, like the tale of the Squire of Dames and the story of Hellenore, were incorporated. A complimentary passage was created for Ralegh, and the Masque of Cupid was revised to make the grand final exploit. No wonder that Spenser's uneasiness over the resulting book makes itself evident in his statement that "many other aduentures are intermedled, but rather as Accidents, then intendments. As the loue of Britomart, the ouerthrow of Marinell, the misery of Florimell, the vertuousnes of Belphœbe, the lasciuiousnes of Hellenora, and many the like." It is a hastily concocted book, and its miscellaneous character brought upon the poet further trouble in the organization of Book IV.

XII
THE SECOND INSTALMENT

> Great wrong I doe, I can it not deny,
> to that most sacred Empresse my dear dred,
> not finishing her Queene of faëry,
> that mote enlarge her liuing prayses dead:
> But lodwick, this of grace to me aread:
> doe ye not thinck th' accomplishment of it,
> sufficient worke for one mans simple head,
> all were it as the rest but rudely writ?
>
> —*Amoretti*, xxxiii

WE HAVE now examined the first instalment of the *Faerie Queene* for evidence of the evolution of the several plot ideas described in the letter to Ralegh and of other plot ideas which guided the poet in various stages of the process of composition. In all this analysis I have assumed that in 1589 Spenser would naturally describe his latest plan and not his earliest and largely abandoned one. Therefore, we have been able to use the letter to Ralegh as a plane of reference.

But we are in a different situation in regard to the second instalment. We have no announced plan in 1596, such as was published in 1590. If the poet had made further modifications in his general structure, we can only discover the fact by observing his practice in the three books of the second instalment. As soon as we begin such an examination, we are struck by the fact that Book IV departs furthest of all from the 1590 plan. It is probably this fact, more than anything else, which has led critics to suppose that the letter to Ralegh describes an old plan which Spenser grew away from as the poem developed. But, if the poet had so far grown away from his plan by the time he came to write Book IV that he failed to supply it with the knightly quest which is the basic plot idea of Books I and II, why did he return to his abandoned plan when he came to write Books V and VI?

As I pointed out in the first chapter, this theory of development away from the plan described in the letter is based on a theory of seriatim composition, and such a theory is initially improbable for so long and complex a set of narratives. Such a theory involves the assumption that all of the second instalment was written after the first instalment and the letter to Ralegh were published. But examination of the structure and subject matter of Book IV strongly suggests that the book was made out of leftovers from the material out of which Book III was hastily constructed.

Spenser's procedure in publishing an original work in instalments was an unusual one. He could hardly have planned to do so from the first. The printing of the letter to Ralegh confesses the difficulty involved in serial publication. The lack of a single basic narrative complicated his problems and encouraged replanning. In the ten years from 1579 to 1589, while he was experimenting, and planning and replanning, it is probable that he was working on an epic, not on a fourth of an epic. That being the case, he would naturally work on various parts of the poem as ideas came to him. If it be granted that in the process of composition his materials underwent considerable revision, corresponding to changes in the general plan for the whole, it is more than likely that when he had completed Books I–III he had quite a large body of verse left over.

Britomart's love story was created before he decided to make her the representative of chastity, yet her meeting with her lover was postponed until the second instalment. When the poet left Florimell in the cave of Proteus in Book III, can we suppose that he had not planned how he was to get her out? On the contrary, the sea cave of Proteus looks like a clever invention to pave the way for the water pageant of the wedding of the Thames and the Medway, which is used as the occasion of Florimell's rescue—and we know that this marriage was an old piece, written in some form by 1580.

The whole relationship between Books III and IV seems to

me to be strong evidence that most of the materials of which they are made up belong to the same period of composition—a period before the twelve-quest plan was decided upon. But, even if Spenser made Book IV largely out of matter on hand, why did he not re-write enough of it to bring it into conformity with his announced plan when he incorporated it in his second instalment?

In the first place, contact with the poetic revival which was in full swing in London in 1590 involved our poet in new poetic interests and ambitions, and these came into conflict with his huge epic undertaking. These new interests are fully demonstrated by the minor works which he published in the 1590–96 period, when, it has been assumed, Books IV–VI were being written. Even if we look upon the *Complaints* volume as made up largely of old pieces, we know that the poet produced *Daphnaïda*, *Colin Clouts Come Home Againe*, probably the *Astrophel*, the *Amoretti* and *Epithalamion*, and at least two of the *Fowre Hymnes*, probably all four,[1] in the period of less than six years when he was getting the second instalment of the *Fairie Queene* ready for the press.

This is the literary output, moreover, not of a professional poet, but of a man who was busy founding a family and a fortune. We know that the estate at Kilcolman involved considerable litigation and that the undertakers were obliged to find and settle English tenants on their lands. Whether or not we consider the *Amoretti* with its account of a protracted courtship to be autobiographical, we know that Spenser arranged a marriage for himself and that his first child was born before he set out on his second visit to England.

The second instalment of the *Faerie Queene* is as long as the whole *Gerusalemme Liberata*, which Tasso took more than fifteen years to write. Yet if we can credit Sonnet lxxx of the *Amoretti*, Books IV–VI were virtually complete by the summer of 1594.[2]

[1] See my articles, "The Theme of Spenser's *Fowre Hymnes*" and "Spenser's *Fowre Hymnes:* Addenda," *Studies in Philology*, XXVIII (1931), 49–57, and XXXII (1935), 152–57.

[2] The *Amoretti* were entered in the Stationers' Register November 19, 1594. If we allow time for the completion of the sonnets and the writing of the *Epithalamion*, we

Even if the enthusiasm with which his first instalment was received set the poet to writing again before his return to Ireland at the end of 1591,[3] he must have completed the second trio of books in less than five years. We can hardly believe that he composed all this verse in so short a time when he was busy with worldly affairs and very active in other poetic undertakings. It seems more probable that the second instalment was partly composed and partly compiled in considerable haste, parts of it in a rather perfunctory way.

Spenser's urgent need to get another section of his long poem in print in 1596 is evident. The sonnet to Lodowick Bryskett indicates the pressure being put upon him by his friends. He could hardly expect to please the aging Queen by publishing other works and delaying the poem which was to "immortalize" her. Prudence might suggest that he had better be getting on with his undertaking if he hoped to finish it before death robbed him of another patron. But the immediate need for a second instalment of the *Faerie Queene* was apparently produced by the storm of criticism which the publication of the *Amoretti* brought upon the poet. We hear of it in the Proem to Book IV, and again at the end of Book VI, where the poet's reply seems to be pointed directly at Lord Burghley. But the sonnet to Lodowick and the dedicatory letter prefixed to the *Fowre Hymnes* indicate that the criticism was fairly general among the poet's friends and patrons.

Everything that we know of Spenser's activities between the publication of the first and second instalments points to preoccupation with other affairs and other types of writing, and

---

cannot date Sonnet lxxx later than the spring of 1594. Probably the statement that Books IV–VI were complete was an exaggeration, as we shall see when we examine the allegory of Book V.

[3] There is some evidence that Spenser's visit to England in 1589–91 was broken into two parts. An advance of money was made to him, apparently in person, in Ireland on May 30, 1590 (see F. P. Wilson, "Spenser and Ireland," *Review of English Studies*, II [1926], 456–57). In May, 1590, Sir John Norris was sent to Ireland with an army of ten thousand men in anticipation of a Spanish invasion, and I believe it is probable that Spenser went with him. Norris stayed all summer but was recalled in the fall, and Spenser may have returned to London with him (see my article on "The Allegory of Sir Artegall in *F. Q.*, V, xi–xii," *Studies in Philology*, XXXVII [1940], 177–200, for Spenser's relations with Norris).

lends support to the hypothesis that the second instalment was got together in haste and that it was by no means all written between 1590 and 1596.

There is, however, one element in the poet's style which must here be taken into consideration. There is only one example of regular feminine rhyme (II, ix, 47) in the first three books of the *Faerie Queene*, but in the last three books and two cantos there are 163 such rhymes.[4] As Professor Stovall points out, Spenser made use of feminine rhymes in his early work, but he seemed to feel that they were not suitable for a serious and exalted style.[5] He concludes that

> Spenser, when he wrote the first three books of the *Faerie Queene*, believed or felt that feminine rimes impaired the dignity of a serious poem..... As the poem progressed, however, his opinion of feminine rimes possibly changed for the better, his style was permitted to become in many ways less serious and elevated; consequently, when he began to write the fourth book after an intermission, he consciously employed feminine rimes in conformity with his general policy of less restraint.

This conclusion seems to be substantially correct, in spite of the fact that it is based upon the usual assumption of seriatim composition. The frequency of this kind of rhyme in Book IV contrasts with the complete absence of feminine rhymes in exactly the same kind of narrative material in Book III.

But even in Book IV such rhymes are too infrequent to prove more about the composition of the book than that the poet added an occasional feminine rhyme when he was putting his material into its present shape. Except for two passages which will be discussed presently, feminine rhymes never occur at a rate of more than one in ten stanzas, and there are four entire cantos in the second instalment which have no feminine rhymes at all.[6] At least two of these cantos, opening Books V and VI, seem to have been entirely, or partly, written after 1590, so that

[4] Floyd Stovall, "Feminine Rimes in the *Faerie Queene*," *Journal of English and Germanic Philology*, XXVI (1927), 91–95. Book IV has an average of one in 10.32 stanzas, Book V of one in 10.46, Book VI of one in 13.85, and the Mutability Cantos of one in 10.36.

[5] The "February," "March," and "May" eclogues have them, but "June" has only one, and "October" and "November" have none.

[6] These cantos, as noted by Stovall, are IV, iv and viii, V, i, and VI, i.

it is evident that Spenser might write long passages containing no feminine rhymes at any time in the whole period of composition of the *Faerie Queene*.

On the other hand, the piling-up of feminine rhymes in the early cantos of Book IV is too striking to be without any significance. The first canto and a half averages more than twice as many per stanza as there are in the book as a whole. The only other passage which has so many feminine rhymes is Scudamour's adventure at the Temple of Love in Canto x. The rest of Book IV has fewer such rhymes than either Book V or Book VI.

The first canto of Book IV must have been written after the ending of Book III was revised, since it opens with the situation as it is in the 1596 ending of Book III, not as it was in the 1590 ending. The number of feminine rhymes drops sharply in the continuation of the *Squire's Tale* (ii, 35 ff.), and they disappear entirely where Braggadochio appears. Such rhymes are rare from there on, except in Canto x. Since both the continuation of the *Squire's Tale* and the episode involving Braggadochio appear, from other evidence, to be older writing, it would seem that Professor Stovall is right in his assumption that about 1590 Spenser changed his mind about the use of feminine rhymes in serious verse.

It is quite possible that here we can detect Ralegh's influence, for, after sedulously avoiding such rhymes for ten years, Spenser suddenly begins to make use of them at a time when we know that he had recently discussed poetry with Ralegh, whose verses show his great fondness for feminine rhymes.[7] However, in 1589–90 Spenser came into immediate contact with what was to him a whole new world of literary fashion, and it is not surprising that some of his poetic practices show the effect of it.

On the other hand, the deterrent influence of habit would certainly be at work on the poet, who had already written from

[7] This characteristic of Ralegh's verse is noted by Agnes M. C. Latham, *The Poems of Sir Walter Ralegh* (London, 1929), p. 17. Harington defended the use of feminine rhymes in his "Apologie of Poetrie" and cited Sidney's use of them (*Orlando Fvrioso* [1607], sig. ¶ 8ᵛ).

fifteen hundred to two thousand stanzas without employing any feminine rhymes. Therefore, it seems quite probable that cantos with feminine rhymes and cantos without might be written in the same year, and nothing more definite can be inferred from their presence in a given passage than that the passage was either written, or revised, after 1590. But since, except in the two passages mentioned, such rhymes are nowhere more frequent than one set in ninety or more lines, we can never be sure that they are not a refinement introduced in the revision of old matter.

Professor Stovall has also considered what he calls "irregular" feminine rhymes, consisting of preterits and past participles in *-ed* "where the suffix is not pronounced as a separate syllable in Modern English but must be so pronounced in the *Faerie Queene* to satisfy the meter." But the pronunciation or elision of the *e* seems to have been regarded as optional by Spenser. He is not consistent in his usage. For example, the latest editors of Book I, in the *Variorum* edition, record *ensewed-ensewd*, *congeald-congealed*, *liued-liu'd*, etc. In the first edition of the first three books the *-ed* spelling is avoided throughout in rhymed words; but there are 22 places in Book I, 58 in Book II, and 62 in Book III where this type of feminine rhyme could be introduced by a mere change of spelling. In some cases the change was actually made in the second edition.[8] Even in the last three books, where most of the past participial rhymes are spelled *-ed*, Book IV has 28, Book V has 5, and Book VI has 14 which are not so spelled and are not counted by Professor Stovall. He counts 125 such rhymes in Books IV–VI, but if we add to these all the possible feminine rhymes which are spelled *-d* instead of *-ed*, the totals for the several books are as follows: Book I, 22; Book II, 58; Book III, 62; Book IV, 71; Book V, 49; and Book VI, 43. The only striking variation here is the small number of such rhymes in Book I. The variation among the other books is not great enough to be significant, especially since Book II is much the longest book of the six, so that the frequency of such rhymes in

[8] In I, v, 29, the third rhyme, *congeald*, *heald*, *conceald*, becomes *congealed*, *healed*, *concealed*, and a similar change was made in st. 37.

Book II is much the same as in Books V and VI. Only Books III and IV show a marked increase in *-ed* rhymes. But in no case, except in Book I, is the presence or absence of such rhymes significant for a study of the history of the composition.

A little can be gathered about Spenser's rhymes from a study of his revisions of the texts of Books I–III in the edition of 1596. After the correction of misprints and the changes in diction, the next most important concern of the poet was with the rhymes. Even while the first instalment was going through the press the poet noted in "Faults Escaped" that *swifte and cruell* in I, vi, 26.6, should read *fiers and fell.* His ear was troubled by the identical rhyme in the series, *compell-cruell-cruell-quell,* and he has eliminated the second *cruell* by the emendation.

There is evidence of a struggle in II, iii, 20.5, which read in 1590 "As ghastly bug does vnto them affeare." "Faults Escaped" corrects *vnto* to *greatly*, which at least makes more sense; but in 1596 the whole line has been altered to read "As ghastly bug their haire on end does reare." Again the problem involved the rhymes. The first set had been *feare-heare-feare-cleare*, and again the emendation got rid of the identical rhyme. In only one instance did the poet alter a whole set of rhymes, but the ingenuity of the change is illuminating illustration of his methods. In II, iv, 17, he introduced a new *c* rhyme without re-writing the lines:

So me weake wretch, of many weakest *wretch*,	one
Vnweeting, and vnware of such mishap,	
She brought to mischiefe through *her guilful trech*,	occasion,
Where this same wicked villein did me *wandring ketch.*	light upon.

In the argument to II, v, the poet re-wrote the second half of the quatrain and so had to change his rhyme word in the first half. And in II, vi, 3.4, "as merry as Pope Ione" became "that nigh her breth was gone," an obvious improvement in taste as well as a change of a rhyme word in a passage which there is other reason to believe represents early writing.

These changes illustrate the poet's care in revision, a subject upon which we have too little evidence at best. But it is a curious fact that all the changes noted occur in Book II.[9] The only similar change in Book I was made when the proof was being read in 1590. In Book III there was only one change to improve the rhyme, where the poet had failed to provide a rhyme for line 1.[10] Changes were made to improve the sense or to smooth up the line, and in III, vii, 50.2, the second edition gets rid of the distortion of a word at the expense of the rhyme. This is in the tale of the Squire of Dames, which I have singled out as part of the early *Sir Thopas* continuation.[11]

In no case did Spenser introduce feminine rhymes in his revisions of Books I–III, but he had trouble with his rhymes, especially in Book II. His rhyme scheme was difficult enough without the further handicap of limitation to masculine rhymes. Younger poets, like Daniel, were using feminine rhymes in serious verse, and Sir Walter Ralegh was especially fond of them. Therefore, Spenser ceased to avoid them, and in two passages he seems to have striven consciously to make use of them; but for the most part habit was against such a practice.

The almost complete restriction of revision in rhyme to Book II supports the conclusion that much of Book II, as well as of Book I, is early writing but that Book I had been worked over thoroughly after the scheme announced in the letter to Ralegh had been adopted, whereas Book II was assembled much more hastily, and Book III was put together out of material written before the final plan was adopted but considerably later than Books I and II, so that the technique of the stanza had become a habit of mind.

Except for the two passages in Book IV (i and x) which other evidence indicates were either newly written or thoroughly worked over after 1590, the occurrence of feminine rhymes is so

[9] In II, x, 19.5, "vpon the present floure" becomes "that impatient stoure" and improves the sense. In II, xi, 9.9, both sense and rhyme were improved by the substitution of "they that Bulwarke sorely rent" for the 1590 reading, "they against that Bulwarke lent." There was also a problem of identical rhymes here, *lent* being rhymed with *bent*, *violent*.

[10] In III, xii, 27.3, "nothing did remayne" becomes "and bore all away."

[11] The poet had written "to quench her flaming thrust," rhyming with *lust*, *trust*, *must*, but 1596 reads *thurst* for *thrust*.

infrequent that an ordinary process of polishing, very little more extensive than is observable in the second edition of Book II, might account for all of them; and therefore they constitute very tenuous evidence, if any, of the date of composition of a given passage.[12] Spenser had definitely decided to make use of them, as his practice in IV, i, indicates, and he would naturally introduce them freely wherever revision involved the finding of a new rhyme.

Before we go on to the analysis of the last three books, let us glance back for a moment. When the poet finally decided upon his plan and his method of publication, he retouched Book I with minute and loving care. Book II may have required extensive revision, especially in the introduction of Arthur, but the poet had little time to work at the smoothing-up of his verses. Book III was put together in great haste partly from old and partly from new materials with something like a scissors-and-paste technique, perhaps partly while the printer waited. It is no wonder that the organization was unsatisfactory and the plan not clear. So the letter to Ralegh was devised, adding to the general plan the culminating device of the twelve days' banquet.

Meanwhile Spenser was in London again, making new friends and learning the new fashions and the new poetic forms—in London when the *Arcadia* came off the press and everybody read what they had longed to see for years. Our poet read it too, as the contents of Book VI demonstrate. I think an examination of Books IV and V will show why it was not until he reached Book VI that the poet was free to give full expression to his enthusiasm for the new Arcadian mode.

[12] See below, Appendix I, for a detailed analysis.

XIII

THE CONTINUATION OF BOOK III: BOOK IV

> After so long a race as I haue run
> through Faery land, which those six books compile,
> giue leaue to rest me being halfe fordonne,
> and gather to my selfe new breath awhile.
>
> —*Amoretti*, lxxx

BOOK IV is almost entirely a continuation of Book III. The story of Britomart had been no more than begun in Book III, since at the end of that book she had not yet caught sight of her lover; and Florimell had been left in the dungeon of Proteus. Amoret's story was sufficiently complete in the 1590 version of Book III, but the poet decided to continue her story in Book IV, and so he altered the ending of Book III in order to continue her separation from her lover and give her a series of adventures in search of him. In addition, Spenser was under some obligation to make a place for Belphoebe in his second instalment, since she was the only representation of the Queen who actually took part in the action. These considerations gave him four heroines for Book IV but no hero and no knightly quest.

The necessity of continuing the stories of Florimell and Britomart and the desire to continue those of Amoret and Belphoebe sufficiently account for the miscellaneous character of Book IV, which has been described, not entirely justly, as "a riot of formlessness."[1] Mechanically, however, it follows a plan which combines features of Books I and III. Arthur is brought in, in

[1] Kate M. Warren, in her edition of the book, says: "It seems as if it may have been pieced together out of fragmentary stories and reflections that he had put by for working up in the future" (see *Variorum*, IV, 282). A. A. Jack, in his *Commentary on the Poetry of Chaucer and Spenser* (Glasgow: Maclehose, Jackson & Co., 1920), p. 221, suggests that the book "was probably not written as a whole, but taken up for a space and then laid down."

Canto viii, as in Books I and II. Florimell is used for the opening and closing sections, as Britomart was used in Book III, and the thread of continuity is provided by Amoret's search for her lover, as in Book III it was provided by the flight of Florimell. Where the houses of Pride and Holiness stand in Book I we have two friendship stories in Book IV, and the grand finale of rescue and reunion occupies the last two cantos as usual. What is lacking is a hero.[2] It is this omission which has obscured the fact that in Book IV Spenser was not drifting still farther from the plan of Books I and II but that he was imitating that structure as well as he could while using materials written for another purpose.

The first four cantos are held together by the device of a cavalcade made up of Blandamour, Paridell, Duessa, and Ate, to which others are added and subtracted from time to time. Into it is interpolated the long story of Cambel and Triamond, and it moves toward the tournament for Florimell's girdle. The episodes of this cavalcade seem to be a composite of old and new matter. It opens with Amoret riding with Britomart, a situation created by the alteration of the ending of Book III. They come upon the cavalcade, and the story is immediately shifted to Duessa and Ate and their companions. Three different accounts of the appearance of Ate occur in this passage. She is first said to be disguised as a fair lady (i, 17), but almost immediately she is made an emblematic figure of discord (i, 27–29), and later (iv, 9–10) she becomes simply an old hag.

These contradictions may be the result of carelessness and confusion on the part of the poet, but there is a corresponding discrepancy in the handling of Duessa which makes probable the alternative hypothesis of replanning and imperfect combination of materials. Duessa is introduced along with Ate, and she is still a member of the cavalcade in ii, 1–10, when Blandamour wins the false Florimell from Ferraugh. But she vanishes almost as soon as the false Florimell appears. There is a vague

[2] H. C. Notcutt has pointed out the balancing of paired episodes in Book IV, such as is evident in the three earlier books ("The *Faerie Queene* and Its Critics," *Essays and Studies by Members of the English Association*, XII [1926], 72–78).

reference to "those dames" who stir up strife (ii, 19), which might apply to either of them, as might the reference to Blandamour's "discordfull Dame" (iv, 3), but five stanzas later Blandamour's lady is the false Florimell, for whom Braggadochio refuses to fight if the loser must take the hag, Ate. Somewhere along the way Duessa has vanished, and her part has been taken over by the false Florimell.

There is still another narrative difficulty in the first canto, where Blandamour is described as hating Scudamour "because his loue he wonne by right" (i, 39). From the conversation we learn that Blandamour was the lover of Amoret and that Scudamour is charged with getting her by a trick. But no such story has been told, and there is no room for such an episode in the account of Scudamour's wooing of Amoret. Taken altogether, these narrative discrepancies suggest that the passage was worked on at different times and that some old matter has been combined with new.

The story of Cambel and Triamond, which has been interpolated into the account of the cavalcade (ii, 30—v, 21), is an attempt to continue Chaucer's *Squire's Tale.* This narrative has been singled out by one critic, because of its style, as perhaps the early fragment sent to Harvey in 1580.[3] While this suggestion is hardly tenable on the basis of what we know about the character of that early fragment, the story obviously belongs to a period when Spenser was trying to combine the matter of Chaucer with the manner of Ariosto. Here he seems to be copying Ariosto's extravagance.

The story of Cambel and Triamond is only an episode or interruption in the narrative sequence of the first five cantos, which are chiefly concerned with the cavalcade which moves toward and takes part in the tournament for Florimell's girdle. Yet whoever wrote the caption seized upon it as the chief illustration of friendship in the book. It seems possible that this heading was supplied by some friend or editor, or even by the

[3] H. E. Cory, *Edmund Spenser: A Critical Study* (Berkeley, Calif., 1917), p. 261, describes the passage as so extravagant, crude, and turgid that "it seems almost boyish and tempts the critic to suggest that this was the early fragment sent to Harvey."

printer, because it names "Telamond" for "Triamond," describing the book as "The Legend of Cambel and Telamond, or of Friendship." The mistake ignores the poet's meaning in his choice of the name (Priamond being the first, Diamond the second, and Triamond the third of the three brothers), and it also shows a lack of comprehension of the structure of the book. The classic treatment of friendship is in the story of Amyas and Placidas, which, in its antecedents, its position in the book (viii–ix), and its relation to Arthur, appears to be the chief exemplum of the titular virtue. Because it is so inept, I suspect that the printer supplied this heading.

The tournament for Florimell's girdle (iv, 13—v, 28), which terminates the movement of the cavalcade, is conducted by the knights of Maidenhead against all comers. It is so closely related to the tournament for Florimell's wedding in Book V that the two will be discussed together in the next chapter.[4]

After the tournament, and as a result of it, Arthegall and Scudamour lie in wait for Britomart, and the ensuing fight and recognition scene between the lovers occupies Canto vi. This scene is an essential part of the story of Britomart, but it is modeled on an episode in the *Gerusalemme Liberata* rather than on Ariosto's Bradamante. If much of Britomart's story had been created before the poet decided to reorient her as the champion of chastity, it would seem that this important event must have been described before Book III was organized. Certainly it was written with a plan in view different from that which made Arthegall the exemplar of justice, for his ambush of Britomart is not just, either in act or in motive.

After a brief love-making, Britomart sets out in search of Amoret, and the poet turns to the adventures of Amoret, which are made to supply continuity to the next three cantos. Cantos vii–ix combine three stories, all of them very important from the point of view of the internal history of this book. They are: (1) the story of Amoret's capture by Lust; (2) her rescue by Timias and Belphoebe, with the subsequent quarrel between Timias and Belphoebe; and (3), interwoven with these, the

[4] A. B. Gough noted the similarity in his edition of Book V (Oxford, 1918), p. 192.

fairly complex friendship story of Amyas and Placidas. These three cantos contain Spenser's best example of friendship, and his narratives of Belphoebe and of Arthur—the only elements in this book which appear to have been written in conformity with the plan announced for the whole poem.

One of these three stories, the Timias-Belphoebe affair (vii, 23—viii, 18), was either entirely written or thoroughly adapted to Ralegh's situation after the scandal over his marriage to Elizabeth Throckmorton occurred in the summer of 1592.[5] Ralegh was in prison from July until September, and he was out of favor and excluded from the court until after the second instalment of the *Faerie Queene* was published. He spent most of this time in retirement at Sherborne.

Spenser represents Timias as retiring to a solitary hermitage when Belphoebe rebuked him for caressing Amoret. If Spenser's first readers associated Ralegh with Timias, as the transparent allegory of Timias' devotion to Belphoebe in Book III would lead them to do, Spenser's account of the hermitage of Timias must have reminded them of Ralegh's very popular poem beginning:

> Like to a Hermite poore in place obscure,
> I meane to spend my daies of endles doubt. . . . .[6]

The topical purport of this passage is hardly subject to question, and it enables us to date the passage as created after the summer of 1592.

The Timias-Belphoebe story is introduced as an episode in the rescue of Amoret from Lust. Another captive of Lust is Aemylia, whose story is closely interwoven with that of Amoret. The three stories—of Amoret, Timias, and Aemylia (whose lover is Amyas)—are so closely interlocked that it seems probable they were worked up together. The change in the ending of Book III seems to indicate that Spenser decided to continue the

[5] All that is known about this affair is reviewed by Fred Sorensen in "Sir Walter Ralegh's Marriage," *Studies in Philology*, XXXIII (1936), 182–202.

[6] The poem was first printed by Richard Jones in *Britton's Bowre of Delights* (1591) and was reprinted in *The Phœnix Nest* (1593) (see H. E. Rollins' edition of the latter [Cambridge: Harvard University Press, 1931], pp. xxxii, 69–70). The poem became a very popular song.

story of Amoret after the first instalment was published, and this is the chief story about her in Book IV (the account of Scudamour's wooing in Canto x is a formal allegory which could have been attached to any heroine). It would seem probable, therefore, that this adventure of Amoret was created after 1590.

There are, however, some indications that the capture of Amoret by Lust is an adaptation of an older story, probably originally told about Florimell. Lust carries Amoret to his cave,

> Ne care he had, ne pittie of the pray,
> Which many a knight had sought so many a day [vii, 8.4–5].

The last line fits the story of Florimell much better than it does that of Amoret. The two names are metrically interchangeable, and the two characters are very similar, so that an old story about Florimell could easily have been converted into one about Amoret.

The account of the giant, Lust, recalls that in the *Sir Thopas* continuation in Book III Sir Thopas and a lady knight called Palladine are said to be the enemies of twin giants, Ollyphant and Argante, representatives of male and female lust. The giant who captures Amoret is a duplicate of Ollyphant. Both giants fear their chaste feminine pursuers (cf. III, xi, 6, and IV, vii, 29.7–9). The description of Lust includes several archaic words, such as are rare in Spenser's later work.[7] The whole description seems to me to be in Spenser's "early" style; yet the account of the rescue, including the stanzas which describe Timias' fondling of Amoret (35–36), are in the voluptuous and suggestive manner which we associate with Spenser's Tasso imitations. It is these stanzas which fit the episode to Ralegh's situation.[8] Perhaps the Diana-like huntress who surprised

[7] *Awhape* (vii, 5.4) and *eft* (9.5) are listed as archaisms, and *mister* (10.5), *affeard* (4.1), *soust* (9.3), and *swelt* (9.4) as dialect words in the study of Spenser's archaisms.

[8] Again, in the account of Timias' retreat (see Appendix I, episode 424) there are five archaic words in eleven stanzas. We are told by B. R. McElderry, Jr., that there are not more than 320 archaisms in all Spenser, of which half occur in the *Calender*. He lists as archaic the following words which occur in this passage (sts. 41–46): *youthly*, *avise*, *lout*, *queint*, and *bestad* ("Archaism and Innovation in Spenser's Poetic Diction," *PMLA*, XLVII [1932], 144–70).

Braggadochio in Book II had rescued a lady from Lust in some earlier story. Arthur's Squire is never called Timias in this passage, perhaps because he was no longer τίμιος to Elizabeth or perhaps because the name did not occur in the episode which Spenser may have been adapting.

Spenser had two good reasons—his duty to the Queen and to Ralegh—for creating this passage. But if he had on hand a passage in which a personification of Lust carried off one of his heroines (and what we can gather of his early plans indicates that he probably did), then this passage represents an adaptation, the preceding part of which had been re-written in order to introduce Aemylia, and perhaps for other reasons.

This entire section is a well-knit story unit, beginning when the poet takes a fresh start at the opening of Canto vii and ending in a bad joint in Canto ix. It includes the only clearly topical matter in this book, the Timias-Belphoebe narrative, which can be dated as written after the summer of 1592. It includes the chief concessions made in Book IV to the general structure of the poem as described in the letter to Ralegh: the parts played by Belphoebe and Arthur. Moreover, the story of Amyas and Placidas, which occurs in these three cantos, is the only real exemplum of friendship, in the Aristotelian sense, in the whole book, since the friendship of Cambel and Triamond is the result of magic.

The story of Placidas' rescue of his faithful friend Amyas would have made an excellent quest motif for the whole Book of Friendship, as the duel between Cambel and Triamond fails to do, if Spenser had set out from the start to write a book illustrating Ariostotle's theory of friendship. As it is, these three cantos are a book of friendship in miniature. Even the intervention of Arthur comes at the right point. But the book remains in miniature. Spenser had sections of the stories of Florimell and Britomart to dispose of, and it was necessary to put them in the books immediately following Book III.

The most confused episode in the whole book occurs in Canto ix, where the poet brings to a hasty conclusion the story of Amyas and Placidas and introduces the account of the Temple of Venus. Craik complains with some justice that this canto has the air of hasty composition, as though it were carelessly thrown together to link unrelated matters. Stanzas 1–16 conclude the Amyas-Placidas story in a most perfunctory way. The giving of the reformed Poeana to the "squire of low degree," who was Aemylia's lover, does not seem like the work of the moralist of II, xii.

Then Arthur rides with Amoret, and we are given a very confused account of a fight involving six knights,[9] during which Amoret disappears without explanation—and we are cheated for the second time of the reunion of Scudamour and Amoret.[10] The absence of the reunion scene is all the more remarkable because a reunion took place in the passage which Spenser is imitating from Ariosto. Amoret has been rescued by Arthur, as Isabella is rescued by Orlando. Both ladies accompany their rescuers until they come upon a fight involving the lover of the lady. Orlando rescues the lover, and a reunion takes place forthwith.[11] But Spenser allows Amoret to vanish so that he can introduce his grand allegory of Scudamour's wooing of her in the Temple of Venus.

Still another narrative difficulty arises from the conversation in which Arthur makes peace among the knights. The four knights accuse Britomart of having taken their lady, the false Florimell. This she denies, entering the counterplea:

> I thereby my former loue haue lost,
> Whom seeking euer since with endlesse paines,

[9] Four are named Druon, Claribell, Blandamour, and Paridell and are said to be the same who recently (v, 24) contended for the hand of the false Florimell; but those four were called Satyran, Eriuan, Blandamour, and Paridell. They set upon Britomart and Scudamour, and then Arthur comes on the scene.

[10] R. W. Church points out that Amoret is spoken of as if she were present in the opening stanzas of the next canto (x, 3–4). John Upton suggests that Spenser intended to insert the reunion scene, which he had removed from the end of Book III, between sts. 39 and 40 of this canto. But st. 40 speaks of Scudamour as still sad; so we cannot look upon the absence of the reunion scene at this point as a mere omission due to the loss of a page of the manuscript or to the neglect of a direction to the printer (see *Variorum*, IV, 215–16).

[11] See *O. F.*, XXIII, 63 ff. The earlier stirring-up of jealousy between the lovers by the false report of a spiteful old hag is reproduced by Spenser (see *O. F.*, XX, 134–42, and *F. Q.*, IV, i, 47 ff.).

> Hath me much sorrow and much trauell cost;
> Aye me to see that gentle maide so tost [ix, 38.2–5].

As the story stands at present the knights were in no way connected with Britomart's loss of Amoret. That may have been another story which was removed when the seizure of Amoret by Lust was put into its present place. Finally, within twenty stanzas, "lewd Claribell" (st. 20) becomes "good Sir Claribell" (st. 40).

Obviously in this canto the poet has hastily patched together a conclusion for one episode and an introduction for another, using materials written for a different situation and doing too little revising as he went. The canto is all the more conspicuous because, as a whole, the book is much better integrated than Book III. Perhaps the confusion arose from the removal of other matters to make room for the Belphoebe and Arthur stories in Cantos vii and viii.

The elaborate allegory of the Garden and Temple of Venus presents a tantalizing problem. There are three reasons for connecting it with Ralegh: the unusually free use of feminine rhymes, the subject matter, and a reference in the *Ruines of Time*. In the *Ruines* Spenser mentions "a pleasant Paradize" which is not surpassed by

> that which *Merlin* by his Magicke slights
> made for the gentle squire, to entertaine
> His fayre *Belphoebe* . . . . [ll. 523–25].

The reference is so like the ones which Spenser puts into *Colin Clout* and elsewhere, calling attention to the Garden of Adonis, that it seems probable the poet was doing the same thing here and that, when he revised the *Ruines* in 1591, he had just created such a garden for Timias and Belphoebe. But Ralegh's disgrace in 1592 would make a topical allegory of that kind undiplomatic. Such a piece would have to be revised so as to eliminate Timias before it could be used in the *Faerie Queene*. The only description of a supernatural garden which appears in the second instalment is this Garden of Venus, which was certainly not written expressly for its place in Book IV.

The reference to "art playing second natures part" fits a

pleasance created by Merlin for Timias and Belphoebe. The very free use of feminine rhymes[12] constitutes delicate flattery of Ralegh, who was very fond of them; and if this allegory was created in 1590–91, that was the period when Spenser had just decided to introduce feminine rhymes and was using them freely, when he began work on the second instalment.

One other element which suggests a connection with Ralegh is the unusual description of Venus, including the translation of the Lucretian hymn to Venus. These elements present parallels to a passage in *Colin Clout* (ll. 800 ff.) and the matter in the first two of the *Fowre Hymnes*. All three pieces seem to belong to the period just after Spenser met Ralegh.[13] It is quite possible that Spenser's sudden interest in Lucretius was the result of contact with Ralegh's speculative and unorthodox mind. At any rate, it seems fairly clear that when he began to write again, after his trip to court with Ralegh, Spenser was much interested in theories about the metaphysical nature of love, and he had been freshly impressed with the beauty of the Lucretian hymn to Venus. If under the impetus of this new interest he created a paradise of love in honor of Timias and Belphoebe, he had to disguise it after Ralegh's disgrace before he could use it in the *Faerie Queene.*

It has been observed that this allegory includes both an island paradise and a temple of Venus.[14] It may represent a combination of two pieces. It may even include parts of an imitation of

[12] There are 9 regular feminine rhymes in 58 stanzas, and 9 rhymes in *-ed.*

[13] See P. W. Long, "The Date of Spenser's Earlier Hymns," *Englische Studien*, XLVII (1913–14), 197–208; and my articles on the *Hymnes*, in *Studies in Philology*, XXVIII, 49–57, and XXXII, 152–57. The relation of the three pieces is discussed at more length in my article on "Spenser's Venus and the Goddess Nature of the *Cantos of Mutabilitie*," *Studies in Philology*, XXX (1933), 165–70.

[14] It has been suggested that the Temple of Venus and not the Masque of Cupid in Book III corresponds to the early *Court of Cupid* mentioned by "E. K.," but the enjambment test shows that the masque is the older piece. There may have been early versions of both pieces among the *Visions* or *Pageants*. Clement Marot, whose works Spenser used when he was writing the *Calender*, has "Le Temple de Cupido" as the first piece in his *Opuscules*, published in *Les Œuvres* (1554, 1557, 1568, 1573, etc.). It describes a lover as searching for Ferme Amour in a temple which "on l'eust pris pour Paradis terrestre." He finds Bel Accueil there, and Fauxdaunger guards the door. Altar, temple, and inhabitants are symbolic and clearly indebted to the *Roman de la rose*, which Marot modernized.

the Garden of Alcina, discarded when the Bower of Bliss was put into Book II, since it presents some parallels with Ariosto.[15] On the other hand, the famous friends, Hercules and Hylas, David and Jonathan, etc. (st. 27), are strange inhabitants for a garden of Venus. They obviously came there when the allegory was being adapted to the friendship theme. But this allegory was hardly created originally for the wooing of Amoret, since it does not agree with the other story of Scudamour's wooing in III, vi, 52–53, and since it is fitted very roughly into its place in Book IV. All things considered, it would appear that this elaborate allegory was put into, rather than written for, its place in the book.

The eleventh canto is devoted to the wedding of the Thames and the Medway. We know that this passage was first planned and probably written as an experiment in "English versifying," or classical meter, in 1580. It was not re-written until after Camden's *Britannia* and the second edition of Holinshed appeared in 1586 and 1587.[16] The *Lay of the Bregog and the Mulla*, which was finally incorporated in *Colin Clout*, was written before the summer of 1589 if, as Spenser says, he read it to Ralegh at Kilcolman. The wedding of the Thames and the Medway draws upon the same material. The organization of Book III could have been much improved by making Florimell, instead of Amoret, the lady rescued by Britomart. These considerations lead me to believe that the rescue of Florimell was already planned and at least partly written before the summer of 1589, when Book III was being completed. That would put the date of composition of the river passage between 1587 and 1589.

One stanza (22), however, bears the mark of Spenser's contact with Ralegh and was probably added to the canto as late as 1595 or 1596. Stanza 21 mentions the Orinoco and Amazon among the famous rivers of the world. The next stanza affirms the English claim to the gold of that region and rebukes the na-

[15] R. E. N. Dodge compares *O. F.*, VI, 19–22, 78, 79, and VII, 2–5, etc. (the general account of the garden and the bridge with a guardian), with Spenser ("Spenser's Imitations from Ariosto," *PMLA*, XII [1897], 185, 202).

[16] See above, chap. viii.

tion for neglecting its opportunity. Ralegh's interest in the Spanish legends of Manoa led him, in 1594, to send an expedition to Guiana. The next year he went himself, returning in August, 1595. His *Discouerie of Guiana*, with its account of the fabulous gold of the Orinoco, was published in 1596.[17] Guiana gold was a long obsession with Ralegh, which was in the end to cost him his life. He may already have been talking of it when he visited Kilcolman in 1589. But 1595 or 1596 seems, from what we know, to be a more probable date for the composition of the stanza, and all that we can learn about Spenser's methods of composition accords with the theory that this topical reference to a current issue was put into an already written canto just before it was published.

Book IV was put together out of the same body of materials which had been drawn upon for Book III, but there are certain striking differences in narrative technique between the two books. In comparison with Book III, Book IV shows a much freer handling of Ariosto's narrative and a much closer imitation of his technique. Even in the stories of Florimell and Britomart, Book IV shows no such dependence on Ariosto for plot as was shown by Book III. But, on the other hand, in Book IV Spenser's characters imitate the character and conduct of Ariosto's characters repeatedly.[18] It would seem that Spenser began with an imitation of Ariosto's narrative and then developed a feeling for character and situation which enabled him to invent stories and develop plots of his own.

In its organization Book IV is more closely imitative of Ariosto than any other book in the poem. Ten of the twelve cantos

[17] See *Variorum*, IV, 248–49, especially the notes by Ray Heffner; and Kathrine Koller, "Spenser and Ralegh," *ELH*, I (1934), 48–49.

[18] Britomart behaves like Marfisa, Ate like Gabrina, Scudamour like Zerbino, and Amoret like Isabella. The Ariosto-like conduct includes Britomart's disclosure of her sex (i, 13), Ate's spiteful false gossip (i, 47 ff.), and Amoret's uneasiness in the company of Britomart and later in that of Arthur. Canto iii contains a direct reference to Ariosto. The offer made in iv, 9–10, is imitated from the *Orlando*, and so is Braggadochio's conduct at the tournament. Amoret's experience in the Cave of Lust is modeled on Isabella's in that of the Orc. The false Florimell's choice of Braggadochio is copied from that of Doralice. Most of these borrowings occur in the early cantos and in passages where early material has been indicated by other considerations.

have characteristically Ariosto-like endings, and there are Ariosto-like transitions at five other points. Only Book VI has more such transitions, and it has only seven such canto endings. Book I has one, Book II has none, and Book III has only two such canto endings.[19] Ariosto's transitions are a simple and uniform trick of always breaking off at an exciting point in the narrative and always recalling the previous situation when he takes up the strand of narrative again. It is not a trick which any writer would fail to observe or find hard to imitate. Therefore, I believe that the many bad joints in Book III, and the failure to tie the book together into a coherent whole, were due less to a failure to understand Ariosto's technique than to a rearrangement of materials so hasty as not to permit a re-writing of linking passages. In Book IV the poet, for the most part, did more revising and took more time to smooth up his links, with the result that, in spite of its miscellaneous character, Book IV is much better integrated than Book III. Except for the account of the cavalcade at the beginning and the confusions in Canto ix, the narrative in Book IV moves smoothly from one episode and set of characters to the next.

In the handling of the allegory, especially in such creations as the houses of Care and of Slander, the Cave of Lust, and the characters of Ate and Corflambo, Book IV is closer to Books I and II than to Book III. These pieces indicate that Spenser had not discarded his moral purpose and perhaps even that he was trying to imitate some passages which had proved successful in Books I and II.

On the whole, Book IV furnishes us with valuable information about the poet's workmanship. He was hampered by the necessity of making use of materials on hand and of continuing the unfinished stories of Britomart and Florimell. He did not succeed in fitting his materials to the hero and quest pattern. These materials, including part of the events of the first four cantos, the story of Cambel and Triamond, the marriage of the

[19] A. H. Gilbert, "Spenser's Imitations from Ariosto: Supplementary," *PMLA*, XXXIV (1919), 225–32.

Thames and the Medway, the Temple of Venus, and perhaps the recognition scene between Arthegall and Britomart, dominate and overbalance the general structure. But the narrative skill with which they are put together is considerable. It illustrates Spenser's tendency to let the parts dominate the whole and to arrange his composition on principles of design rather than of growth and narrative structure, but he follows his principles when he has time to work over his compositions. His failures are not entirely the result, as the critics have assumed, of carelessness, inaccurate memory, and incompetence.

XIV

THE CONSTRUCTION OF BOOK V

> For take thy ballaunce, if thou be so wise,
> And weigh the winde, that vnder heauen doth blow;
> Or weigh the light, that in the East doth rise;
> Or weigh the thought, that from mans mind doth flow.
>
> —V, ii, 43.1–4

BOOK V follows closely the plan announced in the letter to Ralegh and followed in Books I and II. But it has fewer episodes than any other book, and these episodes are more formal and disconnected than is usual in the other books.[1] Not only are they independent beads on the very thin thread of narrative but they are of uniform size, two to a canto. Ten of the cantos break in two in this way. The result is a peculiarly wooden and inflexible structure, especially in the opening cantos, where the episodes are not closely related to one another in subject matter.

The canto introductions show how firmly the poet kept in mind his purpose to illustrate justice, when he was putting this book together. There is an elaborate treatment of justice in the Proem to the book (eleven stanzas, as compared with four, five, and seven in the other books), and, in addition, nine of the cantos have similar introductions. No other book is so treated. These introductions could have been added at the last minute, but, except for the two passages which continue the stories of Florimell and Britomart, the whole book is made up of episodes which are purely exempla of justice.

The book falls into three distinct parts: (1) exempla of jus-

[1] H. S. V. Jones, *A Spenser Handbook* (New York, 1930), pp. 249–50, comments on the "highly episodic arrangement" of the opening cantos (i–iv). He also notices the three sharp divisions of the book and its structural relation to Book II. He observes that it has a more patchwork arrangement than any other book in the poem.

tice and the tournament for Florimell's wedding (i—iv, 20), (2) the Amazon episode which brings Arthegall and Britomart together again (iv, 21—vii), and (3) the purely topical allegory which makes up the last five cantos. These three sections are quite distinct and require separate consideration.

The first section is marked by its disconnected, wooden exempla of justice and (except in the introductory stanzas) by its very sparing use of enjambment. The introductory stanzas are notable for their failure to attempt any connection between the hero of this book and the Arthegall of Books III and IV. Spenser begins all over again with an allegorical account of his upbringing by Astraea, his arming, his quest, and his assistant Talus, who now makes his appearance for the first time. He even adopted "Artegall" as the regular spelling of the name in Book V. It seems that, with the deaths of Leicester, Sidney, and the Earl of Warwick, and the consequent loss of Dudley patronage, Spenser had decided to reinterpret Arthegall. But, on the other hand, much of the first section of this book is comparatively crude in conception and execution, as though it was early work. Perhaps after the death of Leicester the poet combined an early attempt to illustrate justice and to celebrate Lord Grey with the Arthegall romance. Grey also died in 1593, and Artegall becomes Sir John Norris in the closing cantos of this book, as we shall see in the next chapter.

The second half of the first canto consists of a naïve imitation of the judgment of Solomon. The second canto is made up of two exempla of justice: the destruction of Pollente and the Lady Munera and the overthrow of the giant Democracy. Canto iii is devoted to the tournament for Florimell's wedding, but Canto iv opens with one further exemplum of justice, the case of treasure trove.

The mechanical and wooden arrangement of these three and a half cantos has its counterpart in the structure of the verses. The whole section has a lower enjambment ratio than any other group of episodes in the whole poem.[2] Four unrelated episodes

[2] The whole matter of enjambment is discussed, with tables, below, Appendixes I and II.

(all of this section except the introduction and the tournament) were invented purely as illustrations of justice. They are not connected with one another or, except in one case, with the rest of the book. No effort was made to work them into a continuous narrative or to connect them with Artegall's quest. It hardly seems possible that the poet could have created these episodes after he had written the first four books and shortly before he wrote the fine legend of Sir Calidore. It seems much more probable that this section of Book V was created out of some early attempts to make allegories of the moral virtues.

As allegories these stories belong with the cruder parts of the Castle of Alma rather than with such creations as the Bower of Bliss and the Garden of Adonis. Even when we have made full allowance for the unevenness of poetic inspiration, there is a crudity about the first part of Book V which is irreconcilable with the quality of Books IV and VI as well as with most of the contents of the first instalment. Gough comments on the careless rhymes in Book V as "perhaps a sign that Spenser's interest in his work was flagging." In a later chapter (xvii) I shall present some reasons for thinking that an illustration of political justice, such as these allegories convey, was a part of Spenser's early plans.

The tournament for Florimell's wedding was obviously put into this book because it was left over from the story of Florimell and because it shows justice being meted out to both Braggadochio and the false Florimell. It serves as a welcome break in the chain of pure exempla, but the tournament in Book V is suspiciously similar to the tournament in Book IV.[3] The setting and characters involved are much the same in both. Both are three-day affairs. In the first, Satyrane and the knights of Maidenhead hold the field against all comers until they are defeated by Artegall in the disguise of a savage knight. In the second, Marinell and six friends are the challengers, and this time Artegall wins the prize disguised as Braggadochio. In the first, Britomart appears at the last minute and defeats Artegall. Then we have the trial of the girdle (which can only be

[3] Gough notes the similarity (see *Variorum*, V, 182).

worn by a chaste woman) and the foolish choice of Braggadochio by the false Florimell. In the second, Braggadochio attempts to claim the honor due to Artegall and is discovered and disgraced. There is a summary of the trial of the girdle, which entirely ignores the previous trial in Book IV; and the false Florimell is disposed of.

There is reason to believe that the tournament in Book V was created before that in Book IV. The story of Florimell's girdle, told in Book III, agrees with what is said of it in Book V, but not with the account in Book IV. In III, vii, 31.8, Satyrane finds Florimell's golden girdle beside her slain horse, where she lost it in her flight from the witch's beast. He used it to tie up the beast, and when the creature escaped from him it carried the "broken girdle" back to the witch (III, viii, 2.7),[4] who was just then creating the false Florimell. But in Book IV (ii, 25-26) we are told that Satyrane has the girdle and has declared a tournament at which it is to be awarded to the fairest lady. It is awarded to the false Florimell, and she appears wearing it in Book V. It would have been in her possession whether it was bestowed upon her by the witch or acquired at the tournament in Book IV, but in the latter case she should not have been able to wear it. The trial of the girdle in Book V ignores the trial of it in Book IV,[5] and the tournament for it in Book IV ignores the story told of it in Book III.

But if the account of the tournament in Book IV were removed, there would be no inconsistency in the story as told in Books III and V. Therefore, it seems reasonable to suppose that the tournament in Book IV is a late interpolation in the story of Florimell, imitated from the tournament in Book V, and put into Book IV so that Florimell's part in that book would not be limited to the last two cantos.

Both tournaments have their source in a single tournament

[4] He tells Paridell how he found it in III, viii, 49.8. It has not been noted that Satyrane's conquest of the beast is reminiscent of the legend of St. George, where the lady sometimes, as in Lydgate's poem, leads the dragon captive by her girdle (see *Variorum*, I, 388).

[5] Gough noted these inconsistencies (see *Variorum*, V, 190).

in Ariosto (Canto XXVII), at which Doralice, the prototype of the false Florimell, chooses Mandricardo, one of the prototypes of Braggadochio, and Brunello is seized and punished for stealing Sacripant's horse and Marfisa's sword. There are other stolen horses in the *Orlando*, but no others are recovered after a tournament. Braggadochio has both the stolen horse and a stolen sword in common with Brunello, although the theft of the sword is at second hand.[6] The relation of the recovery of Guyon's horse to the theft of it in II, iii, has already been commented upon. I do not think that Spenser would have troubled to pick up the dropped thread if he had not already had the episode on hand.[7]

If the tournament at Florimell's wedding in Book V was a part of the early story of Florimell, the present state of her story is easily explained. Most of it was incorporated into Book III, but room had to be found for such other matters as the romance of Britomart and the Timias-Belphoebe love idyl. Therefore, the rescue of Florimell from the cave of Proteus had to be postponed until another book. It was an ambitious piece, and Spenser decided to use it for the conclusion of Book IV. He could not omit Florimell from the first ten cantos if he was to use her release as his grand finale, and since she was securely locked up and not available for further adventures, he created the tournament for her girdle, imitating the tournament for her wedding, drawing upon the same source in Ariosto, but elaborating it and selecting a different part of the sequel for imitation in Book IV. He has worked it into the structure of the book by making it supply motivation for the subsequent duel and recognition scene between Britomart and Artegall. But, in spite of the

[6] Braggadochio makes use of the magician Archimage (II, iii). Brunello steals by magic. Dodge notices that Braggadochio is a combination of Mandricardo and Martano, but he does not see that Brunello is also included in the matrix. Gough, however, notes the Brunello parallel in Book V.

[7] Cf. chap. viii. V, iii, 31, imperfectly joins the theft of the horse with its recovery, since Guyon says that he challenged "the thiefe to fight" but was refused. Perhaps this episode was lost through the interpolation of the Medina passage between the theft of the horse and Guyon's discovery of his loss.

prominence given in Book IV to the Order of Maidenhead, I believe the tournament in Book V is the older piece.

The central cantos of Book V (iv, 21—vii) add a further section to the Artegall-Britomart story. Artegall is captured by the Amazons, and Britomart rescues him. Britomart's adventures in this book are more constantly indebted to Ariosto's Bradamante than they are in either Book IV or Book III.[8] But her adventure at Isis Church, which connects the love story with the justice theme, is without parallel in Ariosto. The abolition of the Amazon kingdom seems also to belong less to the Artegall-Britomart romance than to the exemplification of justice. It is suggestive of the ruthless destruction of the Bower of Bliss by Guyon. Otherwise, Artegall's encounter with Radigund belongs, not with the Artegall-Justice matter, but to the adventures of the knights of the Order of Maidenhead. Radigund defied the whole order (iv, 29), and Sir Terpin accepted the challenge and was defeated. Artegall, not as Justice, but as a knight of Maidenhead, came to the rescue and was in turn defeated and imprisoned.

It is the first and third sections of Book V which fit it securely into the virtue and quest plot. But the Britomart-Artegall romance is no part of that plot, for, while parts of it appear in Books III, IV, and V, these parts are among the "many other aduentures" intermeddled "rather as Accidents, then intendments." Britomart's quest is not the quest of Artegall but the rescue of Amoret; and Artegall's quest is not concerned with Britomart but is the rescue of Irena. The plot, except for the episode of Isis Church, presents a running parallel to Ariosto which suggests that most of this passage belongs to the period

[8] Her encounter with Dolon occurs at the same point in the narrative as Bradamante's adventure at Tristram's tower. Spenser had already imitated that episode twice in Book III, but he brings it in here because he is now imitating the whole chain of events described by Ariosto. Britomart's encounter with the two brothers on the bridge is an echo of Bradamante's encounter with Rodomont. Artegall had encountered the brothers before her, just as Orlando had encountered Rodomont before Bradamante. After this encounter Bradamante arrives at Arles and fights Marfisa, whom she supposes to be her rival, just as Britomart after her encounter with the two brothers (and her visit to Isis Church) arrives at the Amazon kingdom and fights with Radigund, of whom she is jealous.

when Spenser was imitating the story of Ruggiero and Bradamante as a compliment to Leicester and that it was adapted to, rather than created for, Book V.

The central section of Book V is closely related to the Britomart materials in Books III and IV, while the opening and closing sections are very slightly connected with the Britomart matter. The only link between the two conceptions of Artegall is Talus, who appears in all three parts of Book V, although he does not appear with Artegall at the tournament in Book IV or at the subsequent treacherous ambush of Britomart. He serves merely as a messenger in the central section of Book V, except when he assists in the destruction of the Amazon kingdom.

There are certain inconsistencies between the three parts of this book which point to rearrangements. When Radigund breaks Artegall's sword (v, 21), the poet was not thinking of the magic sword given to him by Astraea in Canto i. That sword is still in use in xii, 23.2. There seems to be another bad joint between the first and second part of the book in the story of Britomart's encounter with Dolon. In the second part we are told (vi, 33) that Artegall had slain Dolon's oldest son Guizor. But in the episode referred to (ii, 7 ff.) the only man slain besides Pollente was "A villaine . . . . with scull all raw"—hardly the son of a knight, however wicked.[9] Evidently there has been some change in the story between the two episodes.

We might conclude that this central section of Book V was created partly out of the older romance of Britomart, with considerable additions such as the allegory of Isis Church, the description of the destruction of the Amazon kingdom, and the part played by Talus. But the lack of correlation between the first section and the second suggests that they were originally written at different times and with different ends in view.

The last section of this book is unique in that it is the only section of anything like equal length which is devoted primarily

[9] Gough identifies Guizor with the "groome of evill guize" of ii, 6.7, whom Artegall slew in 11.9 (see *Variorum*, V, 213). But the identification will not hold, since Guizor is one of the three sons of Dolon, a knight.

to topical allegory. One wonders whether pressure had been put on the poet to make his "colourd showes" and "antique praises" more clearly "vnto present persons fit."[10] At any rate, Cantos viii–xii are distinct from the rest of the book and must be dealt with separately in the next chapter.

In spite of the fresh material in the last third of the book, it is evident that when Spenser wrote Book V he found either his time or his material running short. The books grow progressively shorter after the second, but Book V is more than a hundred stanzas (the length of two cantos in Book I) shorter than the average for the first three books. Moreover, there is a thinness of invention in Book V which suggests a lack of matter. Short as the book is, two episodes seem to have been added after it had been arranged in cantos and the "Arguments" written, since neither the episode of the giant Democracy in Canto ii nor the encounter of Artegall with Envy and Detraction in Canto xii is mentioned in the canto headings.

In this book, perhaps more than in any other except Book I, the poet brought his materials into conformity with his general plan. Artegall represents justice and has a quest. Arthur is introduced as displaying the same virtue as the hero, in accordance with the theory that his virtue includes all the others. Yet it is perfectly clear that Artegall was created as a good knight, but not especially the embodiment of justice, before he became the hero of Book V. On the other hand, the style of the formal episodes in the first section of the book suggests that there was a Knight of Justice before he was named Artegall, or that Artegall was an exponent of justice before he was re-created as the lover of Britomart. The second part of the book, except for its allegory of Isis Church, is less concerned with justice than with the story of love and adventure borrowed from Ariosto. The

[10] Whatever Sidney intended, his contemporary readers found topical allusions in the *Arcadia*, and Harington found them in the *Orlando Furioso* (see E. Greenlaw, "Sidney's *Arcadia* as an Example of Elizabethan Allegory," *Kittredge Anniversary Papers* [Boston, 1913], pp. 327–37; and "The Captivity Episode in Sidney's *Arcadia*," *Manly Anniversary Studies in Language and Literature* [Chicago, 1923], pp. 54–63; see also R. W. Zandvoort, *Sidney's Arcadia* [Amsterdam, 1929], pp. 120–35; Marcus S. Goldman, *Sir Philip Sidney and the Arcadia* ["Illinois Studies in Language and Literature," Vol. XVII (Urbana, 1934)], chap. vii, pp. 168–85).

third section has unity of theme and character, but it is distinct from the other two in subject matter and allegorical method.

The history of the central section seems clear enough because of its relation to the Britomart story in Books III and IV. The condition of the first four cantos (i, 13—iv, 20) suggests that the poet was drawing heavily upon some early experiments in moral allegory and old bits of the Florimell and Braggadochio stories. The closing cantos, on the other hand, refer to events which were recent in 1596 and indicate, as I shall show in the next chapter, that the end of Book V, and not Book VI, was the last part of the second instalment to be written.

XV
THE HISTORICAL ALLEGORY IN BOOK V

But O dred Soueraine
Thus farre forth pardon, sith that choicest wit
Cannot your glorious pourtraict figure plaine
That I in colourd showes may shadow it,
And antique praises vnto present persons fit.

—III, Proem, 3.5–9

THERE can be no question that, in the last five cantos of Book V, Spenser attempted to describe contemporary affairs under a very thin veil of allegory. But justice has not been done him in the interpretation of this historical allegory because it has been dealt with in too piecemeal and dogmatic a fashion. Each episode has been considered without relation to the others, and so the unity of theme of the whole passage has been entirely missed, and the whole interpretation has been twisted to fit a priori and mistaken identifications of Arthur and Artegall.

The material in question consists of six allegories as follows:

Arthur and Artegall rescue Samient, destroy the Soldan, and overcome the household of his wife, Adicia.
They capture Guile.
They attend the trial of Duessa at the court of Mercilla.
Arthur rescues Belge and slays Gerioneo.
Artegall rescues Burbon.
Artegall rescues Irena and is attacked by Envy and Detraction.

The poet leaves us no room for doubt as to the identity of Belge, Burbon, and Irena, and the trial of Duessa was immediately recognized by James VI of Scotland as a reference to the trial of his mother, Mary Queen of Scots, who was executed February 8, 1587.[1] The combat with the Soldan has been recognized as a representation of the defeat of the Spanish Armada in 1588.

[1] *Calendar of State Papers, Scotland*, ed. M. J. Thorpe (London, 1858), II, 723, 747.

This series of allegories represents, therefore, the five great events which marked the years between 1585 and 1595: the defeat of the Armada, the execution of Mary Queen of Scots, English aid to the Netherlands and France in their struggle with Spain, and, finally, the rescue of Ireland from civil war. In every case the strife seemed to Spenser and his contemporaries to be caused by Catholic aggression. These are all parts of the same great religious struggle, and I believe that the poet intended to represent a sixth important phase of that struggle in the pursuit and capture of Guile.

The struggle with Guile is commonly interpreted as having reference to the English efforts to exterminate the Irish rebels in 1580–82, an interpretation which arises out of the identification of Artegall with Lord Grey. But I have shown that this identification has little or no foundation,[2] and, in view of the general purport of this whole section of Book V, I believe that the Guile episode represents a further phase of the religious struggle—that of the English law with the Jesuits and missionary priests who worked in both England and Ireland. The first Jesuit mission to England arrived in 1580, and the first laws were enacted against them in 1581.[3] The elusiveness and shapeshifting of Guile, and the merciless pursuit of him by Talus, represent very graphically the struggle between the militant Catholics and the English law. In view of the succession of plots pre-

[2] See above, chap. vii, and "The Allegory of Sir Artegall in *F. Q.*, V, xi–xii," *Studies in Philology*, XXXVII (1940), 177–200.

[3] Between 1574 and 1580 a hundred priests came to England from the seminaries at Rome and Douay. In July, 1580, Parsons and Campion arrived, and the act of 1581 imposed the death penalty on all Jesuits. The act of 1584 ordered all priests and Jesuits to leave England at once, on pain of death if caught, and it made the act of harboring such persons a capital crime (see Sidney Lee, "The Last Years of Elizabeth," *Cambridge Modern History* [Cambridge: University Press], III [1904], 350). Ireland was a hotbed of Jesuit activity, and Spenser was aware of it as early as 1581/82 (see Raymond Jenkins, "*Newes Out of Munster*, a Document in Spenser's Hand," *Studies in Philology*, XXXII [1935], 125–30). According to Edwin Greenlaw, the Jesuits and priests "swarmed into" Ireland again in 1594 (*Studies in Spenser's Historical Allegory* [Baltimore, 1932], pp. 150, 154–55). In the *View* Spenser mentions the trouble caused by the priests in Ireland (see Renwick's ed., pp. 209–10). But as early as the writing of the "September" eclogue Spenser was aroused to the danger of the Jesuit mission and the seminary priests. In 1591 a royal proclamation (*S.T.C.* Nos. 8207 and 8208) described some of the disguises and subterfuges used by these priests.

ceding the execution of Mary Queen of Scots, it might have occurred to almost any Elizabethan that Catholic intrigue was a Protean monster which assumed a new form whenever it was caught.

It may be that the various episodes which make up these six allegories were written at various times, but the poet put them together with some attention to their order and with a consciousness of the underlying unity of the whole as a great religious struggle. Therefore, I do not believe that we can understand his allegory if we disregard his general topic and his arrangement.

Canto ix deals with the capture of Guile and the trial of Duessa. From the point of view of chronology or causation these two episodes should have preceded the defeat of the Armada alluded to in Canto viii. But strict chronology was impossible in this series of overlapping struggles, and so the poet has arranged them, not in a temporal order, but in an order which indicates the growing strength of the Protestant cause. He begins with the beating-off of a threat of invasion, goes on in Canto ix to describe the internal measures by which Catholicism was defeated in the persons of the Jesuits and of Mary Queen of Scots, and then, having put their own house in order, Arthur and Artegall, representatives of English might, rescue the Netherlands, France, and finally Ireland. It is a logical rather than a temporal order, presenting a sequence of growing strength which begins with the repulse of an attack on England and ends with the expulsion of Spanish and Catholic interests from the surrounding countries.

So interpreted, it is much more than mere "versified politics," as it has been called.[4] It is Spenser's reading of the significance of the age in which he lived. It is, in a sense, a coda to the Book of Redcrosse, bringing the English phase of the religious struggle up to date in 1595.

With the general purport of the whole passage in mind, let us

[4] J. W. Mackail, *The Springs of Helicon* (New York, 1909), p. 110. I cannot agree with the late Professor Greenlaw, however, that the whole book shows "the poet's art at its zenith" (*Studies*, p. 138).

look at the culminating exploits of Arthur and Artegall. Probably because of the preconceived and mistaken notion that Arthur represents the Earl of Leicester,[5] the allegory of the rescue of Belge in Canto x has never been satisfactorily explained. Some of the details have been referred to the events of the 1580's, and it has been assumed that Arthur's taking of the city far upland is a description of a recovery of Antwerp which never took place.[6] But many Dutch cities besides Antwerp had castles or forts built to intimidate the city, and these were regularly razed when the Dutch and English took the city from the Spaniards. While no particular taking of a city corresponds strikingly with Spenser's description of Arthur's feat, the allegory of the rescue of Belge is an apt generalized symbol of the Dutch struggle for freedom, and of English aid to them, as that picture appeared in 1593-95.

The rescue of Belge and the destruction of the monster, Inquisition, which Leicester did not live to see, were accomplished by 1595. But during Leicester's sojourn and immediately afterward the Dutch states passed through their darkest hours, when town after town was betrayed to the Spaniards by both English and Dutch commanders. By 1591 the tide had begun to turn, and by 1595, when Spenser was preparing this book for the press, Holland could truthfully be represented as restored to her sovereignty by English aid. In 1595 Lord Treasurer Burghley pointed out to the Queen that the Netherlands were prosperous and suggested that they be asked to begin the repayment of loans. "The Estates acknowledged and extolled the many and great Courtesies of the Queen, accounting themselves bound to her, next under God, for all their Prosperity."[7] They were, for a time, free from Spanish interference and prosperous. We have only to assume that the Belge episode was written in 1594 or 1595, and it becomes a record of fact instead of a time-serving

[5] See above, chap. vii.

[6] Recently a very interesting argument has been presented that the city referred to is Zutphen and that the appraisal of Leicester's achievements is that of contemporary followers of the Earl (see Mrs. Viola B. Hulbert, "The Belge Episode in the *Faerie Queene*," *Studies in Philology*, XXXVI [1939], 124-46).

[7] W. Camden, *The History of . . . . Elizabeth* (4th ed., 1688), pp. 502-3.

bit of prophetic fantasy. But if it was written six or seven years after Leicester's death, then Arthur does not represent Leicester. His achievement is that of the English people, not that of any one man.

Arthur's rescue of Belge is followed by Artegall's rescue of Burbon and Irena. Artegall's quest is the rescue of Irena from Grantorto (i, 3–4), and he sets out from the court of Mercilla for that purpose (xi, 36) but is turned aside by the need to rescue Burbon, and, having accomplished that good deed, he goes on immediately to rescue Irena. Before he has fully established order, he is called home and assailed on the way by Envy and Detraction.

The rescue of Irena and the encounter with Envy and Detraction have traditionally been interpreted as allegory of the experiences of Spenser's old patron, Arthur Lord Grey of Wilton, with whom the poet went to Ireland in 1580. Like Artegall, Lord Grey restored order and was called home in disgrace in 1582. But the rescue of Burbon, which serves to interrupt and delay the rescue of Irena, does not apply to Lord Grey or to 1580–82. The Burbon episode obviously refers to the English aid furnished to Henry IV of France at the time he deserted the Protestant cause, which Spenser very appropriately symbolizes as his shield, given to him by the Redcrosse knight. Henry IV joined the Catholic communion as the price of Paris on July 25, 1593.

Henry's apostasy was a very serious blow to the Protestants, but the English did not dare to abandon him for fear of thereby forcing him to make a peace with Spain which would be to their disadvantage. They were especially concerned with keeping the armies of the French Catholic League, which was allied with the Spanish interest, out of Brittany and the Channel ports.

It is this Burbon episode which gives us the clue to the identity of Irena's rescuer, since it was not Lord Grey but Sir John Norris who turned aside from the rescue of Irena to go to the aid of Burbon. It was he who was recalled from France to go immediately to Ireland to put down Tyrone's rebellion. He landed at Waterford on May 4, 1595, more than eight months before the second part of the *Faerie Queene* was entered for publication.[8]

Spenser was well acquainted with Sir John Norris, son of Sir Henry Norris of Rycote and his wife, Margery, whom Queen Elizabeth nicknamed affectionately her "black crow." Sir John was the leading general of the day. He had served his apprenticeship under Admiral Coligny in France in 1571, and he had distinguished himself as a commander both in Ireland and in the Low Countries before he became lord president of Munster in July, 1584. At very nearly, or exactly, the same time that Norris was installed in the presidency of Munster, Spenser took over the duties of clerk of the council in that province, an office which made him Norris' secretary for a year.[9] Because of the Dutch crisis of the next summer (1585), when Antwerp was about to fall, Norris was hastily recalled from Ireland and dispatched to the Low Countries with an army. The Earl of Leicester, with superior authority, arrived some months later, but Norris was the able and experienced general selected to cope with the emergency.

His younger brother, Sir Thomas Norris, became his deputy in Munster and continued to fill that position until Sir John's death in 1597, when he succeeded to the lord presidency. Thomas Norris was a member of the literary circle which included Spenser and which is described by Lodowick Bryskett as meeting at Dublin in 1582–84.[10] Both public and private business threw Spenser and Sir Thomas much together. When the plantation of Munster was begun in 1587, they took neighboring estates. It is quite probable that the Norrises helped the poet to his grant, and it is also probable that Sir Thomas promoted Spenser's interest with Sir Walter Ralegh, who was his cousin.[11]

[8] Stationers' Register, January 20, 1595/96.

[9] Raymond Jenkins, "Spenser and the Clerkship in Munster," *PMLA*, XLVII (1932), 109–21; "Spenser: The Uncertain Years, 1584–1589," *PMLA*, LIII (1938), 350–62.

[10] *A Discovrse of Civill Life* (1606), pp. 5–6.

[11] The sister of Sir Henry Norris married Sir Arthur Champernowne, Ralegh's mother's brother. Their mutual cousin, Gawain Champernowne, married Gabrielle de Montgomeri, and both Sir John Norris and Ralegh began their military careers fighting in France for Montgomeri in 1569–71.

In the spring of 1590, when a Spanish invasion of Ireland was threatened, Sir John Norris was sent over with an army and remained all summer but was recalled in the fall to collect troops for an expeditionary force to keep the Spaniards out of Brittany.[12] He arrived in Brittany early in June, 1591, and almost immediately "her majesty was truly comforted" by the news of his successes. For the next three and a half years Norris was almost continuously occupied with the task of preventing the Spaniards from gaining a foothold in Brittany. He was there when Henry IV heard Mass as the price of Paris, July 25, 1593, and thereby undermined the strength of the Catholic League. By the spring of 1594 the League had been dissolved and Henry had been crowned and had gained possession of all the chief cities of France. The Lady Flourdelis had been restored to the arms of Sir Burbon without much of a struggle after Sir Burbon threw away his shield. But the Spaniards, driven out elsewhere in France, undertook to intrench themselves in Brittany; and Norris collected a fresh army in England in the summer of 1594 and conducted a whirlwind campaign which drove them out of the whole peninsula. By November 8 he had captured Brest, and the enemy was in retreat.

At this time, according to Camden, "upon certain Notice that divers Spanish Commanders were come into *Ireland* to raise a Rebellion, *Norris* was called Home again out of *Bretaigne*," and, when Henry IV protested, Elizabeth "shewed him how there was a Necessity" for the recall "in regard Rebellions grew hot in *Ireland*."[13] It was known in Ireland early in December that Norris was to be sent there from Brittany, although the army was not shipped until February and did not arrive until March 20.[14] Sir John Norris was ill, and the whole expedition was de-

[12] There is some evidence that Spenser was with Sir John Norris in the summer of 1590 (see chap. xii, n. 3). I have traced the movements of Sir John Norris in detail in my article on "The Allegory of Sir Artegall in *F. Q.*, V, xi–xii," and there is not room to repeat that matter here.

[13] Camden, pp. 487 and 496.

[14] Lord Deputy Russell knew by December 6, and Tyrone had heard of it by January (see *Calendar of State Papers, Ireland, 1592–96*, ed. H. C. Hamilton [London, 1890], pp. 285, 299).

layed. It finally arrived in the charge of Sir Henry Norris, another of the brothers, and Sir John did not reach Waterford until May 4.

If Spenser wrote his account of the rescue of Burbon and Irena with Norris in mind, he could not have written the Burbon episode before the spring of 1594 or the Irena story before the summer of 1595. But in 1595 the recent achievements and activities of Sir John Norris were just those which Spenser ascribes to Sir Artegall. The only element which is doubtful is the conclusion of the Irena story. When he had slain Grantorto, Artegall

> day and night employ'd his busie paine
> How to reforme that ragged common-weale: . . . .
> But ere he could reforme it thoroughly,
> He through occasion called was away,
> To Faerie Court . . . . [xii, 26.3–27.3].

Sir John Norris had got no further than an unsatisfactory truce with Tyrone when Spenser published this part of his poem. It might seem, therefore, that this part of the allegory fits Lord Grey better than it does Sir John Norris. Other passages in Book V have been interpreted as allegory of Lord Grey as Lord Deputy (also called *Justice*) in Ireland, although with no great certainty. But in the *View* Spenser defends Lord Grey's rule in Ireland, and many readers have seen in the Irena passage a parallel defense of Grey.

Finally we must consider Spenser's assertion in *Amoretti* lxxx that he had by that time completed six books of the *Faerie Queene*. The *Amoretti* were licensed in November, 1594. At that time Sir John Norris had not finished his last campaign in Brittany, and he had certainly not freed Irena from the fear of Grantorto. The Burbon episode could have been inserted after the poet considered Book V completed, but the culminating episode, the rescue of Irena, is an essential part of the structure of the book and so must have been written before the book could be described as completed.

The most reasonable conclusion about this situation seems to be that the Irena episode was originally written with Lord Grey in mind, but that, when the poet was giving the book a final polishing in the summer of 1595, he decided to freshen his rather stale allegory of the rescue of Irena by working it over to fit her new rescuer, Sir John Norris, with whom he was just renewing an old acquaintance. The order established by Lord Grey in Ireland had fallen into chaos again long before his death in 1593, as Spenser observed in the *View*.[15] But what Lord Grey had accomplished in 1580–82, Sir John Norris could reasonably be expected to repeat in 1595–96, since Norris was a much more able and famous general than Grey, and both men believed in strong measures. "Ireland was not to be brought to obedience but by force." Both men were uncompromising Protestants who saw the wars in Ireland as fomented from Spain and Rome.[16] Spenser considered Catholicism the real enemy, for the giant who seduced Flourdelis from Burbon is the same Grantorto who threatened to destroy Irena. The rebellion of Desmond in 1580 and that of Tyrone in 1593 and the following years were parts of the same great, fundamentally religious and ideological conflict. Therefore, it would be natural enough to convert an allegory originally intended for Lord Grey to Sir John Norris by the simple expedient of inserting the Burbon episode so as to represent Artegall as turning aside from his quest long enough to rescue Burbon and then passing directly to the rescue of Irena.

One other figure can be identified. "Good Sir *Sergis*, truest Knight aliue," brings Artegall news of Irena's desperate plight at the beginning of the Burbon episode (xi, 37 ff.) and assists Artegall in the rescue of Irena (xii, 6–10). It has been suggested that Sir Sergis stands for Sir Henry Sidney, who visited Lord Grey in England in 1580 to advise him about the government of Ireland.[17] But that explanation does not account for the part played by Sir Sergis. He warns Artegall of the urgency of

[15] Renwick ed., p. 137.

[16] They were closely connected, since Sir John Norris' elder brother and Lord Grey married sisters, daughters of that distinguished Protestant, Sir Richard Morison.

[17] Upton suggests Walsingham as Sir Sergis but offers no argument (see *Variorum*, V, 302). Walsingham died in 1590.

Irena's need, but he is also represented as going to Ireland with Artegall and providing him with supplies there.

I believe that Sir Sergis stands for Sir Henry Wallop (1540?–99), whose service in Ireland began in 1579. During Lord Grey's deputyship he was made treasurer of the wars for Ireland, and he continued in active service there until 1589, when he retired to his estates in England[18] and carried on his office as treasurer of the wars by deputy. Sir Sergis is "an aged wight" who "long since aside had set the vse of armes"; that is, he had retired. But he comes out of retirement to warn Artegall of the desperate condition of Irena. He seems to be with Artegall when Burbon is rescued, although he takes no part in the rescue; and he goes to the island of Irena with Artegall and assists him there. I can find no evidence that Wallop was with Norris at any time in France, but there is considerable presumptive evidence that he warned Norris about the condition of Ireland, and he certainly went to Ireland about the same time that Norris went (in 1595), to attend to the pay and provisioning of the army.

Wallop was in Ireland in September, 1593,[19] when the rebellion of Tyrone and O'Donnel had flared into the open. He was back at court in April, 1594, acting as an intermediary between Tyrone and the English government in an effort to forestall a war.[20] Sir John Norris was also at court in April to report on the state of affairs in Brittany, and the two men, who had served together in Ireland in 1584–85, and who still held important offices in the government there, would certainly consult together about the state of that country. Wallop's outlook was gloomy. He reported to some of the Queen's council, and no doubt to Norris also, that the impending rebellion in Ireland "will prove the longest, most chargeable, and most dangerous war, that in man's memory, hath happened in Ireland."[21] Old

[18] "Farleigh-Wallop," where he entertained Elizabeth in 1591. Unfortunately, the house and the family papers were burned at a later date.

[19] His deputy died in 1593, leaving his accounts in bad shape, and Wallop's return to Ireland was probably partly to straighten out that business. But when Sir William Russell undertook the deputyship, he demanded Wallop's return to Ireland (see *State Papers, Ireland, 1592–96*, pp. 141 and 274).

[20] *Ibid.*, pp. 230 and 236. [21] *Ibid.*, p. 402; see also p. 345, his letter to Burghley.

Sir Sergis reports to Artegall that Irena "is in wretched thraldome bound" and "death shall by" if she does not find a champion within ten days.

Spenser seems to glance at Norris' desertion of his post in Munster (xi, 38–41), for Sir Sergis tells Artegall that Irena had lost her liberty by

> presuming on th' appointed tyde,
> In which ye promist, as ye were a Knight,
> To meete her at the saluage Ilands syde,
> And then and there for triall of her right
> With her vnrighteous enemy to fight [xi, 39.1–5].

But Artegall had failed of the appointment, and Irena was taken captive as a result. Munster was a key province after Lord Grey had depopulated it in putting down the Desmond rebellion. A scheme for confiscating the land and replanting it with Englishmen was devised, and Wallop was one of the commissioners for a survey of the lands. Later he served on the commission which passed the lands to the undertakers (one of whom was Spenser) in 1587.[22] However, delay and inefficiency largely defeated the purpose of the plantation. Wallop (and Spenser) may well have felt that a firm hand was needed in Munster during the years (1584–89) when the scheme of plantation was being worked out, and that Norris' failure to do his part in Ireland after 1585 had been a serious detriment to the whole enterprise.

The connections between Wallop and Norris and Wallop and Spenser are inferential but clear. When Wallop left Ireland in 1589, he selected Spenser's friend, Lodowick Bryskett, as his steward in Ireland to manage his estate at Enniscorthy. As treasurer for the wars during Lord Grey's regime, he would naturally be brought into close contact with Grey's secretary, Edmund Spenser. Business was transacted between Spenser and Wallop.[23] After Grey's recall, Wallop and Archbishop Lof-

[22] See R. Dunlop, "The Plantation of Munster, 1584–1589," *English Historical Review*, III (1888), 250–69.

[23] See F. I. Carpenter, *A Reference Guide to Edmund Spenser* (Chicago: University of Chicago Press, 1923), pp. 34, 38, 70; and Dorothy F. Atkinson, *Edmund Spenser: A Bibliographical Supplement* (Baltimore: Johns Hopkins Press, 1937), pp. 2, 4–5. See also H. R. Plomer and T. P. Cross, *The Life and Correspondence of Lodowick Bryskett* (Chicago: University of Chicago Press, 1927), pp. 44–59.

tus acted as joint justices for the rule of Ireland (1582–84), and Loftus praised his companion for "sufficiency, carefulness, and perfect sincerity." Spenser calls Sir Sergis "truest Knight aliue." Wallop must have had a high reputation for honesty, since he served for twenty years as treasurer of the Queen's most costly and unsatisfactory enterprise—the wars in Ireland. He must also have had a hand in the passing of Kilcolman to Spenser, since he was on the commission which assigned escheated lands to the undertakers.

Wallop's connection with Sir John Norris needs no demonstration. He was one of the chief officials in the plantation of Munster at the time when Norris was lord president of that province. Moreover, Wallop seems to have helped Norris financially on at least two occasions.[24]

The clearest intimation that Sir Sergis stands for Sir Henry Wallop occurs at the opening of the Irena episode (xii, 10). Spenser says that Artegall pitched his tent "on the open plaine." His friends were forbidden to entertain him (a reference to Lord Deputy Russell's nonco-operation?):

> But yet old *Sergis* did so well him paine,
> That from close friends, that dar'd not to appeare,
> He all things did puruay, which for them needfull weare [xii, 10.7–9].

As treasurer for the wars, Wallop was responsible not only for the soldiers' pay but also for buying food and other supplies. It was his duty to "puruay" all things "which for them needfull weare," and he seems to have exerted himself considerably. He arrived in Ireland on the same day that the troops from Brittany were landed and was very busy through the summer of 1595 in getting money and provisions out of England. There is evidence that he had recourse on at least two occasions to his

[24] In the *State Papers, Ireland, 1592–96*, pp. 302 and 315, there are two entries which require explanation. Under March 8, 1594/95, is recorded a brief of sundry allowances given Norris in the account of Wallop ending September 30, 1586. Since Norris was not in Ireland at that time, the sum may represent a transfer by which services in the Low Countries were paid for out of the Irish funds in Wallop's charge. The other entry is dated April, 1595, and records an allowance of 60*s.* a day to Sir John Norris as general of Her Majesty's armies, allowed in the account of Sir Henry Wallop, 1588–91. The items probably represent back pay. The Queen was always far behind in the pay of her soldiers.

own private resources when public money and stores failed to arrive.[25]

Altogether, the account of Sir Sergis fits Sir Henry Wallop so well that it confirms the identification of the rescuer of Burbon and Irena as Sir John Norris. The chain of events which Spenser is recording seems to be as follows: In April, 1594, when Wallop was at court trying to deal with Tyrone, and Norris was there to report on the state of France, the two men talked over the situation in Ireland. Wallop urged Norris to return immediately, but Norris saw the rescue of Burbon as the more immediate emergency. When he had cleared the Spanish out of Brittany, however, he hurried at once to Ireland, early in 1595, and Wallop accompanied and assisted him during the summer when Spenser was putting the finishing touches on his second instalment.

If this is the purport of the allegory, then the Burbon episode and the first ten stanzas of the Irena episode (Sir Sergis is not mentioned after xii, 10) could not have been written before the summer of 1595. The rest of the Irena story may have been intended originally to shadow forth the deputyship of Lord Grey. The allegory is made up of conventional details of a knightly rescue of a lady in need of a champion—details which by the exercise of a little ingenuity could be fitted to either Grey or Norris, but which are, in fact, conventional and not primarily topical. Only stanzas 26–27 definitely fit Lord Grey better than they seem to fit Norris.

Whether or not the Irena episode was originally written about Lord Grey, there is little question that when the Burbon passage was added, and the whole story (xi, 36—xii) was published early in 1596, Spenser intended that his readers should recognize in Sir Artegall the new champion of Ireland, Sir John Norris. As lord president of Munster he was on a commission from the Faery Queen to rescue Irena, but he turned aside to save

[25] See *State Papers, Ireland, 1592–96*, pp. 305, 325, 330, 342, 345, etc. Provisions for the army were inadequate, as usual, and Norris complained to Sir Robert Cecil, but he blamed Lord Deputy Russell rather than Wallop (see pp. 357, 402–4, 405–6). On one occasion Wallop borrowed in order to pay "victuall money" to the destitute soldiers (p. 360); and he drew upon his own estate to provide the means for brewing beer for the army at the Newry (pp. 397–402, and see p. 387).

Burbon at a critical moment, just after Burbon had abandoned his shield of faith, and then he hurried to Irena's island before it should be too late.

Readers of this allegory in 1596 would easily recognize Sir John Norris in the champion of Burbon and Irena. But what would they make of the allegory which represents Artegall as called home before he had finished his task and attacked by Envy and Detraction? Is this a survival of the state of the composition in which Artegall stood for Lord Grey? Or was it added when the passage was made over to fit Sir John Norris? The answer to this question depends on the date of composition of the passage and on its applicability to Norris as well as to Grey.

For evidence on the second point we must look at Norris' situation in Ireland. He had been sent in response to a request from the lord deputy, Sir William Russell, for "some experienced Souldier . . . . to assist him with his Counsel and what else he should need him in."[26] But Russell wanted a man under his command, not a rival. Norris was appointed with absolute commission in the absence of the lord deputy, and there was trouble from the beginning.[27] During the summer Norris recovered the fort on the Blackwater, but he was not able to crush the rebellion; and, according to instructions from England and against his better judgment, he accepted the submission of Tyrone and established a hollow truce.[28] The two rebels, O'Donnel and Tyrone, signed their submissions on October 18, probably before Spenser left Ireland for London to publish the second part of the *Faerie Queene*. By January, when he was seeing it through the press, Elizabeth was beginning to suspect Tyrone's sincerity.[29] Things were going badly in Ireland, and Norris, who had been given full credit for the truce, would natu-

[26] Camden, p. 507.

[27] *Ibid.*, p. 509; *Calendar of Carew Manuscripts, 1589–1600*, ed. J. S. Brewer and W. Bullen (London, 1869), p. 113; *State Papers, Ireland, 1592–96*, pp. 308, 312, 314, 402–4.

[28] *Historical Manuscripts Commission Report . . . . Penshurst* (London, 1934), II, 167 ff.; *Carew Manuscripts, 1589–1600*, pp. 121–26; *The Edmondes Papers*, ed. G. G. Butler ("Roxburghe Club," No. 164 [London, 1913]), p. 285.

[29] *Carew Manuscripts, 1589–1600*, p. 131.

rally reap the blame for the failure of a policy forced upon him from above.[30] Moreover, he had "many enemies in the Queen's councils," including the Earl of Essex.[31]

When the second part of the *Faerie Queene* was being printed, Norris had disappointed his friends and given the advantage to his enemies.[32] Malicious tongues were free to wag, and unquestionably did. Even Camden was infected with the venom of detraction, for he blamed Norris for a policy which was dictated, as he knew, by the Queen. It would not take much foresight on Spenser's part to see that his fate was to be the same as that of every other commander sent to Ireland by Elizabeth. He would be called home before his task was done to answer charges.

If it can be shown that Artegall's encounter with Envy and Detraction was written after Spenser arrived in England in the winter of 1595–96, then there is no reasonable doubt that the passage was inspired by indignation at the attitude toward Sir John Norris which Spenser found prevalent in London.

There are two indications that a passage was added to the last two cantos of Book V after it was prepared for the printer. There is a mistake in a catchword and a striking dislocation of subject matter in the headings of the last two cantos of this book.

The rescue of Burbon occupies the last thirty stanzas of Canto xi, but it is not mentioned in the verse heading of that canto. Instead, both the Burbon and the Irena episodes are described in the verse heading of Canto xii as if both occurred in that canto. It seems evident that the Burbon episode was shifted, after the canto headings were written, from the beginning of Canto xii to the end of Canto xi. It has been suggested that the Burbon epi-

[30] A. Collins, *Letters and Memorials of State* (London, 1746), I, 363.

[31] The quotation is from the *Dictionary of National Biography*. Essex quarreled with Norris in the spring about the selection of captains for his forces, and the quarrel was still going on by letter in the fall (see *Historical Manuscripts Commission: Calendar of the Manuscripts .... at Hatfield House* [London, 1892], V, 413–14).

[32] As early as September 27, 1595, Norris wrote to Burghley asking to be recalled. He says that the lord deputy is not furnishing him with the necessary supplies, and he doubts the sincerity of the rebels' submission, although he will follow instructions (*State Papers, Ireland, 1592–96*, pp. 402–4, and Collins, I, 344).

sode was an afterthought,[33] and I have indicated how it may have been added to the older Irena episode in such a way as to convert the latter into an allegory of Sir John Norris. But that does not account for the dislocation in the canto headings. The heading of Canto xii must have been written after the Burbon episode had been put in, but before it was shifted from Canto xii to Canto xi.

If we look for an explanation of this shift, we shall observe that the meeting of Artegall with Envy and Detraction is not mentioned in the heading of Canto xii, although it constitutes about half of the subject matter of that canto. Evidently it was this passage, and not the Burbon episode, which was added after the canto headings were written. The addition of this passage gave Canto xii seventy-two stanzas, whereas Canto xi had only thirty-five stanzas.[34] The shifting of the Burbon episode from the beginning of Canto xii to the end of Canto xi gave Canto xi sixty-five stanzas and Canto xii forty-three, bringing both cantos to a more normal length.

Evidence of the very late date at which this readjustment was made is provided by the catchword on the page (332, misnumbered 342) on which the Burbon episode begins. According to Dr. J. G. McManaway's excellent "Critical Notes on the Text,"[35] the catchword at the foot of this page indicates that Canto xi ended with stanza 35 when the page was set by the compositor. The catchword is "Canto," which was the usual sign that a new canto was to begin on the next page. It appears that, after the page had actually been set up, stanza 36, which opens the Burbon episode, was added to that page, and the

[33] J. C. Smith, Introduction to his edition of *Spenser's Faerie Queene* (Oxford, 1909), p. xiii. The suggestion has been generally accepted.

[34] W. L. Renwick, in his review of *Variorum*, Vol. V, in *Modern Language Review*, XXXIII (1938), 62–64, expresses the opinion that Canto xi must have been more than 35 stanzas long before the Burbon episode was added, and therefore he thinks the Burbon episode may be a substitution rather than an addition. But since Canto i of this book has only 30 stanzas, and Canto ii had only 28 when the canto heading was written, the argument that 35 stanzas is too short for Canto xi has no force.

[35] *Variorum*, V, 372–73.

catchword, which usually followed closely the end of the text, was moved to the foot of the page without being corrected.

Both the heading of Canto xii and the catchword just described indicate that the Burbon episode was shifted from Canto xii to Canto xi in the process of printing. I suggest that this change was made because the poet was adding Artegall's encounter with Envy to the end of Canto xii. But before the suggestion can be accepted, we must consider the relation of the ending of Book V to the opening of Book VI.

Spenser links Books I and II and Books II and III by making the retiring knight encounter the hero of the next book. He does not use the device again until he reaches Book VI, where Calidore encounters Artegall and is put on the trail of the Blatant Beast. If the ending of Book V, which describes Artegall's encounter with Envy, Detraction, and the Blatant Beast, was an afterthought, then this opening of Book VI, which represents Artegall as telling Calidore of the Blatant Beast, must have been added at the same time. It involves the insertion of seven stanzas near the beginning of Book VI. These stanzas make an effective link between Books V and VI, but they are not an essential part of the structure of Book VI. Artegall tells Calidore where he has recently encountered the Beast, but the Blatant Beast is already the object of Calidore's quest, and he does not act on the information supplied him by Artegall. The quest was assigned by the Faery Queen, and no more than a stanza was required to mention it and bridge the gap between stanzas 1–3, which describe Calidore's character, and stanzas 11 ff., which take up his first adventure.

If Calidore's quest of the Blatant Beast was already written when the poet added his account of the attack on Artegall by Envy and Detraction to the end of Book V, it must have occurred to him that he could link Books V and VI together by adding the Blatant Beast to the attackers of Artegall. Only two stanzas at the end of Book V (xii, 37 and 41) mention the Blatant Beast. These two stanzas interrupt rather than promote the account of the attack on Artegall. Stanza 38 follows naturally after stanza 36, and stanza 37 definitely looks like a patchwork intrusion. Both stanzas could have been inserted as an afterthought at the same time that stanzas 4–10 were put into VI, i.

It cannot be demonstrated that all these steps were taken, but the evidence that the passage on Envy and Detraction was a very late addition to the end of Book V is strong enough to create a presumption in favor of it. The whole situation looks like a brilliant bit of patching by which the poet gave expression to his indignation at the talk about Sir John Norris, and then saw the chance to relate the new close of Book V to the subject of Book VI. By inserting two more stanzas at the end of Book V and seven stanzas at the opening of Book VI, he could provide a very effective link between the two books.

According to this analysis, the history of the composition of this passage (xi, 36—xii) is about as follows. Some time between 1582, when Lord Grey left Ireland, and 1593, when he died, Spenser perhaps wrote the account of Artegall's rescue of Irena (xii, 11–26, or 27). But while he was giving a final polishing to the second instalment, in the summer of 1595, he inserted the Burbon episode at the beginning of Canto xii, introducing Sir Sergis and fitting the two stories together in such a way as to convert the whole canto into an allegory of the exploits of Sir John Norris. While it was in this form, he wrote the canto headings and took the manuscript to London to be published. There he heard criticisms of Norris' conduct of the war, which aroused his indignation. At a white heat he wrote his account of the attack on Artegall by Envy and Detraction,[36] and then, seeing an opportunity to connect Books V and VI, he introduced the Blatant Beast into the new passage by inserting stanzas 37 and 41 and wrote and put into the opening of Book VI a description of the meeting of Calidore and Artegall. Meanwhile the printer had got deep into Book V, and there was barely time to insert the new passage at the end of Book V and to adjust the length

[36] This passage has a more rapid movement than the preceding ones because there are many more run-on lines in it than is the average for the book (see the tables in Appendix I).

of the last two cantos by shifting the Burbon episode from Canto xii to Canto xi. According to the evidence of the catchword, the change was made after page 332 had been set up.

Contemporary readers would undoubtedly understand and relish the scornful satire of the closing stanzas in which the poet foresees for Norris the envy and detraction which met all commanders upon their return from Ireland. That had been the fate of Lord Grey, and more recently Sir John Parrot had died in the Tower after coming home from Ireland to face a trial for treason.[37]

If this brilliant and caustic allegory was written, as it appears to have been, when the poem was passing through the press, then it is obvious that the poet was stirred to write it not so much by the long-past wrongs of the dead Lord Grey as by fresh indignation at the current attitude toward Sir John Norris. What he wrote was a prophecy which did not happen to come true. Norris died in Ireland in 1597. But in 1595–96 the poet had every reason to expect that history was about to repeat itself, and his allegory gains in satiric force from the fact that it has a basis in a general situation which prompted and justified the prophecy.

The highly topical character of the last third of Book V enables us to date and trace the history of its composition with more assurance than we can that of almost any other part of the poem, except possibly the Timias-Belphoebe matter. For that reason it is of the very first importance both for an understanding of Spenser's method of handling topical allegory and for a study of his methods of composition. Here, more clearly than anywhere else in the poem, we can see the poet at work, revising, adapting, bringing into conformity with his latest plans, and adding by interpolation as new ideas occurred to him and new situations arose. Here, if anywhere, we can study the actual process by which the poem was written.

[37] By an unhappy stroke of fortune the passage also fits the fate of the Earl of Essex, but we can hardly suppose that Spenser foresaw in 1595 the events of four years later. I have discussed the suggestion that Artegall stands for Essex in this passage in my article on "The Allegory of Sir Artegall in *F. Q.*, V, xi–xii," pp. 179–83.

XVI
THE EXCURSION INTO ARCADIA: BOOK VI

> The waies, through which my weary steps I guyde,
> In this delightfull land of Faery,
> Are so exceeding spacious and wyde,
> And sprinckled with such sweet variety,
> Of all that pleasant is to eare or eye,
> That I nigh rauisht with rare thoughts delight,
> My tedious trauell doe forget thereby.
>
> —VI, Proem, 1.1–7

THE organization of Book VI has a strong superficial resemblance to that of Book V. Like Book V, it falls into three distinct parts, of which the first and third are concerned with the knightly quest of the hero, while the central section describes the adventures of two lovers and has nothing to do with the quest. But, unlike Book V, Book VI does not make use of the same hero throughout the three sections.

Cantos i—iii, 26, are concerned with the character, quest, and exemplary conduct of Sir Calidore. At the end of this section he departs in pursuit of the Blatant Beast, and we hear no more of him until he reappears at the beginning of the ninth canto and becomes the central figure in the romance of Pastorella, which occupies the rest of the book. The five and a half central cantos form a continuous account of the adventures of Calepine and Serena and do not mention Calidore. Instead, Prince Arthur takes a considerable part in the rescue of Serena.

Apparently the part of Arthur in Book VI represents a further evolution in the poet's manipulation of his plot. In Books II and V the titular hero appears throughout, and Arthur is added in the last third of each book to assist the hero and duplicate the allegory. Obviously that is not a very satisfactory arrangement, since it necessitates two culminating episodes. In Book VI Arthur is used, not to duplicate the moral achievement of the hero, but to alternate with him. He appears only in the central section of the book, from which Calidore is absent, and the two heroes never meet.

In addition to this important change in the organization of Book VI, there are important stylistic differences between Book VI and the other books. Throughout Book VI the scenes are elaborated, especially in the matter of conversation, and in the first and third sections there is a good deal of moralizing. Many of the cantos have formal introductions, but these are usually linked to the following matter by the application of the general observation to the character or situation under discussion, whereas in Book V these introductions were less closely joined to the following matter. Book VI has a more reflective tone than is apparent in the other books.

In every respect Book VI is of better quality than either Book IV or Book V. The first section, while it parallels the first section of Book V, is not so bald and mechanical, both because it is better written and because it is much shorter, being confined to three examples of courtesy, where Book V has five examples of justice. The Calepine-Serena story in the middle of the book (iii, 20—viii) has the most elaborate and well-managed plot of any part of the poem except Book I, where the story is told in the same way. In both cases, after an adventure, a knight and his lady are separated, and the story moves back and forth from one to the other until they are brought together again. The wooing of Pastorella in the last third of the book is also a well-managed and fairly elaborate narrative.

Not only in its management but also in its subject matter, Book VI shows a fresh approach. It displays a consciousness of the new vogue for pastoral romance, inspired by the publication of the *Arcadia* just after the first instalment of the *Faerie Queene* appeared. In every respect Book VI appears to have been written after 1590 and to have incorporated only a minimum of old material.[1]

[1] For statistics on style see Appendix I and the discussion of the significance of the enjambment ratios in Appendix II. Mackail particularly admires the Pastorella story. He says: "In the beautiful pastoral incident which fills several cantos of the sixth book,

In this book, as in all previous ones, Spenser levies upon Ariosto for materials. Most of the borrowings are in the central section, but a few occur in the last section. The material so borrowed is handled more nearly in the free manner of Book IV than in that of the other books. There is an important borrowing from Tasso in the last section of the book, and, in addition, Spenser began in this book to draw upon two or three fresh sources of narrative. While the *Arcadia* is the most pervasive influence, there is very little actual borrowing of plot from it.[2] But Malory contributes to the first two cantos in a direct and undisguised way which is new in the *Faerie Queene*. The character of the savage man and the episode of the infant being carried away by a bear seem to come from the late medieval prose romance of *Valentine and Orson*.[3] The need for new story material may have arisen partly because of the exhaustion of the Florimell and Britomart matter which forms so large a part of Books III, IV, and V, but the poet was moving in the direction of a more free and frankly romantic style of narrative which required a new kind of story material.

In structure, style, and subject matter Book VI represents a fresh approach which seems clearly to reflect the literary stimulus of the visit to England in 1590. But we must not fail to notice that this fresh approach does not involve any change in

---

Spenser reverts not only to the free romantic manner of the *Arcadia*, but to simpler, fresher style and language" (*The Springs of Helicon* [New York, 1909], p. 115).

[2] E. Greenlaw in "Shakespeare's Pastorals," *Studies in Philology*, XIII (1916), 122–29, has made a study of Spenser's debt to Sidney for the plot of *F. Q.*, VI, ix–xii—the Calidore-Pastorella story. He considers the indebtedness "beyond question," but the value of his study would have been much enhanced if he had given the sources of the "composite plot" which he constructs as the basis of Sidney's plot (p. 123). See also M. Y. Hughes, "Spenser's Debt to the Greek Romances," *Modern Philology*, XXIII (1925), 67–76.

[3] H. J. Todd noted a parallel to the latter incident in *Palladine of England* (1588); see his edition of *The Works of Edmund Spenser* (London, 1805), VI, 427–28. Arthur Dickson, in his edition of *Valentine and Orson* for the "Early English Text Society: Original Series," No. 204 (London, 1937), pp. li–lix, notices these and many other parallels. He presents an imposing list of parallels for every book of the *F. Q.*, but he recognizes that some of them are weak and superficial. Except for the name "Trompart," which might have been an independent etymological creation, or a current name for a braggart, the parallels seem to me to be more apparent than real until we come to the sixth book.

the fundamental plot of the poem, since Book VI fits the plan outlined in the letter to Ralegh better than any other book except Book I and perhaps Book V.

Calidore is on a quest assigned to him by the Faery Queen. His behavior is designed to illustrate courtesy. The central sections of the book also work out a varied illustration of courtesy, although Calidore does not appear there and although Arthur is an avenger of discourtesy more often than an example of courtesy. Discourtesy is illustrated in the behavior of Sir Turpine, native or savage courtesy in the savage man, humanity in Calepine's rescue of the babe, etc. In fact, the moral purpose to illustrate courtesy is kept so firmly in hand throughout the book that it seems evident that Spenser was writing throughout with his mature plan fully in view. There is no such evidence of adaptation of already written material and rearrangement of stories as appears in Books III and IV and parts of V.

Especially in the second and third sections the strands of narrative of a fairly complicated plot are kept in good order. Except for a slight confusion in names by which Serena is once called Crispina and once Matilda, the stories are smoothly and coherently told. Only one strand in the narrative suggests by its style and subject matter an adaptation of old matter, and this strand, curiously enough, concerns Timias and makes further apologies for Ralegh.

Timias appears in the central section of the book and is involved in three episodes. At the opening of Canto v, Serena and her savage host set out to look for Calepine and meet Arthur and Timias. The poet stops at once to explain how Arthur found Timias again after their separation at the opening of Book III, which was continued by Arthur's failure in Book IV to recognize his squire in the solitary hermit who was mourning the loss of Belphoebe's love. In Book IV Timias and Belphoebe are reconciled by means of a bird and a ring, but, says the poet in VI, v, 12,

> After that *Timias* had againe recured
> The fauour of *Belphebe*, (as ye heard)
> And of her grace did stand againe assured . . . . ,

he fell into an ambush prepared for him by "three mightie enemies," Despetto, Decetto, and Defetto. There he was bitten by the Blatant Beast (Slander or Scandal)[4] before Arthur came on the scene and rescued him (sts. 12–24). Since Ralegh seems at all times to have had plenty of enemies, the reference of this particular episode is not certain.

When Arthur and Timias come upon Serena, she also is suffering from the bite of the Blatant Beast, and Arthur takes the two to a hermitage where their wounds are treated (allegorically) and finally healed. This second episode clearly alludes to the disgrace of Ralegh and Elizabeth Throckmorton and their retirement to Sherborne. It has been objected that Serena is not Timias' lady but Calepine's and that she therefore cannot stand for Elizabeth Throckmorton; but the rescue of Amoret in Book IV is open to exactly the same objection as allegory of Ralegh's love affair, and yet its application to Ralegh has not been seriously questioned.[5]

The Mirabella story is the third allegory involving Timias in Book VI. Mirabella represents an image of Pride, written in the manner of Books I and II. She bears a strong resemblance to the proud Rosalind of the *Calender*,[6] and her story is connected with the court of Cupid, an institution which reminds us of the early lost *Court of Cupid*.[7] It seems quite possible that

[4] For contemporary interpretation of the Blatant Beast see the *Return from Parnassus*, cited by Greenlaw, *Studies in Spenser's Historical Allegory* (Baltimore, 1932), p. 215.

[5] R. W. Church accepts the Timias-Ralegh reference for all three of the episodes involving Timias in Book VI as well as for the Timias-Belphoebe episode in Book IV (*Spenser* [London, 1886], p. 163). Ray Heffner objects that if Calidore is Sidney, then the Serena affair cannot apply to Ralegh's disgrace, because Sidney was dead before Ralegh's marriage in 1592. But since Calidore does not appear at all in this part of the book, the time element is hardly significant ("Essex, the Ideal Courtier," *ELH*, I [1934], 7–36).

[6] Church (p. 129) describes Mirabella as "Spenser's long fostered revenge" on Rosalind.

[7] In most cases we can only guess at the nature of Spenser's lost works, but we know that he was a devoted student of Chaucer, and therefore it is worth noting in connection with his *Court of Cupid* that the 1561 edition of *Chaucer* contains a *Court of Love* which describes Cupid's court beside Mount Citherea and which contains a set of statutes which might have suggested legal formalities such as Mirabella's indictment in VI, vii, 33–37. Helen E. Sandison, "Spenser's 'Lost' Works and Their Probable Relation to His *Faerie Queene*," *PMLA*, XXV (1910), 145–47, discusses this possibility.

Mirabella is a survival of early work, either an independent piece or a part of the early *Faerie Queene*.

In the latter connection it should be noted that Mirabella's story is complementary to the story of the Squire of Dames in Book III, which I have singled out as perhaps the oldest fragment of plot in the poem. The Squire is condemned by his lady to wander until he has found as many chaste women as he had found unchaste ones. Cupid condemns Mirabella to wander through the world "till she had sau'd so many loues, as she did lose."

The whole story is out of key with Book VI, and I think it would not be hard to persuade a careful reader that it was an early invention, interpolated here in order to give the poet still another opportunity to make an allegorical apology for Ralegh. Mirabella is accompanied by Disdain and Scorn, who punish her as she rides along. Timias is moved by her plight and attempts to rescue her from her tormentors. Instead he is captured and tormented in turn until Arthur rescues him. The poet seems to be saying that Ralegh had attempted to rescue Elizabeth Throckmorton and had involved himself in her punishment. Elizabeth had been a Maid of Honour for at least twelve years when Ralegh married her. Whatever her conduct may have been during that time, it would be conventional to treat her as a scornful maid who had flouted Cupid and must pay the penalty. It is not possible to judge fully the applicability of these three allegories to Ralegh's affairs as long as we lack information as to the exact nature of his offense.[8] But the misfortunes of Timias and Serena and Timias and Mirabella bear too strong a family resemblance to the Timias-Belphoebe-Amoret affair in Book IV to be dissociated from it.[9]

One other topical problem presents itself in connection with

[8] See Fred Sorensen, "Sir Walter Ralegh's Marriage," *Studies in Philology*, XXXIII (1936), 182–202.

[9] The battle between Arthur and Disdain is very like the battle between Arthur and Orgoglio in I, viii, 7–14. Spenser says that Disdain was "sib" to Orgoglio (VI, vii, 41.8). He is either imitating himself or employing an old passage which was thriftily saved and used when a combat between a knight and a giant (Disdain is not named during the fight) was needed.

this book. Until 1910 it was traditional to regard Calidore as patterned on Sir Philip Sidney, but in that year Professor Percy W. Long advanced the theory that Calidore was intended to represent, not Sidney, but Essex.[10] His argument was reviewed, point by point, by Dr. K. T. Rowe, who argued that Sidney stood for the ideal of courtesy in his day and that he had some notable encounters with Slander (the Blatant Beast). He pointed out that Essex, on the other hand, was neither above the reach of scandal in his personal conduct, nor was he a model of courtesy.[11] The late Professor Ray Heffner replied in defense of Essex. He cited some praises of Essex, mostly written after his death, which describe him as an able courtier. He also cited some instances in which praise of Essex was couched in the popular pastoral form and some evidence that Essex was looked upon as Sidney's successor.[12]

There is abundant evidence of the almost universal fascination which Essex exercised over the younger courtiers of his day. He seemed by the time of his return from Cadiz, in the summer of 1596 just after the publication of the second part of the *Faerie Queene*, to be the morning star heralding a new age. In spite of his most unchivalrous attempts to bully the old Queen, he might have seemed to enthusiastic followers to be a model of courtesy, although why his quest should be the Blatant Beast is not clear. But we have nothing to connect Spenser with Essex before the legend of Sir Calidore was published except the commendatory sonnet printed in 1590. It is one of sixteen, some of which are addressed to people for whom there is no reason to suppose that Spenser had any great admiration. Spenser's connection with Ralegh put him squarely in the opposite camp, and we cannot assume, without more evidence than the sonnet provides, that he either enjoyed or courted Essex' patronage before 1596.[13]

10 "Spenser's Sir Calidore," *Englische Studien*, XLII (1910), 53–60.

11 "Sir Calidore: Essex or Sidney?" *Studies in Philology*, XXVII (1930), 125–41.

12 "Essex, the Ideal Courtier," pp. 7–36.

13 See my article on "The Allegory of Sir Artegall in *F. Q.*, V, xi–xii," *Studies in Philology*, XXXVII (1940), 179–83, for further discussion.

On the other hand, the combination of the courtesy theme with Arcadian romance would naturally suggest Sidney to those who had known him, and in his dedication of the *Shepheardes Calender* Spenser had given public notice of his relation to Sidney. Sidney crusaded against slander most of his adult life. He defended his father's government of Ireland, he replied to the libel on his uncle, called *Leicester's Commonwealth*, and he defended poetry against the attacks of the Puritans. He was also a conscious model of knightly courtesy throughout his life and in his last hours. He abandoned his cuisses because his companion had none, and after he was wounded he gave his cup of water to another wounded man.

But there is no personal allegory of Calidore, such as we have of Artegall at the end of Book V. The wooing of Pastorella has been interpreted as shadowing Essex' courtship of Sidney's widow,[14] but we can hardly distinguish between Sidney and Essex on that basis, since both men married the same woman. The Queen objected to both marriages on the same grounds—disparity of rank. Neither the wooing of Pastorella nor her captivity nor her discovery of her true parents has been shown to resemble any event in the life of Frances Walsingham, and there seems to be no reason to attempt to read allegory into the story, as distinct from the character, of Sir Calidore.

There is topical reference in the legend of courtesy, but it is pointed, not at the life of Sidney or Essex, but at the *Arcadia*. There can be little question that when he wrote Book VI Spenser was not only under the influence of the *Arcadia* but that he intended to remind his readers of it, and for that purpose he introduced two passages which are so strongly reminiscent of the prose romance that they amount to allusions. One of these passages (x, 34–36) closely parallels an episode in the *Arcadia* where one of the heroes rescues his lady from a wild animal. The other (x, 5–32) is the passage in which Colin sees the Graces dance. Sidney brings himself into his story under his pastoral name of Philisides (Book II, chap. 21), and here Spenser is doing the same thing. Sidney makes reference to his love for

[14] Long, pp. 58–59; and Heffner, pp. 32–33.

Stella, and Spenser celebrates Amoretta. Sidney represents himself in the characteristic activity of tilting, and Spenser assumes the posture conventional for a poet, the shepherd's.

When we take into account these deliberate and allusive echoes of the *Arcadia*, the elegies for Sidney which Spenser was writing about 1590–91, and his known relations with Sidney and with the Dudley family, the presumption seems to be strongly in favor of Book VI having been written in compliment to Sidney and of its being so understood by contemporaries.

But the commemoration is of Sidney's character, not of his life. Surely we must recognize that Spenser did not try to drive a three-horse team all the way through the poem. He had a narrative to handle, and he usually framed it so as to convey a moral allegory. He sometimes added, or substituted for the moral allegory, a topical allegory. But if we are to study the methods and processes of composition, we must distinguish between what an ingenious interpreter can make of a given passage and what the poet most clearly had in mind when he wrote it. His attention focuses now on the story and now on the allegory; and if we are to read the poem intelligently, we must be able to follow these shifts in attention.

Sir Calidore represents the ideal of knightly courtesy. In so far as Sidney, or Essex, or Ralegh, or any other contemporary figure exhibited courtesy, he is celebrated in Calidore; but unless contemporary incidents and events have clearly influenced the form of the story, I believe it is a mistake to try to give the story topical import. The effort to find Essex in Calidore must be considered in conjunction with efforts to find Essex in Artegall and even in Prince Arthur.[15] He has also been identified as Guyon and as Scudamour. The same kind of case could be made for Essex as Redcrosse. But unless it can be shown that Spenser was courting Essex' favor when this passage was written, we cannot assume that he was and proceed to interpret the allegory on that basis. On the other hand, we know that Spenser admired and was concerned with celebrating Sidney. We know that

[15] Ray Heffner, "Essex and Book V of the *Faerie Queene*," *ELH*, III (1936), 67–82; I. E. Rathborne, *The Meaning of Spenser's Fairyland* (New York, 1937), pp. 235–40.

Sidney was recognized as pre-eminent in knightly courtesy and that he had some notable bouts with the Blatant Beast of slander. Allusive imitations of the *Arcadia* in Book VI indicate not only that Spenser had that work in mind when he wrote but that he intended to remind the reader of the *Arcadia* and so, presumably, of its author. But courtesy still lived at the court of Gloriana. It lived in Sidney's book and in the imitation of his character which his friends (including Essex) attempted. And Sir Calidore (from the Latin *calidus?*) is not the dead knight but the living idea of courtesy. His adventures do not, so far as we know, represent anybody's life, but they illustrate courtesy, and in so far as Sidney was famous for that virtue they commemorate him.

Both in subject matter and in style Book VI shows the effect on Spenser of his contact with the literary ferment in London in 1590. It shows not only a fresh attack upon his problems and materials but also the impact of a fresh point of view on the country-staled and overbookish poet. The passage in which Colin sees the Graces dance is emblematic of a conscious maturity, a new urbanity. Here, and in *Colin Clouts Come Home Againe* and in the marriage hymns, we have the easy wearing of poetic greatness like that which graces Chaucer's mature style.[16] In this book Spenser records his understanding of Tasso's disgust with the life of courts (VI, ix). Ireland had never been "home" to him until he had been a part of the court, a suitor kept waiting. Then he came to the full maturity of wisdom—to the knowledge of the mutability of all things, the vanity of all shows, and the sober peace of contentment with a humble life.

It is not in Book IV, or in Book V, but in Book VI that this new spiritual growth manifests itself. It was into Book VI that Spenser poured the matured and seasoned wisdom which the visit to court with Ralegh had brought him.

[16] W. L. Renwick makes this observation about *Colin Clout* (see his edition of *Daphnaïda and Other Poems* [London: Scholartis Press, 1929], p. 180).

XVII
THE ILLUSTRATION OF THE VIRTUES

Reuele to me the sacred noursery
Of vertue, which with you doth there remaine,
Where it in siluer bowre does hidden ly
From view of men, and wicked worlds disdaine.
Since it at first was by the Gods with paine
Planted in earth, being deriu'd at furst
From heauenly seedes of bounty soueraine,
And by them long with carefull labour nurst,
Till it to ripenesse grew, and forth to honour burst.
—VI, Proem, 3

IT WAS Spenser's understanding, as it was that of his age, that the inculcation of morality was the chief purpose and justification of poetry. Therefore, it is reasonably certain that whether he began with Sir Thopas or with Redcrosse, or even with Guyon or Arthegall, he had a moral purpose in mind from the first. But none of his epic models provided him with a systematic treatment of virtue such as he was undertaking. Ulysses had been made by some interpreters into a consistent model of prudence, and some of the other epic and romance heroes had been marked out for pre-eminence in some one virtue, but nothing like Spenser's formal scheme for the illustration of each of the virtues had been attempted.

Yet, from their inception, at least Books I, II, V, and VI were created to illustrate particular virtues. Book VI is not significant for a study of Spenser's beginnings, since there is every reason to believe that it was almost entirely written after 1590. The two Ariosto-like books, III and IV, resemble Ariosto also in their more casual and miscellaneous treatment of morality. But Books I and II and the first section of V were clearly planned and written as illustrations of holiness, temperance, and justice.

It is equally clear that in these books the illustration of twelve moral virtues *according to Aristotle* was not the basic or formative idea. The poet was not writing with Aristotle at his elbow. Holiness is not an Aristotelian virtue, temperance has been much enlarged from Aristotle's definition, and justice is a political virtue and not one of Aristotle's private moral virtues.[1] Aristotle is not sure that chastity is a virtue at all, and he says nothing about chaste love, such as Britomart has been supposed to represent.[2] The Book of Friendship is not Aristotelian but largely chivalric in its antecedents.[3] Even courtesy, treated in a book begun after Spenser had announced his obedience to Aristotle, is a chivalric virtue, both in its fundamental conception and in its illustrations. These books have been "justified" out of Aristotle by the exercise of some ingenuity, but we are here concerned with creative processes, not with apologetics. In dealing with the inner history of the poem, we must distinguish between formative ideas and critical rationalizations, as far as that is possible. We are not concerned with whether Spenser's virtues can be defended as Aristotelian or even with whether he intended them to be so interpreted. We are here concerned with an attempt to follow his mental processes and to discover the creative ideas which produced the poem.

It is clear that, when he wrote the Book of Holiness, Spen-

[1] See the discussions by J. J. Jusserand, "Spenser's 'Twelve Private Morall Vertues as Aristotle Hath Devised,' " *Modern Philology*, III (1905–6), 373–83; W. F. DeMoss, *The Influence of Aristotle's "Politics" and "Ethics" on Spenser* (Chicago: Private edition, 1918); and Viola B. Hulbert, "Spenser's Twelve Moral Virtues 'According to Aristotle and the Rest,' " *University of Chicago Abstract of Theses, Humanistic Series*, V (1928), 479–85; and H. S. V. Jones, "The *Faerie Queene* and the Mediæval Aristotelian Tradition," *Journal of English and Germanic Philology*, XXV (1926), 283–98.

[2] Spenser may have got the hint for his association of Britomart and Florimell with chastity from Ariosto, who in his stories of Bradamante and Angelica makes use of a magic ring, of which Thomaso Porcacchi says, in his explanation of the allegory in *O. F.*, Canto IV: "Bradamante, che per uertù dell'anello lo uince, & libera tanti prigioni; significa la pudicitia, che uince ogni amor lasciuo, & leua di seruitù coloro, che francamente si dispongono di seguir piu tosto la ragione, che l'appetito" (*Orlando Furioso di M. Lodovico Ariosto* [Venetia: Domenico & Gio. Battista Guerra fratelli, 1582]).

[3] C. G. Smith, *Spenser's Theory of Friendship* (Baltimore: Johns Hopkins Press, 1935), shows that Spenser's ideas about friendship were commonplace and not especially Aristotelian. He thinks that they were based on a conception of the universe which was more Platonic than Aristotelian.

ser's mind was focused on the idea of combining the legend of St. George with the story of the Revelation in such a way as to create an allegory of Everyman. The parts of the Revelation selected indicate that he was also thinking of the Protestant Reformation. Aristotle's ethical theory could have no real place in such a book.[4] The story of Guyon probably had its beginning in an Ariosto-like romance in which Guyon (as the lover, or a lover, of the Faery Queen, and perhaps as the Sir Thopas–like representative of chastity) vanquished Acrasia. The book developed into a continued allegory of temperance in a much wider sense than Aristotle's definition of that virtue allows.[5] An Aristotelian cast was given to the book by the insertion of the allegory of Medina in Canto ii, but Aristotle's doctrine of the golden mean, which is the touchstone of all virtue, had long been associated with temperance in the larger and more popular sense in which Spenser illustrates temperance, and therefore the association of the golden mean with temperance is really evidence that Spenser's concept was popular rather than Aristotelian throughout.

Moreover, there are two reasons for thinking that the allegory of Medina was a very late addition to the book. The closing stanzas, which record Guyon's praises of the Faery Queen, tell also of the annual banquet, which seems to have been a very late elaboration added to the plot; and it also describes the initiation of Guyon's quest in a way which agrees with the statement about it in the letter to Ralegh but not with the events described in the preceding canto. If the death of Amavia was an early part of the book and if the allegory of Medina was a finishing touch, then the failure of two successive cantos to agree about the initiation of Guyon's quest is understandable. It would seem that Guyon displayed temperance before Medina was his mis-

[4] This is Jusserand's view. DeMoss tries to get Redcrosse into Aristotle's list by identifying him with high-mindedness or magnanimity. Mrs. Hulbert finds little resemblance between Spenser's list of virtues and Aristotle's. F. M. Padelford, "The Spiritual Allegory of the Faerie Queene, Book One," *Journal of English and Germanic Philology*, XXII (1923), 1–17, thinks that holiness is the Christian counterpart of the Greek high-mindedness.

[5] See *Variorum*, Vol. II, Appendixes III and IV.

tress, just as Redcrosse illustrated holiness without benefit of Aristotle. In fact, not one of Spenser's virtues can be fitted into Aristotle's list without Procrustean operations.

There was another and much more popular system of morality which distinguished four cardinal virtues, and Spenser's holiness, temperance, and justice are three of these cardinal virtues. This ethical scheme was commonplace to medieval and Renaissance morality. It had been expounded by both Platonic and Stoic philosophers and taken over into Christian ethics, and as a system it was much more widely known than Aristotle's more elaborate and indefinite scheme.

In several of his dialogues Plato puts into the mouth of Socrates a list of four cardinal virtues: wisdom, temperance, justice, and courage.[6] The Stoics took over Plato's system but substituted prudence for wisdom and fortitude for courage.[7] In the Renaissance every schoolboy knew about the cardinal virtues from the opening lines of Cicero's *De officiis*, which begins:

> My Son Marcus, you here perceive at least a sketch, and, as it were, the outline of virtue; which, could we perceive her with our eyes, would, as Plato says, kindle a wonderful love of Wisdom. But whatever is virtuous arises from some one of these four divisions: for it consists either in sagacity and the perception of truth; or in the preservation of human society, by giving to every man his due, and by observing the faith of contracts; or in the greatness and firmness of an elevated and unsubdued mind; or in observing order and regularity in all our words and in all our actions, in which consists moderation and temperance.[8]

This system had been known throughout the Middle Ages, partly through Cicero and partly through St. Ambrose's *De officiis ministrorum*, which Christianizes Cicero.[9] In addition, there were two popular tracts, specifically on the cardinal vir-

[6] See *Euthydemus*, *Republic* iv, and *Laws* i. In the *Protagoras* he adds holiness, making a list of five, but in the *Euthyphro* Socrates examines the nature of holiness and fails to arrive at a definition.

[7] Perhaps the identification of prudence with wisdom goes back to Aristotle, who seems to identify prudence with reason (see the *Nicomachean Ethics*, II, vi, trans. J. E. C. Welldon [London: Macmillan & Co., 1920], p. 47).

[8] *Cicero's Three Books of Offices*, trans. Cyrus R. Edmonds (London, 1850), p. 11.

[9] H. O. Taylor, *The Classical Heritage of the Middle Ages* (New York: Columbia University Press, 1901), pp. 74–78; St. Ambrose, *De officiis ministrorum*, in J.-P. Migne, *Patrologiae cursus completus*, Series I: *Latina*, XVI (Paris, 1845), 23–185.

tues, in general circulation. St. Martin of Brecara's *Tractatus de quattuor virtutibus* was understood to be excerpted from a lost work of Seneca. It was well known in sixteenth-century England.[10] Dominicus Mancinus' *De quattuor virtutibus* was translated into English by Alexander Barclay and later by George Turberville.[11]

From these and other sources the concept of ethics as organized into the four cardinal virtues passed into the conduct books of the sixteenth century. Sir Thomas Elyot in *The Boke Named the Gouernour* (1531) treats the four virtues.[12] *The Institucion of a Gentleman* (1555) follows Cicero.[13] Cornelius Valerius' *The Casket of Iewels* (1571) mentions and treats the cardinal virtues, although he does not confine himself to that system. *A Moral Methode of Ciuile Policie*, translated and abridged by R. Robinson out of the commentaries of Francesco Patrizi (1576), identifies the virtues as the usual four. *The Maner To Dye Well*, by "W. B." (1578), represents the thoughts of a man as a household. The house is his conscience. The father of the house appoints Prudence, Fortitude, and Justice to watch. Temperance also takes part in the dialogue. Thomas Pritchard, in *The Schoole of Honest and Vertuous Lyfe* (1579), uses both Cicero and Macrobius in his discussion of the four virtues. Jacques Hurault, in *Politicke, Moral, and Martial Discourses*, translated by Arthur Golding in 1595, makes his moral virtues the four cardinal ones. Simon Harward, in his *Encheiridion Morale* (1596),

[10] The Latin text was printed by W. de Worde in 1516 and 1523. An English translation appeared about 1538, and another, by R. Whyttyngton, was printed in 1546 and again, with the Latin for use as a schoolbook, in 1547.

[11] Mancinus was printed in 1484, and at Paris, 1488, and Leipzig, 1516. *The Englysshe of Mancyne upon the Foure Cardynale Vertues* appeared about 1520, and Barclay's *The Myrrour of Good Maners* was printed in 1523(?) and again in 1570 with Barclay's eclogues. Turberville's *A Plaine Path to Perfect Vertue* appeared in 1568.

[12] In the curious excursus on dancing in Book I, chaps. 21–25, he explains the Aristotelian principle of the mean and then divides "the first moral vertue, called prudence" into eight parts, or figures, of the dance. In Book III he takes up the cardinal virtues in a more systematic way, beginning with justice (chaps. 1–7), and fortitude (8–19), under which he treats magnanimity, which he identifies with courage, abstinence, and continence. Next he takes up temperance (20–22), and finally sapience (23 ff.), which he defines after Cicero as "the science of things diuine and humaine," and which he quite properly makes antecedent to prudence, its practical manifestation.

[13] Reprinted in 1568 and again in 1839.

collects his commonplaces under the heads of the four virtues, identifying fortitude with magnanimity.

Writers on gentility and heraldry regularly began their works with an account of the cardinal virtues. Gerard Legh, in his popular *Accedens of Armory* (1562, 1568, 1576, 1591, etc.), describes them in his prefatory matter and gives their heraldic emblems. John Bossewell, John Ferne, and Sir William Segar all describe these virtues as requisites of a gentleman.

Whether or not Spenser had studied Aristotle's ethical treatises, he and his contemporaries were thoroughly familiar with the Platonic-Stoic-Christian list of four cardinal virtues. The first of these four was the Platonic and Christian wisdom, or the Stoic prudence.

Plato himself made knowledge, or wisdom, the basis of all virtue, and he thought that it was of divine origin. Aristotle distinguished between speculative and nonspeculative virtues, making knowledge or wisdom a speculative virtue. This distinction anticipates the medieval one between the contemplative and the active life and the virtues of each.[14] St. Thomas Aquinas describes four cardinal or moral virtues and four intellectual virtues, making prudence common to both groups. The other intellectual virtues are *sapientia*, *intellectus*, and *scientia*.[15]

The close connection between wisdom and prudence and the transcendental character of wisdom to Platonists and Christians were commonly recognized in Spenser's day.[16] Such popularizers as Bossewell and Ferne mention the relationship. Bossewell equates prudence with the Greek *Sophia* and the Hebrew Wisdom.[17] Ferne makes wisdom, or sapience, the "soueraigne queene to all vertues,"

much more excellent, then Prudence, that communicateth some portion of her operations, to brute beastes, as Philosophye hath tolde. But wisedome

[14] See Jones, *op. cit.*, note 1, pp. 283–92.

[15] See H. O. Taylor, *The Mediaeval Mind* (London: Macmillan & Co., 1911), II, 326.

[16] Marsilio Ficino, in his discussion of the *Philebus* (chap. viii), says: "Ex diuinis primum prudentia, id est, sapientia, secundum, moderatus animi habitus, tertium, Iustitia, fortitudo, quartum, omnia illa humana ad diuina referri vult" (*Opera* [Paris, 1641], II, 178B).

[17] *Workes of Armorie* (London, 1597, reprinted from 1572), fol. 4v. He treats all four virtues, following Legh.

instructing both soule and body, what to follow, and what to eschew, reuealing the knowledge of hidden secreats, subsisting of the quintessence, and beste refined part of reason, illuminated by deuine graces, wherein we seeme like to our God: is more noble, then all nobilitie, yea better then precious riches, & nothing to be desired of man, able to stande, in the degree of her comparison. Which attendeth as a hand-mayde, at the throne, and supernall seat of *Iehouah*. By her, Kinges doe rule, and law-makers determine, that is iust: by her, princes commaunde, and Iudges be instructed, how to administer iustice. Hence is it, that all the learned, haue borrowed their knowledge and artes. From her, the sage & pollitique Counsailors of states, receaue the wisedomes of their gouernmentes. Yea, vnder this title of *Sapience*, let all vertues be couched.[18]

Jacques Hurault, in his book on ethics, which Arthur Golding translated as *Politicke, Moral, and Martial Discourses* (1595), summarizes the various modifications of this system as follows:

Some diuide vertue into two parts, that is to wit, Contemplatiue, and Morall; we cal that vertue Contemplatiue, which consisteth in well vnderstanding, and well considering, that is to say, in the inward minding and reasoning, whereout springeth discretion and wisedome. And we call those vertues morall, which belong to manners, and not alonely to vnderstanding. . . . .

For Wisedome is a certain hauior of vertue, which consisteth in the wit and vnderstanding; but Temperance belongeth to a mans actions and manners, and in respect thereof wee terme it Morall. . . . .

Others make foure principal vertues, the which they terme Cardinall, vnder which, all other vertues are comprehended: namely, Wisedome, which teacheth what is to be done; Hardinesse, or Valeantnesse, which teacheth what is to be indured; Temperance, which teacheth what is to be chosen; and Iustice, which teacheth what is to bee yeelded vnto euery man. Othersome do lodge wisdome in the vnderstanding and the wit; Iustice, in the will; Hardines in that part of the mind which conceiueth anger; and Temperance, in the lust of the sensitiue appetite [pp. 57–58].

For a Christian, wisdom was synonymous with religion. In his second book, Hurault takes up the cardinal virtues in a systematic way, beginning with "Of Wisedome, and Discreetnesse." He starts by quoting the Greek precept, "Know thyself," and he says:

Therefore when we say, a man must know himselfe: it is as much to say, as hee must haue a care of his soule, to prepare it to the knowing of God his maker, after whose image it is created, that hee may, as it were in a looking glasse behold the inuisible Godhead, the efficient cause of wisedome, and of

[18] *The Blazon of Gentrie* (1586), pp. 30–31.

all good things; and that by the knowledge of the vertues which God hath giuen vnto him, he may consider how greatly he is indetted vnto God. . . . .

Those then which refer al their actions to the said first cause, we call Wise men, according to the writings both of the Bible, and also of the Heathen authors, specially of the great *Mercurie*, *Plato*, and *Cicero*, who affirme, that the first point of wisedome, is to know a mans selfe [p. 150].

This is the virtue which Spenser is illustrating in his story of Redcrosse,[19] whose beloved and helper is a symbol of religious truth, and who is accompanied by her dwarf, Prudence.

Several modern critics have recognized that Spenser's temperance is also a cardinal virtue,[20] commensurate with that moderation in all things which Aristotle makes the ground of all virtue, but which Plato distinguishes from courage, wisdom, and justice. Cicero makes temperance synonymous with "the ordre, and measure of all thinges, that are done, and saide."[21] Bossewell quotes Plotinus' definition that "the propertie and office of Temperance, is to covet nothing, which may be repented, also not to exceede the bounds of Mediocrite, and to keepe desire vnder the yoke of reason." John Higgins, in his address "To the Nobilitie" prefacing his addition to the *Mirour for Magistrates* (a work which Spenser used), discusses the four cardinal virtues and quotes the same definition of temperance from the same source.[22] It is a characteristic combination of Aristotelian

[19] See J. S. Harrison, *Platonism in English Poetry of the Sixteenth and Seventeenth Centuries* (New York, 1903). His discussion of Book I is reprinted in *Variorum*, Vol. I, Appendix VIII. See also Miss Winstanley's edition of Book I (Cambridge, 1915), pp. lix–lxvi. Macrobius, in his discussion of the four cardinal virtues, identifies prudence with contemplation of divinity, asserting that the highest prudence is in the divine mind (*In Somnium Scipionis* [Paris, 1585], pp. 36–38; see also H. S. V. Jones, *A Spenser Handbook* [New York, 1930], pp. 159–62).

[20] Viola B. Hulbert, "A Possible Christian Source for Spenser's Temperance," *Studies in Philology*, XXVIII (1931), 184–210, shows that Spenser's temperance is a Christian virtue with a medieval tradition behind it and a considerable debt to Cicero. She finds that even Medina belongs in the Christian tradition. Greenlaw says: "Fundamentally, Guyon's story is an exposition of the Platonic ideal, but certain Aristotelian elements are present" notably, the theory of the mean (*Variorum*, II, 427–31). Harrison and Miss Winstanley both comment on the Platonic character of Spenser's temperance. DeMoss defends its Aristotelian character, but Padelford betrays the weakness of such a defense by arguing that "Spenser's Temperance is really Aristotle's Continence . . . . contrasted with Temperance . . . . in the *Ethics* 7" (*Variorum*, II, 420–22).

[21] Nicholas Grimald's translation of the *De officiis*, published many times between 1553 and 1600. I quote from the edition of 1574, fol. 7.

[22] This address appeared in the edition of 1575 and in subsequent editions.

and Platonic principles, one in all probability known to Spenser, and one which might almost serve as an outline of the Book of Guyon.

The first two books of the *Faerie Queene* fall naturally and fully into the system of the four cardinal virtues, and Thomas Keightley once suggested that the twelve moral virtues were intended to be grouped around the cardinal virtues.[23] It seems more probable that Spenser began with a plan to illustrate the cardinal virtues than that he began, as Miss Janet Spens suggests, with the illustration of the seven deadly sins. Her hypothesis fails to take into account what we know about Spenser's plans and beginnings. It entirely neglects the place both of the titular heroine and of the Ariosto imitation in the early plot. Her presentation of evidence that the narrative has been revised and rearranged is sound and valuable, but her attempt to reconstruct the original plot is at variance with much of the evidence and is supported only by the flimsiest of arguments.[24]

So far as we can tell, Spenser began with the Faery Queen created as a compliment to Queen Elizabeth. The redaction of *Sir Thopas* seems to indicate that chastity was the first of the Queen's virtues to be celebrated, but, as the poet's ambitions mounted, it would be natural for him to celebrate her greater virtues.

The enumeration of Queen Elizabeth's virtues began at least as early as the coronation pageants where her devotion to true religion was commemorated. But in many conspicuous instances she was credited with the four cardinal virtues. The Bible of 1569 has on its title-page a picture of the Queen with Justice and Mercy (in place of Temperance) supporting her crown, and Fortitude and Prudence supporting the throne.[25] William Patten, in *The Calender of Scripture* (1575) gives the Queen seven virtues by adding Faith, Hope, and Charity to the

[23] "Plan of the 'Faerie Queene,'" *Notes and Queries*, IV (4th ser., 1869), 211–12.

[24] See *Spenser's Faerie Queene* (London, 1934), chap. i, esp. pp. 27–28.

[25] Reproduced in E. C. Wilson, *England's Eliza* ("Harvard Studies in English," Vol. XX [Cambridge, Mass., 1939]), opposite p. 366.

conventional four.[26] F. Zuccaro's portrait of Elizabeth, drawn in 1575, shows in the background the animal symbols of the cardinal virtues.[27] Even before her accession, her brother Edward had nicknamed her "his sweet Sister Temperance."[28] The Queen herself, in her speech in defense of her treatment of Queen Mary (1586), says: "Nothing is more necessary [for rulers], then to be plentifully furnished with the predominant Vertues of *Iustice*, *Temperance*, *Wisedome*, and *Fortitude*."[29] Again, in *The Copie of a Letter to the Right Honourable the Earle of Leycester* (1586), she says that she has considered "what it fitted a King to do: and there I saw, he scant was wel furnished, if either he lacked Justice, Temperance, Magnanimitie [i.e., fortitude], or Judgement."[30] About 1582 the town hall at Kingston was provided with the inscription: "Vivat Regina Elizabetha, in qua fides, Prudentia, Fortitudo, Temperantia, et Justicia elugent [*sic*! elucent?] luculente."[31]

Maurice Kyffin, in *The Blessednes of Brytaine* (1587), credits the four cardinal virtues to the Queen (st. 5), and so does Sir William Leighton in his *Vertue Triumphant, or A Lively Description of the Foure Vertues Cardinall* (1603). Sir Henry Lee, in 1590, celebrated the Queen as a crowned pillar, in allusion to the fact that the heraldic symbol of fortitude was a pillar.[32]

It was inevitable that the most familiar list of moral virtues—

[26] Wilson, p. 367 n. This combination goes back at least to Aquinas (see Taylor, *The Mediaeval Mind*, II, 326).

[27] Described in J. Nichols, *Progresses and Public Processions of Queen Elizabeth* (London, 1823), I, xiv–xv n. and reproduced in *A Collection of Prints in Imitation of Drawings*, ed. Charles Rogers (London, 1778), I, opposite p. 89.

[28] W. Camden, *History of . . . . Elizabeth* (1688), "The Introduction," sig. Bi^{v}.

[29] Camden, *Annales* (1625), III, 176. The edition of 1688 translates Camden's Latin as "those prime capital Vertues, Justice, Temperance, Prudence, and Magnanimity" (p. 367).

[30] Pp. 30–31, quoted in Greenlaw's *Studies in Spenser's Historical Allegory* (Baltimore, 1932), p. 203.

[31] Wilson, p. 86. See also pp. 87, 362 n., and 388–92 for other listings of the Queen's virtues.

[32] See E. K. Chambers, *Sir Henry Lee* (Oxford, 1036), pp. 137–40. The pattern poem quoted on p. 140 is from *The Arte of English Poesie*, II, xii. See also G. Legh, *The Accedens of Armory* (1562), "The Description of the Viniet"; and Bossewell, pp. 4^{v}–7^{v}.

the list which Sir Walter Ralegh identified with the four rivers of Eden[33] and Sir John Harington with the four ladies sent to rescue Ruggiero[34]—should be the list most frequently attributed to the Queen, and therefore the natural one for Spenser to use when his tribute to his Augustus took on a more serious moral tone.

The theory that Spenser began with the illustration of the four cardinal virtues does much to explain the curious state of the fifth book. As I have pointed out, the four formal exempla of justice in the first section of it are crude and stiff both in narrative and in style.[35] They contrast with the second and third sections of the book, which can be shown by their contents to belong to late plot ideas and materials. This first section is either a deplorable piece of hack work or it is a survival of an earlier and cruder attempt to illustrate justice.

In so far as these episodes—of the beheaded lady, of Pollente and the Lady Munera, of the giant Democracy, and of the case of treasure trove—have been given topical interpretation, they have been applied to the events of Spenser's first two years in Ireland. Actually they present academic problems of justice, and I seriously doubt that any topical application was intended. But, in any case, there is nothing in any of them which could not have been written by 1582.

I suggested in an earlier chapter that the name of Arthegall came into the *Faerie Queene* out of Spenser's studies in the *Stemmata Dudleiana*. If these illustrations of justice were early work, the hero of them might have been called Arthegall out of compliment to the Dudleys, or he might have been called by some other name which was changed to that of Britomart's lover when Book V was put together. It is not very probable that the name of the first Earl of Warwick was used to "shadow"

[33] *History of the World*, Book I, chap. iii, sec. 2. He cites Du Bartas as his authority (*The Works of Sir Walter Ralegh* [Oxford, 1829], II, 66).

[34] *Orlando Furioso* (1607), p. 80.

[35] See Appendix I. The reader will note the contrast in enjambment ratio between the opening stanzas (i, 1–12) and the rest of the section (i, 13—iv, 20) as well as between that section and the other two. There are only eleven feminine rhymes in Cantos i—iv, 20, as compared with ten in Canto v alone.

Arthur, Lord Grey of Wilton. If the early representative of justice was meant to compliment Lord Grey, he probably had some other name; but I believe there was no conscious intention to represent Grey, except possibly in the quest of Irena, and that the Arthegall-Justice theme came by another series of associations.

Arthegall is linked with Guyon, the other famous Earl of Warwick, both in II, ix, 6, and in the story of the recovery of Guyon's horse in V, iii. If Books II and V once stood in immediate sequence, these links would be more significant and useful than they are in their present state.

There is one further suggestive situation which seems to point to a four-book scheme to illustrate the cardinal virtues—a scheme which had progressed as far as the opening of the Book of Justice before it was expanded to twelve books. In his letter to Ralegh, Spenser makes the amazing offer, when he had finished only a quarter of his enormous undertaking, to write a second such work. He says:

> I haue followed all the antique Poets historicall, first Homere, who in the Persons of Agamemnon and Vlysses hath ensampled a good gouernour and a vertuous man, the one in his Ilias, the other in his Odysseis. . . . . By ensample of which excellente Poets, I labour to pourtraict in Arthure, before he was king, the image of a braue knight, perfected in the twelue priuate morall vertues . . . . which if I finde to be well accepted, I may be perhaps encoraged, to frame the other part of polliticke vertues in his person, after that hee came to be king.

As I have pointed out, the whole idea of making Arthur the chief hero was a late addition to the omnibus plan. But Arthegall and Guyon may represent the original conception of the Agamemnon and Ulysses of his plot. The association of Guyon with Ulysses is made explicit in the voyage of Guyon to the Bower of Bliss, which clearly echoes the wanderings of Ulysses. The formal exempla at the opening of Book V show Arthegall as a "good gouernour," and I suggest that they had long been written when Spenser composed his letter to Ralegh. They did not fit into his recently adopted Aristotelian system, but he thought that he might eventually illustrate the political virtues when he had finished the private moral ones. In the end he made use of this justice material to fill up his fifth book.[36] The result is a book which illustrates the cardinal rather than the private moral virtue described by Aristotle.[37]

It may be no more than a coincidence that four books of twelve cantos each, illustrating the cardinal virtues, would just equal the length of the *Iliad* and *Odyssey* together, which total 48 books. Tasso has 20 cantos, Vergil 12 books, and Ariosto 46 cantos. It hardly seems probable that Spenser's initial plan called for a poem of 144 cantos, not to mention the proposed continuation. It is longer, in its present state, than *Paradise Lost*, the *Aeneid*, and the *Gerusalemme Liberata* all put together.[38]

The fourth cardinal virtue was the Platonic courage, or Stoic fortitude. Gerard Legh says that "fortitude is magnificence, with a ioyfull cleare courage. . . . . Fortitude is perseuerance." Cicero defined it as "the greatness and firmness of an elevated and unsubdued mind." It was associated with both constancy and magnanimity. The *Oxford English Dictionary* says of magnanimity that

> in scholastic descriptions the notion [Aristotelian] was modified in accordance with Christian ideals, and blended with elements suggested by the etymology of the Latin word (*animus* being capable of the sense of "courage"); hence "magnanimity" is often classed as a subdivision of "fortitude" (so Aquinas, following Macrobius, *In Somnium Scipionis*, I, viii, 7).

Mancinus and Sir Thomas Elyot identify magnanimity with fortitude.

[36] Not Agamemnon but the much more spectacular Hercules is Spenser's model of the good governor (see V, i, 2–3). Rosemond Tuve compares Arthegall's captivity among the Amazons to that of Hercules ("Spenser's Reading: The *De claris mulieribus*," *Studies in Philology*, XXXIII [1936], 147–65). M. Y. Hughes has called my attention to the comparisons between Arthur and Hercules, a point made also by Isabel E. Rathborne in her chapter on "Gods and Heroes," in *The Meaning of Spenser's Fairyland* (New York, 1937). Both of these critics see in Arthur Spenser's copy of Hercules. But the comparisons between Arthur and Hercules are concerned with the twelve labors, and similar comparisons are made with Redcrosse, Guyon, Arthegall, and Calidore. The specific comparison between Arthegall and the Hercules who was the exponent of justice seems to me to be more significant. There were several Herculeses, according to the mythologists (see Rathborne, pp. 94 ff.).

[37] That is the opinion of Kate M. Warren in her edition of the book (*Variorum*, V, 272). A. B. Gough comes to the same conclusion (*Variorum*, V, 311).

[38] The *F. Q.* has about 34,200 lines, while *P. L.* has only 10,565; the *Aeneid* about 9,500; and *G. L.* 14,096. The whole *Orlando Furioso* has only 37, 000.

This conception of fortitude reminds us at once of the existence of two cantos "of some following Booke of the *Faerie Queene*, vnder the Legend of Constancie." I do not subscribe to the theory that these two cantos represent early writing;[39] but they are numbered vi and vii, which suggests that Spenser may have had on hand when he wrote them a beginning of a book of constancy in about five cantos. At any rate, they illustrate the influence of the current conception of the cardinal virtues on Spenser's poem. The cardinal virtues are fundamental. The expansion of the list to twelve and the mention of Aristotle are late and superficial additions. Perhaps, as J. J. Jusserand suggested, the expansion was prompted partly by Lodowick Bryskett's translation of the second part of G. B. Giraldi's *De gli hecatommithi* (1565).[40] Bryskett supplements Giraldi's account of the virtues from Piccolomini, as follows:

There are then by the generall consent of men foure principall vertues appertaining to ciuill life, which are, Fortitude, Temperance, Iustice, and Pru-

[39] Miss Evelyn Albright argued that these cantos were written in the spring of 1580 ("Spenser's Reason for Rejecting the Cantos of Mutability," *Studies in Philology*, XXV [1928], 93-127). Her argument has been refuted on five different grounds (see H. M. Belden, "Alanus de Insulis, Giles Fletcher, and the *Mutabilitie* Cantos," *Studies in Philology*, XXVI [1929], 131-44; Douglas Bush, "The Date of Spenser's *Cantos of Mutability*," *PMLA*, XLV [1930], 954-57; F. M. Padelford, "The *Cantos of Mutabilitie:* Further Considerations Bearing on the Date," *PMLA*, XLV [1930], 704-11; Edwin Greenlaw, "Spenser's '*Mutabilitie*,'" *PMLA*, XLV [1930], 684-703; and my "Spenser and Gabriel Harvey's *Letter-Book*," *Modern Philology*, XXIX [1931], 163-86). Miss Albright has offered two replies: "On the Dating of Spenser's 'Mutability' Cantos," *Studies in Philology*, XXVI (1929), 482-98, and "Spenser's Connections with the Letters in Gabriel Harvey's 'Letter-Book,'" *Modern Philology*, XXIX (1932), 411-36. Her case rests on some material in Harvey's *Letter-Book*, which she contends is a copy of a letter seen by Spenser, and which I have shown is an unfinished literary exercise and not a genuine letter. W. W. Greg says of my article: "I do not think her conclusions are seriously invalidated by E. M. Albright's reply." Since Professor Greg has examined the original manuscript, while Miss Albright relies entirely on the careful but misleading edition in the "Camden Society Publications," Professor Greg's verdict carries considerable weight (see *English Literary Autographs, 1550-1650*, selected and edited by W. W. Greg and others [Oxford: Oxford University Press, 1932], Part III, Art. LXXI). J. M. Purcell's "The Date of Spenser's *Mutabilite* Cantos," *PMLA*, L (1935), 914-17, is an attempt to illustrate the inconclusiveness of J. V. Fletcher's evidence for "Some Observations on the Changing Style of the *Faerie Queene*," *Studies in Philology*, XXXI (1934), 152-59. His argument has no real bearing on the dating of the *Cantos*.

[40] Jusserand suggests that Spenser's idea of the moral virtues was derived from this work rather than from Aristotle. Bryskett says that he got his account of the virtues from Piccolomini, who claims that he is following Aristotle. But Spenser's list does not agree with Bryskett's any better than it does with Aristotle's. Since Bryskett's transla-

dence; from which foure are also deriued (as branches from their trees) sundry others to make vp the number of twelue, and they are these ensuing, Liberalitie, Magnificence, Magnanimitie, Mansuetude, Desire of honor, Veritie, Affability, and Vrbanitie.[41]

The idea of four cardinal virtues as fundamental, and eight other virtues as springing from them like branches or subdivisions, can be found in other discussions of the virtues. Bryskett's list, aside from the cardinal virtues, is not Spenser's list. But we can see how, when Spenser decided to extend his number from four to twelve, he was only shifting from the traditional Platonic to the traditional Aristotelian number, without much reference to Aristotle directly. His reason for making the expansion seems clear from the character of the third book. He wished to compliment the Queen's favorite virtue, and he also wished to include in his first instalment some part of the story of his lady knight, Britomart.

The importance of the cardinal virtues in Spenser's thought and in his plans can hardly be overemphasized. His obeisance to Aristotle in the letter to Ralegh has confused and misled many of his critics. But the moral scheme of the poem is best understood by beginning with wisdom, temperance, justice, and fortitude.

---

tion does not seem to have been made before 1582, Jusserand suggests that perhaps Spenser's general plan of the virtues developed slowly and had not been fully formed by that date (*op. cit.*, n. 1, above). That is my conclusion, but on other grounds.

[41] *Discovrse of Civill Life* (1606), p. 214.

XVIII
THE PROGRESS OF THE COMPOSITION

> Guyde ye my footing, and conduct me well
> In these strange waies, where neuer foote did vse,
> Ne none can find, but who was taught them by the Muse.
>
> —VI, Proem, 2.7–9

ACCORDING to my analysis of the evidence, the history of the composition of the *Faerie Queene* was something like this. Sometime during the fruitful period of hope and ambition, just after the poet left Cambridge (1576–80), he began, among other undertakings, a poem called the *Faerie Queene* (and therefore probably about that character), in which he "wil needes seeme to emulate, and hope to ouergo" Ariosto. Gabriel Harvey's comments seem to indicate that this work was comparable in scope to the writing of comedies. It could hardly have been any part of the story of Redcrosse, which is in no Renaissance sense an imitation of Ariosto, which could not, by itself, have gone under the title of the *Faerie Queene*, and which makes extensive use of the Revelation of John, a model which Harvey praised in the same letter in which he disapproved of the *Faerie Queene*.

If that early *Faerie Queene* is still a part of the poem, it must be some part in which the titular heroine figures; that is, either the redaction and continuation of Chaucer's *Sir Thopas* or the adventures of the knights of Maidenhead who belong to the court of the Faery Queen. I have pointed out a passage in Book III which, in conjunction with Arthur's story in Book I, constitutes evidence that Spenser at one time undertook to continue *Sir Thopas*, perhaps in imitation of Ariosto's continuation of the *Orlando* of Boiardo.

I have argued that this was the poem, or beginning of a

poem, which met with Gabriel Harvey's disapproval in the spring of 1580. Harvey's censure came just at a time when the poet was suffering a setback in his hopes, including the loss of Leicester's patronage, abandonment of the projected publication of the *Dreames*, and departure for Ireland and the rigors of attendance on a general during an active military campaign. Into his "exile" the poet took not only his *Dreames* and his first *Faerie Queene* but also several other manuscripts, including the *Stemmata Dudleiana*, the *Epithalamion Thamesis*, his translations for Van der Noot's *Theatre*, and perhaps a revised version of the four apocalyptical sonnets in it (possibly the same as the *Dreames*) out of which the legend of Redcrosse eventually developed.[1]

Whether or not the first version of the *Faerie Queene* was intended as an epic, we know that Spenser was fired with the ambition to be an English Vergil, as well as an English Ariosto, and that he looked upon the writing of an epic as the next logical step when he had completed the pastorals required of an apprentice according to Vergilian tradition. He was profoundly uncertain, however, of his theme. His conception of the epic was fundamentally governed by his understanding of Vergil's procedure. The poet must have a great patron and a great theme which provided opportunity for flattery of that patron,

> But ah *Mecœnas* is yclad in claye,
> And great *Augustus* long ygoe is dead:
> And all the worthies liggen wrapt in leade,
> That matter made for Poets on to play.[2]

He lacked a Maecenas, he wavered in his choice of an Augustus between the Queen and Leicester, and he could find no satisfactory heroic action. He lacked a legend which would serve as a medium through which he could "antique praises vnto present persons fit." If he ever seriously entertained the idea of celebrating Leicester as his Augustus, the notion probably van-

[1] We hear of *Dreames*, *Visions*, *Pageants*, *Legends*, and *Sonnets*. Eventually the translations were broken up into three parts: *Visions of Petrarch*, *Visions of Bellay*, and the "visions of St. John," which found their way into Book I.

[2] "October," ll. 61–64.

ished with the loss of the Earl's favor. Queen Elizabeth was the only really possible choice, and yet her sex presented an insurmountable difficulty. Her heroic action must be performed vicariously, through her band of knights, if he was to "sing of bloody Mars, of wars, of giusts"; but, even so, "present persons" failed to fit "antique praises" until it was much too late to make their actions the basis of his epic. Their "woundlesse armour rusts, and helmes vnbruzed wexen dayly browne." The poet struggled mightily, but the great theme would not come, and the history of the composition of the *Faerie Queene* is largely a history of his effort to find a substitute for that missing heroic action.

It is a little hard for us to see, from our point of vantage in time, why neither Arthur nor St. George was made the central figure from the first, why Spenser planned neither an epic of national greatness based on Arthurian legend nor an epic of the religious struggle. I have suggested that he began to write too soon—that the vogue for Arthur and the celebration of national greatness began in the eighties, just too late to provide him with a fundamental theme, although he attempted late in the development of his plans to repair the oversight. But the consciousness of national greatness and the triumph of Protestantism both came too late to provide the epic theme he wanted.

Confronted with the lack of suitable historical action[3] and the problem of celebrating a feminine Augustus, the poet seems to have turned to moral allegory as a substitute for "bloody Mars."

If Spenser's tentative beginning was in the tone of personal flattery of the "Aprill" eclogue and celebrated the Queen's private moral virtue of chastity, it would be a very natural step, when he attempted a more serious vein, to substitute the four cardinal virtues for the chastity motif. Sir Thopas was the

[3] Professor Draper notes Spenser's fundamentally historical concept of the epic ("The Narrative-Technique of the *Faerie Queene*," *PMLA*, XXXIX [1924], 319–20). For his choice of Clio as his muse see my article on "Spenser's Muse," *Journal of English and Germanic Philology*, XXXI (1932), 200–19. The abstract of this article in *Variorum*, I, 514–15, is too brief to be useful. F. M. Padelford's argument that Spenser's muse is Calliope is there reprinted in full (pp. 506–14).

enemy of lust, and when Guyon's chief exploit turns out to be the punishment of Acrasia we may venture to suspect that this knight, whose name suggests the *Stemmata Dudleiana* and the intention to celebrate Leicester, and who is singularly devoted to the Faery Queen, may have supplanted Sir Thopas early in the process of development of the poem.

Arthegall seems to have come through the same channel. Redcrosse, on the other hand, could hardly have been one of the first of these knights, since he is not a knight of Maidenhead. If the development was from Ariosto emulation and (what emulation usually meant to an Elizabethan) imitation, through the moral allegory of Alcina and Logostilla, to the moral virtues of temperance and justice, then the addition of a knight to illustrate wisdom, "the science of things both human and divine," is a logical development. On the other hand, if the poet turned from his Sir Thopas–Faery Queen story directly to the Book of Redcrosse, there must have been a sharp break and a fresh start, for the two subjects are very far apart in tone and treatment. But if the legend of Redcrosse was a fresh start, it is a little hard to see why the poet did not extend it to full epic length. It is his one real success in his struggle for an epic theme. Since he did not do so, probably he had already created his larger frame plot of the court of the Faery Queen and the Order of Maidenhead.

The illustration of virtue was as much an essential part of Spenser's conception of the epic as were an Augustus and a historic action. And it is not in the exemplification of virtue but in the systematic treatment of the virtues that he departs from his models. If he began to write with Ariosto in mind, then it is probable that this systematic treatment of the several virtues was the product of an effort to introduce order and significance into Ariosto's studied disorganization.

We know little enough of his poetic activities during the early years in Ireland, but it seems reasonable to suppose that during his secretaryship to Lord Grey he had little time for composition. On the other hand, constant personal contact with this stern Protestant whom he admired must have had a sobering influence on the young poet, and it would not be surprising if the celebration of the four cardinal virtues was undertaken as soon as he had a little leisure, perhaps in the two years (1582–84) between Lord Grey's departure from Ireland and Spenser's assumption of the duties of the clerkship of Munster.

We have only one piece of information, and that of doubtful authenticity, about the progress of the *Faerie Queene* during these years. Lodowick Bryskett, in the Introduction to his *Discovrse of Civill Life: Containing the Ethike part of Morall Philosophie*, represents himself as asking Spenser to

> spend this time . . . . in declaring vnto vs the great benefites which men obtaine by the knowledge of Morall Philosophie, and in making vs to know what the same is, what be the parts thereof, whereby vertues are to be distinguished from vices.

To this request he represents Spenser as replying:

> Though it may seeme hard for me to refuse the request made by you all, whom, euery one alone, I should for many respects be willing to gratifie; yet as the case standeth, I doubt not but with the consent of the most part of you, I shall be excused at this time of this taske which would be laid vpon me. For sure I am, that it is not vnknowne vnto you, that I haue already vndertaken a work tẽding to the same effect, which is in *heroical verse*, vnder the title of a *Faerie Queene*, to represent all the moral vertues, assigning to euery vertue, a Knight to be the patron and defender of the same: in whose actions and feates of armes and chiualry, the operations of that vertue, whereof he is the protector, are to be expressed, and the vices & vnruly appetites that oppose themselues against the same, to be beatẽ downe & ouercome. Which work, as I haue already well entered into, if God shall please to spare me life that I may finish it according to my mind, your wish (M. *Bryskett*) will be in some sort accomplished, though perhaps not so effectually as you could desire.[4]

Unfortunately, there is some question about the historicity of this narrative. It purports to describe a three days' meeting taking place near Dublin in May, 1582, but the third day must have been after June, 1584.[5] The whole *Discovrse* is a transla-

[4] Edition of 1606, pp. 25-27.

[5] For discussions of this matter see H. R. Plomer and T. P. Cross, *The Life and Correspondence of Lodowick Bryskett* (Chicago, 1927), pp. 77–84; John Erskine, "The Virtue of Friendship in the *Faerie Queene*," *Variorum*, IV, 291–93, includes a résumé of the discussions of the historical character of this meeting and concludes that the meeting was imaginary because the whole work is a translation, except for such "dramatic trimming" as the reference to the *Faerie Queene*. But, so far as Bryskett's evidence

tion from G. B. Giraldi except where Bryskett has substituted his friends for the original speakers. The complete work was not printed until 1606, and it seems impossible to determine just when any part of it was written.

It can be noted, however, that Bryskett's description of the *Faerie Queene* is in no sense an echo of the letter to Ralegh, printed at the end of the third book in 1590, as we should expect it to be if it had been written after the letter appeared. It mentions the knights who illustrate virtues but does not specify twelve, or mention Aristotle, or say anything about their setting out on quests; nor does it make any mention of the machinery of the annual banquet or of the all-virtuous Arthur. The argument from silence is of little force, but the contrast between Spenser's letter, which so strongly emphasizes Arthur and Aristotle, and Bryskett's account of the *Faerie Queene*, purporting to describe the poem in 1582 and not mentioning either, is worth noting. We cannot be sure of the authority of Bryskett's statement, but my analysis of the process of composition of the *Faerie Queene*, arrived at from a study of the poem itself, corresponds closely with Bryskett's representation of what Spenser said of it in 1582–84.

In the summer of 1584 Sir John Norris arrived in Ireland to take up his duties as lord president of Munster. Lodowick Bryskett was clerk of the council in that province but discharged his office by deputy, and at just about the time of Norris' arrival Spenser became his deputy.[6] It seems to have been the duty of the clerk to attend upon and act as secretary for the president, and it is probable that during the year Norris

---

of the nature of the *F. Q.* in 1582 is concerned, the pertinent fact is not whether the meeting took place but when the translation was made and this account of the *F. Q.* was written. Janet Spens, *Spenser's Faerie Queene* (London, 1934), pp. 139–44, argues that the *Discourse* is an imitation of the *Courtier* and that the preliminary matter was not written until most of the people represented in it were dead. Her argument rests solely on the parallel with Castiglione, however. It assumes (*a*) that Bryskett knew that Castiglione's characters had all died before the *Courtier* was *published* and (*b*) that, therefore, he waited until his characters were dead before *writing* about them.

[6] Raymond Jenkins, "Spenser and the Clerkship in Munster," *PMLA*, XLVII (1932), 109–21; "Spenser: The Uncertain Years, 1584–1589," *PMLA*, LIII (1938), 350–62.

spent in Ireland Spenser was kept fairly busy by the duties of his new office. But in midsummer of 1585 Norris was recalled hastily to England to take charge of the army which was being sent to the Low Countries and over which Leicester was given supreme command. Sir John's younger brother, Sir Thomas Norris, became acting president of Munster, and Spenser continued to discharge the duties of the clerkship. But the colonization of Munster by the English proceeded very slowly, and during the next four years Spenser found leisure for reading and opportunity for replanning and continuing his *Faerie Queene*.

On the basis of Harvey's letter criticizing the 1580 version of the poem, I have postulated a beginning which was largely under Ariosto's influence. The formal illustration of the virtues which grew out of it, as it is preserved in the first two books of the poem, seems to represent a period of composition during which Ariosto gave way to older models. The structures of the books of Redcrosse and Guyon are nearer to Vergil than to Ariosto. But before 1589 the poem underwent another change which brought Ariosto again into view as Spenser's chief model and source of material. To this second period of Ariosto imitation belongs the romance of Britomart and probably much of the elaboration of the story of Florimell.

As I pointed out at the beginning, Florimell's story has been broken up and added to. It is used as filler in books which are nominally about other heroines. Therefore, it seems probable that some of it was written before the final plan for the poem was adopted. Florimell is strongly connected with the Order of Maidenhead and the court of the Faery Queen. Her chief enemy is lust, in various forms, and the general outlines of her story may go back to the early celebration of chastity. But parts of the Florimell plot, especially the elaborations which concern the creation of the false Florimell and the tournament for her girdle, appear to be mature in style, and it seems safe to say that if Florimell was created early, her story was added to and elaborated at the same time that the story of Britomart was being created.

It seems evident that after he had made a beginning at the

illustration of holiness, temperance, and justice, Spenser read the *Gerusalemme Liberata* for the first time and re-read Ariosto. It is tempting to see a connection between his intimacy with Lodowick Bryskett and his return to Italian models.[7] But two other important elements besides the return to Ariosto went into the creation of Britomart. Since both Britomart and Arthegall could be taken as complimenting the house of Dudley, it seems probable that there was a connection between Leicester's appointment to supreme command in the Low Countries and Spenser's undertaking to imitate Ariosto's story of Ruggiero and Bradamante—the story which Ariosto had used to flatter his patron. The English poet probably anticipated a new period of greatness for Leicester, and he may have hoped for a return of the Earl's favor. These hopes died, of course, with Leicester, in the fall of 1588, and it became expedient to convert his heroine and his genealogy alike, into flattery of the Queen.

The third element in the creation of Britomart was a revival of interest in British chronicle history. Since this interest led to a revision of old matter, apparently after Camden's *Britannia* (1586) came into the poet's hands, we have a fairly well-established date *post quem* for the creation of the Britomart love story. I believe that it was this revived interest in the chronicles which brought Arthur into the poem also. But it is hard to see how, when he wrote the Britomart romance, Spenser expected to fit it into his scheme of virtues. Perhaps he intended her story to illustrate fortitude, or constancy. A love story is hardly the medium for the illustration of either chastity (in Queen Elizabeth's sense) or justice.

But the striking difference in structure and narrative method between Books I–II and III–IV suggests that the poet was still wavering, when he created the materials of Books III and IV, between the formal illustration of the virtues and an Ariosto-like romance. When he finally made his decision, he revised Book I by adding Arthur to it, and the traces of Tasso's in-

[7] Bryskett kept in touch with Italian literary developments. Besides translating Giraldi, he imitated the elegies by Torquato Tasso's father in his elegies for Sidney (see W. P. Mustard, "Lodowick Bryskett and Bernardo Tasso," *American Journal of Philology*, XXXV [1914], 192–99).

fluence and the loose end in Canto vi in a story borrowed from Ariosto suggest that this revision was made during the second period of Ariosto imitation. The Book of Guyon probably needed much more revision to bring it into structural conformity with Book I. Arthur and the British chronicle seem to have been added, and perhaps the Tasso imitation in Canto xii came at that time. The legend of Britomart had to be replanned and rearranged in great haste, probably after Leicester's death late in 1588, in order to alter it from compliment to Leicester to flattery of the Queen. As much as possible was done to celebrate the Queen, both by stressing her chosen virtue of chastity and by converting the chronicle into an account of her great ancestry. The fairy genealogy was added to Book II to bridge the gap in her genealogy, and the Timias-Belphoebe passage was created to please Ralegh.

Meanwhile at least the first book and a half of the work had been seen by Abraham Fraunce, who quotes II, iv, 35, in his *Arcadian Rhetorike*, entered in the Stationers' Register June 11, 1588.[8] His citation of book, canto, and stanza shows that he had seen a manuscript of the poem, complete through at least II, iv. As to just when and how Fraunce saw the manuscript, an important piece of evidence has been overlooked. The recent biographers of Lodowick Bryskett[9] have failed to record the important fact that he was at court in the late summer of 1587,

[8] E. Koeppel in "Sidneiana," *Anglia*, X (1888), 523, and R. W. Zandvoort in *Sidney's Arcadia* (Amsterdam, 1929), p. 3 n., raise the question whether the *Arcadian Rhetorike* actually appeared in 1588, since it was licensed to Thomas Gubbin and Thomas Newman, but the only surviving copy is undated and printed by Thomas Orwin. However, two other works by Fraunce, the *Lawiers Logike* and the *Insignivm Armorvm Emblematvm*, were entered to Gubbin and Newman on May 20, 1588, just three weeks before the entry of the *Rhetorike*. Of these two books, the *Logike* was printed by William How for Gubbin and Newman in 1588. There are three issues, in one of which Gubbin and Newman are not mentioned. The *Insignivm* was printed by Orwin for Gubbin and Newman in 1588. The evidence seems to indicate that the owners of the publication rights divided the work between How and Orwin. Perhaps Orwin got the *Rhetorike* as pay for printing the *Insignivm*. At any rate, there is no reason to suppose that the publication was delayed or that Orwin's was an unauthorized edition.

[9] See Plomer and Cross, *op. cit.;* and Deborah Jones, "Lodowick Bryskett and His Family," in *Thomas Lodge and Other Elizabethans*, ed. C. J. Sisson (Cambridge, Mass.: Harvard University Press, 1933), pp. 242–361.

but his friend, Captain Nicholas Dawtrey, mentions his being there in a letter dated August 26, 1587.[10] Bryskett's elegies for the death of Sir Philip Sidney had been entered in the Stationers' Register just four days before Dawtrey wrote. Spenser's good friend was not only in London but was undoubtedly in close touch with the Sidney family, to whom Fraunce was closely attached,[11] at just the time when the final draft of the *Rhetorike* must have been under way.[12] If he had with him a manuscript of the first two books of the *Faerie Queene*, or some part of it, it is easy to see how Fraunce, and perhaps others of the Sidney circle, came to see it.[13] His object in carrying the manuscript to England must have been either to look for a publisher or to solicit patrons for Spenser. What evidence we have seems to point to the latter undertaking. Bryskett's contacts were with the Sidney family, and with the literary circle which centered in the Countess of Pembroke after the death of Sir Henry and Sir Philip Sidney.

Fraunce's citation not only gave notice of the *Faerie Queene* to the literary world, but it also served to connect Spenser's name, for the first time in print, with the *Shepheardes Calender*.[14]

[10] John Dawtrey, *The Falstaff Saga: Being the Life and Opinions of Captain Nicholas Dawtrey* (London, 1927), pp. 184–87.

[11] See Kathrine Koller, "Abraham Fraunce and Edmund Spenser," *ELH*, VII (1940), 108 ff.

[12] The quotation appears on sig. E3, about halfway through the book.

[13] George Peele imitates I, v, 2.1–5, in *David and Bethsabe*, and Christopher Marlowe borrows two epic similes and perhaps other things from Book I, in the second part of *Tamburlaine* (see *Variorum*, II, 399; Georg Schoeneich, *Der litterarische einfluss Spensers auf Marlowe* [Halle: Hohmann, 1907]; Douglas Bush, "Marlowe and Spenser," [London] *Times Literary Supplement*, January 1, 1938). Both plays were acted, but neither play was printed, before the first instalment of the *Faerie Queene* appeared, early in 1590. We cannot be sure, therefore, whether or not either playwright saw the poem in manuscript. For their connection with the literary circle of the Countess of Pembroke see Mark Eccles, *Christopher Marlowe in London* ("Harvard Studies in English," Vol. X [Cambridge, Mass., 1934]). F. S. Boas, *Christopher Marlowe* (Oxford: Clarendon Press, 1940), pp. 72–73, thinks that the Spenser borrowings were added to *Tamburlaine* in the eight and one-half months between the publication of the *F. Q.* and the entry of *Tamburlaine* in the Stationers' Register. An extract from Paul Ive's *Practise of Fortification* (1589) also occurs in the play, and it seems unlikely that Marlowe used two works in manuscript.

[14] Sig. c4 cites "Immerito: Spencer" and quotes the *S. C.* William Webbe, whose *Discourse of English Poetrie* was printed in 1586, evidently was a friend of Harvey's

It is quite possible that Bryskett's efforts in 1587, giving rise to Fraunce's advertisement of the *Faerie Queene* in 1588, led to Ralegh's visit to the poet in the summer of 1589 and so accomplished its object of finding Spenser a patron and sponsor.[15]

The twelve virtues according to Aristotle were incorporated in the growing plot in the final reorganization, when Medina and probably Arthur and the Bower of Bliss were added to Book II, and Book III was planned as a book of chastity, supplanting the old justice material and perhaps a beginning of a book of constancy or fortitude. Bryskett gives the number of virtues as twelve, and it has been suggested that this number had more to do with Spenser's plans than did Aristotle's theory of ethics. Vergil had established twelve as the proper number of books for an epic. The Italians used a canto division, and Spenser's combination of the two, so as to make a plan of twelve books of twelve cantos each, probably represents a combination of two structural plans, one, evident in the first two books, following Vergil, and the other, dominating the structure of Books III and IV, following Ariosto. Whenever the combination of the two systems was made, the poet committed himself to the Herculean task which he was destined never to finish. The combination was effected by the summer of 1587, but I cannot believe that in the beginning Spenser set out to write 144 cantos of approximately 50 stanzas each.

I have pointed out abundant evidence that Book III was organized very hastily, partly out of materials created for another purpose; and certain features of the allegory show that this "last minute" was the last half of 1589. The introduction of the topical Timias-Belphoebe love idyl makes it probable that

---

and knew the secret of the authorship of the *S. C.*, but he limits himself to references to "Master *Sp.*" (see G. G. Smith, *Elizabethan Critical Essays* [Oxford: Clarendon Press, 1904], I, 232, 242, 245, 247, 263–65, 270–73, 276, 283, 286–90).

[15] Spenser seems to hint in *Colin Clout* that Ralegh had heard of his poetry before he visited him in Ireland. He says:

> There a straunge shepheard chaunst to find me out,
> Whether allured with my pipes delight,
> Whose pleasing sound yshrilled far about,
> Or thither led by chaunce, I know not right [ll. 60–63].

this book was not put into its present form until after Ralegh visited Kilcolman.[16]

Certainly the Proem of Book III, and probably also those of Books I and II, were written after Ralegh arrived in Ireland. There may even have been some touching-up of Books I and II, if I, xi, 7, has reference to the Armada. It is just possible that Ralegh was responsible for the enlarged plan which attempted to combine two books of moral allegory with one of Ariosto-like romance. Certainly the letter to Ralegh, which was published in 1590, was the outcome of discussions of epic theory and of the poet's plans for the whole.

But the illustration of "Aristotle's" twelve virtues is a natural enough enlargement of Spenser's formal moral scheme. The conflict between his two chief models, Ariosto and Vergil, coupled with his struggle for an epic theme, furnishes an adequate basis for an understanding of his structural difficulties without postulating other influence.

He understood the principle of opening *in medias res* and then of giving an account of the previous action "by some *Nuntius*," as his handling of Arthur in Book I, for example, shows. Professor M. Y. Hughes has called attention to the close imitation of Vergil's management of his narrative, even to the banquet scene, in the second book.[17] The idea of postponing this necessary exposition until the very end of the poem was not so

[16] Ralegh went on the expedition to Portugal which sailed in April and returned in June. Then he went into the west of England and on to Ireland (see W. Stebbing, *Sir Walter Ralegh* [Oxford, 1891], pp. 67–69). It is quite possible that the two poets met in Ireland in the autumn of 1588. Ralegh went with Sir Richard Grenville to Ireland to destroy the remnants of the Armada and seems to have been busy there with the Spanish survivors for about three months (see G. H. Bushnell, *Sir Richard Grenville* [London: George G. Harrap & Co., 1936], pp. 204 ff.). Spenser seems to have accompanied Sir Thomas Norris on the same mission to Connaught and Ulster at the same time (see Jenkins, "Spenser: The Uncertain Years, 1584–1589," pp. 350–62). Ralegh and Grenville operated on land as well as at sea, and the two expeditions probably co-operated with each other. I believe that Jenkins is mistaken in suggesting the possibility of a meeting at Youghal in 1588, since, by his own account, Spenser could not have spent much time there in that year, and neither could Ralegh have been there for more than a brief visit. If he was mayor of Youghal in that year, it must have been by courtesy only (see Stebbing, pp. 64–67).

[17] II, ii, 38 ff. (see *Virgil and Spenser* ["University of California Publications in English," Vol. II (Berkeley, 1929)], pp. 330–32).

much the result of Spenser's holding mistaken and false theories of epic structure as of his having allowed his poem to grow by a process of accumulation of materials, so that by the time the unifying, master-plot was decided upon there was no place left in which to work out the explanatory matter except at the end. There was no time to write an account of Gloriana's feast and put it near the beginning of the poem where it belonged. And so, at long last, it was never written at all. In Book I the introductory matter connecting Redcrosse with the master-plot was put into the letter to Ralegh, and in Book II the necessary exposition was combined with a hasty attempt to make temperance appear to be an Aristotelian virtue by creating the allegory of the house of Medina. But, by the time he came to assemble Book III, the poet had too little time left to make the necessary extensive changes.

I believe that when Books I–III were ready for the press he had left over much of the first part of the Book of Justice and a considerable volume of Ariosto-like material such as he had drawn upon for Book III. This he made use of in Books IV and V and even in the Mirabella section of Book VI.

The second instalment, like the first, was partly written with the final plan in full view and partly put together in haste out of old materials of varying quality. Book VI is made up of what seems to be almost entirely fresh material, inspired by new sources of narrative and especially by enthusiasm for the *Arcadia.* It may have been the first book undertaken after the poet returned to Ireland in 1591. Most of the material for Book IV, on the other hand, was already in existence in the form of the adventures of Florimell and parts of the Arthegall-Britomart romance which could not be used in Book III. Because of their narrative relation to Book III, these must be used in Book IV; but Spenser need not have gone to work on them at once. The Timias-Belphoebe section of Book IV could not have been put in its present form until after Ralegh's disgrace in the summer of 1592.[18] As I have pointed out, it is part of a larger section

[18] F. M. Padelford and W. C. Maxwell, on the basis of their study of "The Compound Words in Spenser's Poetry" (see below, Appendix III), conclude that perhaps Book VI

which includes both Arthur's appearance and the best example of friendship in this book. This whole section is closely interwoven and was probably created as a whole after the summer of 1592, when Spenser set to work to weld his old materials into a book of friendship.

When Book IV was roughed out, there was still left over the tournament at Florimell's wedding and probably some early moral examples of justice. Possibly there were also some topical allegories of justice, including perhaps an early version of the Irena episode. But, whatever the history of the materials in the first two sections of Book V, the closing allegories of Burbon and Irena were completed last of all, late in 1595, just before the second instalment was published.

The datable allegories in the second instalment furnish us with some important evidence that the poet not only did not write the books seriatim, in their present form and order, but that he did not finish one before he began another. The Timias episodes in Book VI, like those in Book IV, must be dated after Ralegh's disgrace in 1592, but we cannot therefore assume that neither book was begun before 1592. The ending of Book V seems to have been added after Spenser reached England in the autumn of 1595. Book VI must have been fully completed at that time. The poet planned and wrote in episodes and narrative sequences[19] which he fitted into his larger plans as best he could, replanning the whole, probably more than once, and rearranging and revising his materials as his plans matured.

---

was written before Book IV. As a general proposition, I believe that this is untenable, but much of Book VI may have been finished before the materials of Book IV were put in their present state. They also suggest that Book V was written before IV, i–x, but I do not believe that we can treat Book V as a unit. Its three parts probably represent three distinct periods of composition.

[19] See below, Appendix II.

XIX
THE NEW POINT OF VIEW

I well consider all that ye haue sayd,
And find that all things stedfastnes doe hate
And changed be: . . . .
But by their change their being doe dilate:
And turning to themselues at length againe,
Doe worke their owne perfection so by fate.
—VII, vii, 58.2–7

I BELIEVE that much new light is thrown on every aspect of the poem by the recognition that the plan outlined in the letter to Ralegh was an omnibus scheme, which attempted to systematize the product of ten years of experimentation, rather than a preconceived working plan according to which the poet began to write in 1580. I think it is fairly clear that neither Arthur nor Aristotle was an early plot ingredient. But, in attempting to trace the exact process by which the poem developed, we have had only such guides as could be derived from a study of Spenser's use of his sources, his conduct of the narrative, and his use of enjambment.

Obviously, without further clues, the history of the composition of individual episodes must remain largely in the realm of conjecture. But I have suggested certain general outlines of development which seem to be at least logical and plausible, and which accord with what evidence of the progress of the poem can be gleaned from biographical sources.

This is a necessary first step. Before we can discover further details of the poem's development, we must recognize not only that it had a development but also the general outlines of the process by which it took on its present form. It is with these general outlines that this study has been concerned. The failure on the part of Spenser's critics to imagine a process of composition has resulted in the general assumption that the poet began to write *after* he had made the elaborate plan outlined in the letter to Ralegh and that he began with the first line of Book I and wrote straight through. This assumption has led to ineffective studies of the technique of the poem, to false estimates of the constructive ability of the poet, and even to some superficial and unsound discussions of his poetic theories and his plans for the whole.

It has also led to misapprehensions of the extent and character of the allegory, both moral and topical. There can be no question that Spenser occasionally wrote with a particular person or event or situation in mind; but, if there has been anything like as much replanning and consequent rearrangement of the materials of the poem as I have suggested, it is obviously futile to look for consistent and continued historical or topical allegory. If the poet's general plans for the poem and his conceptions of most of the characters underwent changes in the process of composition, it is obviously a mistake to expect each character to represent consistently some one historical figure.[1]

On the other hand, the very definiteness with which Spenser tells us that the Faery Queen and also Belphoebe represent Queen Elizabeth, the thoroughness with which he indicates in Book III that Timias stands for Ralegh, and the completeness of the correspondence between the rescuer of Burbon and Irena and Sir John Norris ought to warn us against ingenious and oversubtilized interpretations and identifications.

The student of moral allegory is on somewhat different ground. Moral teaching was a part of Spenser's initial conception of the function of poetry, and we need not question that, throughout the evolutionary process by which the present poem was created, he had some moral purpose fairly consistently in

[1] Arguing from entirely different evidence, E. Greenlaw adequately pointed out the fallacy of equating Spenser's characters consistently with real people (see *Studies in Spenser's Historical Allegory* [Baltimore, 1932], chap. ii). H. C. Notcutt warns that there are no standing personal equations in the *Faerie Queene* (*Essays and Studies by Members of the English Association*, XII [1926], 70–72); and A. B. Gough, in his edition of Book V (Oxford, 1918), asserts that "one real person appears under several disguises, and, what is more confusing, one allegorical figure represents several persons" (p. xxx).

mind. We must, however, put aside such apologetics as attempt to equate everything with the ethics of Aristotle and look more widely among the theories of the age, and more openmindedly at Spenser's handling of his materials, if we are to arrive at a full understanding of his ethical teaching. We must not attempt to force consistency where it is not in evidence. Because Books I and II are essentially moral in their inception and in their growth, we must not overstress the importance of the moral in the development of Books III and IV.

If we bear in mind the main strands out of which the poem is loosely knit together, we are in a position to evaluate more justly the significance of various episodes as they are presented to us. There were at least two periods of Ariosto imitation, the first of which probably saw the creation of Florimell on the pattern of Angelica, and the second of which gave us Britomart on the model of Bradamante. There seems also to have been a change in the tone of the poem, but in the opposite direction from the one which a theory of seriatim composition suggests. There seems to have been a development in the illustration of moral virtue from chastity, through the four cardinal virtues, to the twelve virtues which the poet associates with the name of Aristotle.

In studying the various books, perhaps the most important principle to keep in mind is Spenser's method of revision and development by elaboration. It is the same method which produced the second version of Sidney's *Arcadia*, and which was advocated by Spenser himself, according to Lodowick Bryskett. We must recognize that as a result of this method of composition no one book, and probably no one thread of narrative, belongs to a single period of composition, with the possible exception of Book VI and the Mutability Cantos. The poem grew, not as a chain grows by the addition of links at one end, but rather as a plant grows, the older parts increasing in bulk and development as new branches are added and new directions taken. It is a paradox of some interest that, while Spenser's conception of structure was symmetrical and schematic rather than organic, his method of composition shows an interplay of planning and growth, in which each influences the other in a thoroughly organic fashion.

An understanding of the processes of composition, at least in general outline, is of primary importance in the interpretation of the poem; but it is, if possible, of even more importance for our understanding of the poet. It is customary to think of Spenser as a "sage and serious" moralist, and his high conception of the function of poetry certainly led him to write in that spirit. But a somewhat different light is thrown on his temperament by a consideration of what the beginning of the *Faerie Queene* was probably like. If we put what we know of his early liking for Lucian, his taste for jestbooks, and his admiration for Ariosto together with what Gabriel Harvey says of his "hobgoblin" beginning, we get an entirely new impression of what the *Faerie Queene* ("that *Eluish queene*") was like in 1580. It is an impression which suggests the tale of the Squire of Dames, the seduction of Hellenore, and the exploits of Braggadochio rather than the sage and serious pageant of Redcrosse.

Spenser was ambitious to be the English Vergil, but he also had a strong desire to be the English Ariosto. He intended to write the great epic of England, but he was in doubt about both the matter and the manner. It is clear that he did not begin with the idea of writing an Arthurian epic but seems to have thought rather of continuing one of Chaucer's unfinished stories or of creating an imitation of Arthur's court as the court of the Faery Queen. His great problem, stated clearly in the "October" eclogue, was the choice of an Augustus and a heroic action. In the irregular development of the poem we can trace the progress of his struggle with that dual problem, and his very irregularities and inconsistencies, his narrative and structural failures as well as his successes, become interesting in the light of that struggle.

His difficulty in selecting a hero and a theme was further complicated by his uncertainty about his model. He was not equipped to write the great epic of England precisely because he was so much a product of a Renaissance which was international. He recognized that the choice of a national hero was essential, but his admiration for and sympathy with Ariosto and Tasso and the fact that his culture was as much Italian as English confused his genius. Redcrosse is a native product of England, and the borrowings from Ariosto in Book I have been thoroughly assimilated to an essentially English theme. But in the other books the poet too often yielded to the temptation to import the Italian poets into English poetry. His emulation too often descends to the level of adaptation.[2] It is this fact, coupled with the recognition of the late and superficial addition of Arthur to his growing plans, which gives us insight into the weaknesses as well as the successes of the *Faerie Queene*.

Spenser's desire to emulate Ariosto dates, as we know, from the inception of the poem. But during the early years of his exile he turned to the illustration of virtue as a solution of his problem of theme and subject matter. The formative plots of the first two books were produced at this time and prove that the poet could create great poetry even out of the most artificial and unpromising of moral allegories. But the manufacture of such allegories seems to have taxed his ingenuity and patience, and sometime along the way he turned back to Ariosto for story material.

We know too little of the extent of his friendship with Lodowick Bryskett to estimate its influence on Spenser. But we know that this Italian was interested in his native literature and in poetry and that he communicated with relatives in Italy and probably had in his library in Ireland some of the important Italian books of the day. We cannot estimate the degree to which he stimulated and directed Spenser's reading. But the fact that Spenser came into close contact with Bryskett is well established and strongly suggests a connection between Bryskett and the second period of Ariosto imitation in the *Faerie Queene*. For some reason, after a struggle to create an allegorical epic in illustration of the virtues, Spenser turned back, in a more mature spirit, to his early model. The history of that wavering course is the history of an artist searching for a suitable

[2] H. Maynadier, *The Arthur of the English Poets* (Boston, 1907), pp. 273 ff. remarks on "Spenser's extreme catholicity of taste" and his neglect of traditional Arthurian matter in favor of Renaissance materials.

medium, not the history of a melancholy Puritan moralist struggling to make an epic out of Aristotle's ethics.

Indeed, it is the lack of this, or any other, singleness of purpose which is responsible for the structural failure of the poem. While the native color of the poet's imagination was able to effect the transformation into pure poetry of individual episodes, the general structure of the whole is too much the product of reason and expediency. It is schematic rather than organic, the product of careful planning and replanning against a background of international Renaissance culture. Except in Book I, and in isolated passages elsewhere, there is little of the essential temperament of Spenser to be discerned in the Renaissance poet. We might say that Spenser is the perfect, limpid, reflector of the tastes, ideas, and ideals of his age, in somewhat the same way that Shakespeare is the perfect reflector of its characters and emotions. But it is no longer good criticism to produce Shakespeare's personality out of *Hamlet*, and it seems an extremely questionable undertaking to discover Spenser's personality in the *Faerie Queene*. Was he a "sage and serious" man, or was "sage and serious" merely his conception of the proper tone for great poetry?

What we can learn of his friends suggests the latter conclusion. Gabriel Harvey was an egocentric college teacher of limited culture and perhaps some Puritan leanings. But he was a considerable scholar whose taste ran to Lucian, Aretino, and apparently Rabelais. His ambitions, like Spenser's, took the direction of the court, not of the church. And Spenser's gift to him of Scogan, Skelton, and Lazarillo de Tormes, with the proviso attached, suggests that the poet was not too serious to plague his teacher by insisting on his doing some very light reading.

We do not know to what extent Spenser was acquainted at court and in the circle about Sir Philip Sidney during the years before he went to Ireland. But he made a friend of Lodowick Bryskett, Sidney's traveling companion on his Continental tour. Bryskett gives us a glimpse of the society which he frequented in 1582–84. He represents the poet as one of a group which included a clergyman, a lawyer, an apothecary, and four captains—altogether five professional men and five soldiers. Whether or not the group is a historical one, it includes men who were prominent in Dublin when Spenser was there and who were all undoubtedly known to him.

In spite of the serious, moral tone of the *Discovrse* which Bryskett represents himself as reading to this group, we can hardly suppose that the English colony in Dublin was habitually serious and moral in tone. There were too many practical soldiers in it for that. Bryskett mentions among his guests Captain Nicholas Dawtrey. A descendant of the Captain's has given us a biography of him, written in the belief that Captain Dawtrey was the original of Falstaff. Whatever this thesis may be worth, the Elizabethan soldier of fortune whose life-history he has traced certainly had more of Falstaff than of moral philosophy about him. Since Dawtrey's character is established by other contemporary evidence, it is worth noting that Bryskett represents him as interested only in the wine, not in the moral conversation. Evidently Bryskett assigned parts to the historical figures in his dialogue with some regard for character, whether or not he had in mind a particular meeting of this particular group. For Spenser's acquaintance with Dawtrey there is direct evidence of a characteristic kind,[3] although it is insufficient to establish the nature of their personal relations. But the very thought of Spenser's having shared the same circle of friends (for Dawtrey was a friend of Bryskett's) with this Falstaffian soldier is a healthy corrective to the current conception of Spenser as a melancholy and disappointed introvert who wrote poetry about fairies as an escape from reality.

Spenser also made a friend of Sir Walter Ralegh, one of the most sophisticated men of his time, a free thinker, and a man of decisive action, of whom there are many traces in the *Faerie*

[3] See John Dawtrey, *The Falstaff Saga* (London, 1927), for Captain Dawtrey's life. Ray Heffner has discovered a record that Dawtrey owed Spenser money, as he owed all his friends and even some of his enemies (see *MLN*, L [1935], 194). From other records of the same kind it seems probable that Spenser's loan was rather an advance in wages than a personal accommodation (see Dorothy F. Atkinson, *Edmund Spenser: A Bibliographical Supplement* [Baltimore, 1937], pp. 3 ff.).

Queene.[4] The interplay of personalities which determines friendships is an incalculable factor in human relationships. But the little we can learn about the poet's social life, the few glimpses of him we can get from his letters, his friendships, and contemporary comment, and the character of his mind as it is revealed by a careful study of the sources and the problems of the *Faerie Queene*, all suggest that the secretary and clerk who built for himself a comfortable fortune in Ireland was not out of touch or out of tune with reality.

When we are told that "the violent fluctuation of his temper between extremes of enthusiasm and disillusion betray the restlessness of the thwarted idealist" who "turned to poetry as a refuge from actuality,"[5] we suspect the critic of reading into a sixteenth-century situation a nineteenth-century attitude on the part of the poet. Such a dichotomy between poetry and life is not in accord with Spenser's conception of the poet's function, which was to record the virtues of the active life, and so perpetuate them by inculcating virtue in later generations by the power of example.[6] We should not confuse Spenser's conception of the high seriousness essential to epic poetry with the personality of the poet. Nor must we assume that the irregularities of tone observable in his longest work are the product of "violent fluctuations of temper." They are rather the product of replanning and rearrangement over a period of many years.

In the absence of further biographical information an effort to reconstruct the process of composition of the poet's principal work offers the best prospect of reliable guidance toward a sound conception of his temperament and personality.

Such a study will certainly prove a corrective for the usual criticism about his workmanship, that he lacked the power to construct a coherent long narrative.[7] Any considered judgment

[4] I propose to treat this subject in a separate study.

[5] B. E. C. Davis, *Edmund Spenser: A Critical Study* (Cambridge: University Press, 1933), p. 1.

[6] See E. Dowden's excellent essay on "Spenser, the Poet and Teacher," in A. B. Grosart, *The Complete Works . . . . of Edmund Spenser* (Privately printed, 1882–84), I, 304–39.

[7] R. W. Church, *Spenser* (London, 1886), p. 125; E. de Sélincourt, *Oxford Lectures on Poetry* (Oxford, 1934), p. 110, and Introduction to the *Oxford Spenser*, pp. l–li; and

of Spenser's constructive ability must take into account the way in which the existing part of the *Faerie Queene* came into being. It must also take into account the schematic rather than the organic character of his conception of structure. A recognition of the apologetic nature of the letter to Ralegh should prove a useful corrective to the critical tendency to judge the structure of the poem on the basis of the letter rather than on its own merits. The satisfactory organization of the first and sixth books is sufficient demonstration that Spenser could handle the organization of a large structure with complete mastery, albeit in his own way, when he had time to revise and polish it sufficiently. It is not incompetence but HASTE that is writ large over the face of the poem's narrative technique.

We know so little about Spenser's literary life that it is hard to estimate just how vacillating his course may have been. It should be recognized that any attempt to retrace that course is likely to be both too simple and too logical. But I believe it is worth while to make the attempt, because such an investigation puts us so much nearer the poet and the act of poetic creation than any reading of the poem as a simple *fait accompli* can bring us.

It is too easy for the critic to patronize his author, sitting in judgment, and taking it for granted that whatever imperfections he finds must be due to the weakness of the author and never to the failure of the critic's own imagination to reconstruct the conditions of composition. It is at least salutary to reverse the perspective, for once, and to look at the work as a product of the poet's mind working rationally at a difficult problem; attacking it now from one angle, and now from another; attempting to create an original work of art on a new pattern; wavering between the ancients and the moderns in his choice of a model; and, in the end, being partly defeated by the press of time and the distractions of a busy life, but still showing himself to be a rational and a not incompetent workman.

William Minto and F. J. Snell, in their article on Spenser in the *Encyclopaedia Britannica* (11th ed.).

APPENDIX I

ANALYSIS OF THE POEM BY EPISODES

As one of the first steps in the analysis of the poem, I found it necessary to divide the narrative into episodic units following the lines of transition—lines which are more clearly evident than a casual reader who has not looked for them might suppose. These units represent single episodes and short narratives such as the poet must almost certainly have planned and written at one time, although he might revise or adapt at another time, and although he might incorporate in the unit previously written material which happened to suit his purpose. However, these units of narrative come much nearer to the actual units of composition than do the cantos, and therefore it seemed desirable to make statistical studies on that basis.

I am presenting my analysis here because I hope that it will serve as a basis for further studies of the structure and techniques of the poem and because it presents briefly the facts commented upon in Appendixes II and III. For convenient reference, I have arranged my materials in the form of a table, describing each episode briefly, and assigning a number to each unit of narrative in each book, thereby making it possible to refer to an episode briefly by number, using the hundreds column for the number of the book. Where a passage is merely transitional and too short for the application of style tests, I have marked it with an asterisk. I have indicated the end of each canto by a bar (/).

In the computation of enjambment ratios I have followed the punctuation of the Cambridge edition, edited by R. E. N. Dodge, rather than that of any of the editions which attempt to reproduce the Elizabethan punctuation. I have done so because I believe that Dodge's careful and scholarly modernization of the punctuation is more consistent and more nearly representative of the actual phrasing of the verse than is the original punctuation. Moreover, the editors of the *Variorum* came to the conclusion that the original punctuation was the work of the printer rather than of the author,[1] and therefore it has no great authority. Since Dodge's text is consistent and, so far as any theory of the order of composition of the poem is concerned, impartial, it seems to me to be the best one for the present purpose.

[1] See *Variorum*, VI, 480 ff.

BOOK I

THE LEGENDE OF THE KNIGHT OF THE RED CROSSE, *OR* OF HOLINESSE

1 Redcrosse and Una are described. i, 1–6
2 Redcrosse slays Error in his den. 7–28
3 Redcrosse and Una meet Archimage and are separated. 29–55/ii, 1–6
*4 Una sets out alone, and Archimage disguises himself as Redcrosse. 7–11
5 Redcrosse slays Sansfoy and rides with Duessa. 12–27
6 They hear Fradubio's story. 28–45/
7 Una finds a lion who befriends her. iii, 1–9
8 Una sleeps with Ignorance and Blind Devotion. 10–25
9 Archimage, disguised as Redcrosse, overtakes Una and is overcome by Sansloy, who siezes Una. 26–44/
10 Redcrosse comes to the House of Pride. iv, 1–17
11 He sees the procession of the seven deadly sins. 18–37
12 Sansjoy challenges Redcrosse and is visited by Duessa. 38–51/
13 Redcrosse overcomes Sansjoy, who is rescued by Duessa. v, 1–18
14 Duessa and Night carry Sansjoy to Aesculapius. 19–44
15 Redcrosse flees from the House of Pride. 45–53/
16 Una is rescued from Sansloy by the satyrs. vi, 1–19
17 Satyrane, whose origin is recounted, learns of Una's plight. 20–32
18 Satyrane assists Una to escape and encounters Sansloy. 33–48/
19 Orgoglio overcomes Redcrosse and makes Duessa his mistress. vii, 1–18
20 The dwarf finds Una and tells her all that has happened to Redcrosse since they separated. 19–28
21 Una meets Arthur, and he undertakes the rescue of Redcrosse. 29–52/
22 Arthur slays the giant, wounds the beast, and punishes Duessa. viii, 1–50/
23 Arthur and Redcrosse make friends, and Arthur tells his story. ix, 1–20
24 Redcrosse and Una visit the Cave of Despair. ix, 21–54/
25 Redcrosse and Una visit the House of Holiness. x, 1–68/
26 Redcrosse overcomes the dragon and sets Una's parents free. xi, 1–55/
27 Redcrosse is betrothed to Una. xii, 1–42/

BOOK I

Episode	No. Sts.	Ratio of Run-on	No. Compounds	Fem. Rhymes	Possible *-ed* Rhymes
101*.........	6	6.75	2	....	....
102.........	22	7.615	6	....	3
103.........	33	4.95	9	....	....
104.........	5	7.5	5	....	....
105.........	16	4.645	4	....	....
106.........	18	5.4	1	....	....
107.........	9	7.363	0	....	....
108.........	16	6.545	2	....	....
109.........	19	4.384	5	....	....
110.........	17	5.84	4	....	....
111.........	20	8.571	3	....	....
112.........	14	5.727	1	....	....
113.........	18	6.75	5	....	....
114.........	26	4.775	4	....	3
115.........	9	4.764	1	....	2
116.........	19	9.0	4	....	....
117.........	13	6.5	2	....	....
118.........	17	4.5	1	....	....
119.........	18	7.715	3	....	....
120.........	10	18.0	2	....	....
121.........	24	6.967	4	....	1
122.........	50	7.5	9	....	3
123.........	20	7.5	1	....	....
124.........	34	7.116	8	....	2
125.........	68	6.725	12	....	1
126.........	55	6.266	26	....	5
127.........	42	7.56	13	....	2

* The figure in the hundreds column indicates the book.

BOOK II

THE LEGEND OF SIR GVYON OR *OF TEMPERANNCE*

1 Archimage sets Guyon on Redcrosse; they make friends and part. i, 1–34

2 Guyon and the Palmer find Amavia and her babe. 35–61/

3 The fountain refuses to cleanse the babe's hands. ii, 1–11

4 Guyon visits the Castle of Medina and leaves the babe. 12–46/ iii, 1–3

5 Braggadochio steals Guyon's horse and meets Trompart and Archimage. 4–19

6 Belphoebe encounters Braggadochio and Trompart. 20–46/

7 Guyon binds Furor and stops Occasion, rescuing Phedon. iv, 1–15

8 Phedon tells his tale. 16–36

9 Atin announces the approach of Pyrochles. 37–46/

10 Pyrochles fights Guyon and releases Furor. v, 1–24

11 Atin finds Cymochles in Acrasia's bower and incites him to avenge his brother. 25–38/

12 Cymochles is induced to visit Phaedria's isle. vi, 1–18

13 Phaedria conducts Guyon to her isle. 19–26

14 Guyon and Cymochles fight. Phaedria parts them. 27–37

15 Guyon meets Atin while Pyrochles burns in water and is saved by Archimage. 38–51/

16 Guyon visits the Cave of Mamon. vii, 1–50

17 Guyon visits the Garden of Proserpine. 51–66/

18 Guyon is saved by Arthur from Pyrochles and Cymochles. viii, 1–56/

19 Guyon regales Arthur with praises of the Faery Queen. ix, 1–9

20 Arthur and Guyon drive off the besiegers of the Castle of Alma. 10–16

21 They explore the Castle of Alma. 17–60/

22 Arthur reads the history of the kings of Britain. x, 1–69

23 Guyon reads the chronicle of fairyland. 70–77/

24 Arthur battles with Maleger. xi, 1–49/

25 Guyon voyages to the Bower of Bliss. xii, 1–37

26 Guyon destroys the Bower of Bliss. xii, 38–87/

BOOK II

Episode	No. Sts.	Ratio of Run-on	No. Compounds	Fem. Rhymes	Possible *-ed* Rhymes
201	34	7.458	3	....	3
202	27	6.0	6	....	1
203	11	4.95	2	....	2
204	38	5.842	4	....	....
205	16	5.333	5	....	2
206	27	7.568	4	....	3
207	15	6.38	2	....	2
208	21	7.826	3	....	3
209	10	5.625	1	....	....
210	24	5.684	7	....	5
211	14	4.5	2	....	1
212	18	4.526	2	....	2
213	8	9.0	....	....	1
214	11	4.5	1	....	2
215	14	7.0	2	....	2
216	50	5.625	11	....	1
217	16	7.584	4	....	....
218	56	5.793	5	....	2
219	9	5.062	1	....	....
220	7	4.5	1	....	1
221	44	7.452	6	1	3
222	69	6.21	3	....	13
223	8	3.794	....	....	2
224	49	5.653	7	....	5
225	37	4.757	9	....	2
226	50	5.696	8	....	....

BOOK III

THE LEGEND OF BRITOMARTIS OR *OF CHASTITIE*

1 Guyon and Arthur encounter Britomart. i, 1–13
2 All four (counting Arthur's squire) are separated in the pursuit of Florimell. 14–18
3 Britomart comes to the Castle Joyeous and meets Redcrosse. 19–67/
4 Britomart tells of her quest for Arthegall. ii, 1–16
5 Britomart tells how she fell in love. 17–52/
6 Britomart visits Merlin and is told of her descendants. iii, 1–50
7 Britomart sets out as a knight-errant. 51–62/ iv, 1–4
8 Britomart laments on the beach. 5–11
9 Britomart overcomes Marinell. 12–17
10 Marinell's story is told. He is rescued by his mother. 18–44
*11 The situations of Britomart, Archimage, Guyon, Arthur, and Timias are reviewed. 44.6–47
12 Arthur pursues Florimell and is benighted. 48–61/
13 Arthur meets her dwarf and hears the story of Florimell. v, 1–12
14 Timias, pursuing the forester, is ambushed and wounded. 13–26
15 He is rescued and healed by Belphoebe. 27–41
16 Timias falls in love with Belphoebe. 42–55/
17 The birth of Belphoebe and Amoret is described. vi, 1–10, 27
18 Venus searches for the lost Cupid. 11–26
19 The Gardens of Adonis are described. 28–50
20 The upbringing of Amoret is recounted. 51–53
21 Florimell takes refuge in a witch's hut and is wooed by the witch's son. 54/ vii, 1–18
22 Florimell flees and is pursued by the witch's beast. 19–28
23 Satyrane subdues the beast and binds it with Florimell's girdle. 29–36
24 Satyrane encounters a giantess who has captured a squire. 37–46
25 The squire explains his mishap and tells his story. 47–61/
26 The witch creates a snowy replica of Florimell. viii, 1–10
27 The false Florimell is stolen from the witch's son by Braggadochio, who loses her to a stranger. 11–19
28 Florimell is rescued by Proteus and imprisoned. 20–43
29 Satyrane tells Paridell of the supposed loss of Florimell. 44–50
30 Satyrane, Paridell, and the Squire of Dames are refused shelter in Malbecco's castle. 51–52/ ix, 1–11
31 Britomart arrives and forces entry for all. They are entertained, and Paridell tells his ancestry. 12–53/
32 Paridell seduces Hellenore, Malbecco's wife. x, 1–60/
*33 Jealousy is apostrophized. Britomart and Satyrane are separated while pursuing Ollyphant. xi, 1–6
34 Britomart meets Scudamour and undertakes to rescue Amoret. 7–55/
35 Britomart sees the Masque of Cupid and frees Amoret. xii, 1–45/

BOOK III

Episode	No. Sts.	Ratio of Run-on	No. Compounds	Fem. Rhymes	Possible -*ed* Rhymes
301	13	7.312	1		2
302	5	9.0	1		
303	49	5.959	5		2
304	16	5.192	3		1
305	36	4.955	7		5
306	50	4.205	5		2
307	16	4.114	1		1
308	7	5.727	2		2
309	6	3.6			
310	27	3.983	3		1
311	3½	3.857	1		
312	14	3.818	3		1
313	12	5.142	1		
314	14	4.152			
315	15	4.5	3		3
316	14	5.04	3		1
317	11	3.333			1
318	16	3.891			4
319	23	5.5			2
320	3	3.0			
321	19	3.446	1		2
322	10	6.0			4
323	8	4.8	1		
324	10	5.0	1		1
325	15	7.411			1
326	10	3.451	1		4
327	9	4.05			1
328	24	5.837	1		2
329	7	4.5			
330	13	4.714	1		1
331	42	4.395	5		5
332	60	6.428	6		6
333	6	4.5	1		
334	49	4.877	9		4
335	45	6.130	10		3

BOOK IV

THE LEGEND OF CAMBEL AND TELAMOND OR OF FRIENDSHIP

1 Amoret rides with Britomart and distrusts her. i, 1–8
2 A custom of a castle reveals Britomart's sex to Amoret. 9–16
3 Duessa and Ate ride with Blandamour and Paridell and encounter Britomart and Amoret. 17–37
4 The party encounters Scudamour and Glaucè, and a fight ensues. 38–54/
5 The party next encounters Ferraugh and the false Florimell. ii, 1–10
6 Paridell and Blandamour fight over the false Florimell. 11–19
7 The Squire of Dames makes peace with the news of Satyrane's tournament. 20–29
8 The cavalcade overtakes Cambell and Triamond and their wives. 30–34
9 We are told the story of Triamond and his two brothers. 35–54/
10 The battle for Canacee is described. iii, 1–52/
*11 The story returns to the cavalcade. iv, 1–5
12 Braggadochio joins the cavalcade and attempts to claim the false Florimell. 6–12
13 A tournament is held for Florimell's girdle. 13–48/
14 After the tournament the false Florimell chooses Braggadochio. v, 1–28
*15 Britomart and Amoret continue the search for their lovers. 29–30.6
16 Satyrane visits the House of Care. 30.7–46/
17 Scudamour joins Arthegall against Britomart. vi, 1–8
18 Britomart fights with Arthegall. 9–33
19 Britomart tells of the loss of Amoret. 34–38
20 Arthegall woos Britomart. 39–41
*21 Arthegall sets out on his quest. Britomart and Scudamour go in search of Amoret. 42–47/
22 Amoret is seized by Lust and hears Aemylia's story. vii, 1–22
23 Amoret is rescued by Belphoebe and Timias. 23–36
24 Timias retreats to a hut and is not recognized by Arthur. 37–47/
25 A dove brings about Belphoebe's reconciliation with Timias. viii, 1–18
26 Arthur finds Amoret and Aemylia, and they lodge with Slander. 19–37
27 Arthur rescues a squire and overcomes Corflambo. 38–49, 63–64/
28 He learns of the friendship of Amyas and Placidas. 50–62
29 Arthur captures Corflambo's castle and reforms Poeana. ix, 1–16
*30 Arthur and Amoret set out again. 17–19
31 Arthur comes upon six knights fighting. 20–27
32 The situation is explained. 28–31
33 Arthur settles the quarrel, Scudamour is asked about his wooing. 32–41/
34 How Scudamour wooed Amoret in the Temple of Love. x, 1–58/
*35 Florimell's imprisonment and Marinell's cure related. xi, 1–7
36 The marriage of the Thames and the Medway. 8–53/, xii, 1–3
37 Marinell falls in love with Florimell, and she is released. 4–35/

BOOK IV

Episode	No. Sts.	Ratio of Run-on	No. Compounds	Fem. Rhymes	Possible *-ed* Rhymes
401	8	4.5	2	4	1
402	8	4.235	....	2	1
403	21	7.269	2	4	....
404	17	4.371	....	1	2
405	10	5.0	1	4	1 and 1*
406	9	6.75	....	3	....
407	10	5.625	1	2	....
408	5	5.625	1	1	1
409	20	7.2	4	2	1
410	52	6.728	....	5	3 and 3
411	5	7.5	1	....	....
412	7	7.0	....	....	....
413	36	6.0	5	1	3 and 2
414	28	4.754	....	2	1 and 5
415	2	....	....	....	....
416	16	6.230	2	1	3 and 1
417	8	6.0	....	....	1
418	25	6.818	3	2	2 and 5
419	5	3.733	....	....	1
420	3	4.5	....	1	....
421	6	5.4	1	....	3
422	22	5.351	1	1	1 and 1
423	14	8.4	2	2	2
424	11	14.157	....	1	1
425	18	4.05	2	....	2
426	19	5.181	2	....	1
427	14	5.04	....	....	1
428	13	5.571	....	....	2
429	16	5.438	1	1	2
430	3	3.857	....	....	....
431	8	6.0	1	....	1
432	4	4.5	....	....	....
433	10	5.0	....	....	2
434	58	6.868	6	9	8 and 1
435	7	5.25	....	....	1
436	49	5.25	12	4	1 and 1
437	32	7.2	2	4	2

* The second figure represents consistent rhymes in *-ed* which are not so spelled and therefore not counted in Professor Stovall's list.

BOOK V

THE LEGEND OF ARTEGALL *OR* OF IVSTICE

1 Astraea brings up Artegall, and he sets out on his quest. i, 1–12
2 Artegall overthrows Sir Sanglier and punishes him. 13–30/
3 Dony brings news of Florimell's wedding and of the evil bridgekeeper, who is promptly punished. ii, 1–28
4 Artegall overthrows the giant, Democracy. 29–54/
5 A tournament is held at Florimell's wedding. iii, 1–26
6 The story of Florimell's girdle is retold. 27–28
7 Guyon's steed is recovered and Braggadochio is punished. 29–40/
8 Artegall judges the case of treasure trove. iv, 4–20
9 Artegall rescues Sir Terpin from the Amazons. 21–51/
10 Artegall is overcome by Radigund and imprisoned. v, 1–54/
11 Talus brings news to Britomart of Artegall's mishap. vi, 1–18
12 Britomart encounters Dolon and his sons. 19–40/
13 Britomart visits Isis Church. vii, 1–24
14 Britomart slays Radigund and rescues Artegall. 25–45/
15 Artegall and Arthur rescue Samient and make friends. viii, 4–14
16 Samient tells her story, and Artegall and Arthur punish the Soldan and Adicia. 15–51/
17 Arthur and Artegall catch Guile, whom Talus punishes. ix, 4–19
18 They visit the court of Mercilla and see the trial of Duessa. 20–50/
19 Belge appeals to Mercilla for aid. x, 5–17
20 Arthur rescues Belge and takes the city on the peninsula. 18–39/
21 Arthur slays Gerioneo and destroys the beast. xi, 1–35
22 Artegall learns of Irena's plight and rescues Burbon. 36–65/
23 Artegall rescues Irena. xii, 1–27
24 Artegall meets Envy, Detraction, and the Blatant Beast. 28–43/

BOOK V*

Episode	No. Sts.	Ratio of Run-on	No. Compounds	Fem. Rhymes	Possible *-ed* Rhymes
501	12	5.4	2	....	2
502	18	9.529	1	....	1
503	28	8.129	1	2	5
504	26	10.565	1	3	1
505	26	7.312	6	3	1 and 1
506	2	6.0	....	....	....
507	12	9.0	1	....	3 and 1
508	17	10.928	1	3	3
509	31	6.136	2	4	2 and 1
510	54	6.75	10	10	10
511	18	5.225	2	1	....
512	22	3.96	....	1	2
513	24	4.408	6	2	1
514	21	5.727	....	3	1
515	11	3.535	2	1	....
516	37	5.225	8	2	2
517	16	6.84	3	3	....
518	31	4.894	4	3	2
519	13	4.034	1	1	1
520	22	6.6	2	3	3
521	35	5.526	1	....	1
522	30	6.136	3	2	2
523	27	6.075	4	1	....
524	16	4.114	2	2	2 and 1

* Introductory stanzas have been omitted as follows: iv, 1–3; viii, 1–3; ix, 1–3; x, 1–4.

BOOK VI

THE LEGEND OF S. CALIDORE *OR* OF COVRTESIE

1 Calidore's character and quest are described. i, 1–10
2 Calidore saves a damsel and punishes Maleffort and Briana. 11–47/
3 Calidore sees Tristram slay the discourteous knight and dubs him "squire." ii, 3–39
4 Calidore rescues the wounded knight and protects his lady's reputation. 40–48/ iii, 1–19
5 Calidore saves a lady from the Blatant Beast. 20–26
6 Calepine rescues Serena and is afflicted by Sir Turpin. 27–51/
7 A savage rescues Calepine and Serena from Turpin. iv, 1–16
8 Calepine rescues a babe from a bear and loses his way. 17–25
9 Calepine gives the babe to Matilde. 26–40/
10 Serena and the savage set out to find Calepine and meet Arthur and Timias. v, 1–11
11 We are told how Arthur found Timias, who had been beset by three foresters. 12–24
12 The party travels, and Serena tells her story. 25–34
13 Timias and Serena are left at a hermitage and cured of their wounds. 35–41/ vi, 1–16
14 Arthur and the savage punish Turpin. 17–44/
15 Turpin again attacks Arthur and is again punished. vii, 1–27. 6
16 Mirabella tells her story. 27.7–38
17 Mirabella's party meets Timias and Serena. Timias is captured and Serena flees. 39–50/
18 Arthur comes upon the party and overcomes Disdain. viii, 1–18
19 Mirabella repeats her story. 19–30
20 Serena falls prey to cannibals and is rescued by Calepine. 31–51/
21 Calidore, pursuing the beast, comes upon Pastorella. ix, 1–12
22 Calidore is entertained by Meliboe. 13–33
23 Calidore courts Pastorella, and Corydon is jealous. 34–46/
24 Calidore sees the Graces dance and talks with Colin. x, 1–31
25 Calidore rescues Pastorella from a lion. 32–38
26 Calidore wins Pastorella, and she is captured by brigands. 39–44/
27 Pastorella is wooed by the robber captain. xi, 1–8
28 The captain resists an attempt to sell her, and many are killed. 9–24
29 Calidore learns from Corydon of the disaster. 25–35
30 Calidore disguises himself and rescues Pastorella. 36–51/
31 We learn of Claribell, Bellamour, and their lost child. xii, 1–10
32 Pastorella is recognized as the lost child. 11–22
33 Calidore overtakes and conquers the Blatant Beast. 23–41/

BOOK VI

Episode	No. Sts.	Ratio of Run-on	No. Compounds	Fem. Rhymes	Possible *-ed* Rhymes
601.........	10	5.0	....	....	1
602.........	37	5.123	3	....	2
603.........	37	4.060	1	1	3 and 1
604.........	28	4.5	1	2	1
605.........	7	5.727	....	2	....
606.........	25	5.743	1	1	2 and 2
607.........	16	6.260	1	1	1
608.........	9	6.230	....	....	....
609.........	15	4.354	1	2	1
610.........	11	7.070	....	....	....
611.........	13	7.8	2	2	1
612.........	10	6.0	....	....	....
613.........	23	4.813	2	1	....
614.........	28	5.860	1	5	3 and 1
615.........	27	5.785	2	....	3
616.........	11	9.0	1	....	2
617.........	12	4.5	....	1	1
618.........	18	7.363	1	....	....
619.........	12	6.75	....	....	1
620.........	21	4.5	....	4	1 and 1
621.........	12	4.0	4	....	3 and 1
622.........	21	4.395	....	3	1 and 1
623.........	13	4.171	2	3	....
624.........	31	4.573	3	1	3
625.........	7	7.0	1	2	....
626.........	6	3.857	....	2	....
627.........	8	6.544	....	....	3
628.........	16	6.0	1	3	1
629.........	11	7.615	1	....	....
630.........	16	6.260	....	....	....
631.........	10	4.090	....	1	1
632.........	11	3.666	....	....	....
633.........	20	5.625	4	2	1

APPENDIX II

THE IMPORTANCE OF THE ENJAMBMENT TEST

It is unfortunate that the technical criteria of recognized value in determining periods of composition are few. Professor F. M. Padelford, in his argument for the late composition of the *Cantos of Mutabilitie*, discusses the use of (1) compound words, (2) run-on lines, (3) feminine endings, (4) certain rhetorical devices, and (5) adjectival relative clauses interposed between subject and predicate.[1] Of these five tests, there are no statistical studies available for the last two, and therefore their value remains problematical. The third is of use only in a study of the relation of the first instalment to the second, and in the second instalment, since feminine endings are confined to that instalment. I have already discussed their significance in chapter xii. The occurrence of compound words is too infrequent and uncertain in significance to be useful in an analysis of any but a few long passages. The significance of this type of rhetorical ornament will be discussed in Appendix III. Only the enjambment test promises to be useful for the study of the progress of the *Faerie Queene*.

There is need for the development of further criteria for the study of Spenser's technique, including a more complete study of his vocabulary, a dictionary of his rhymes, and studies of his rhetorical devices, such as his use of proverbs, imagery, cadences, phrasing, etc. Such studies must be made, however, in such a way that they can be brought to bear on the historical problem before us. Any statistical summaries presented on the basis of book and canto divisions merely obscure any progressive development which the materials in the poem may show. Such studies should be based on the narrative episodes and units of allegory which, by their coherence, stand out as natural units of composition.

The enjambment test has been developed chiefly in connection with the study of blank verse, and its close correlation with the chronology of Shakespeare's plays has been demonstrated. But the use of this test in the *Faerie Queene* is conditioned by the intricate organization of the Spenserian stanza. The nine-line unit, while it limits the opportunity for run-on lines, since Spenser almost invariably comes to a full stop at the end of the stanza, makes the frequency of such lines within the stanza unit more significant. The difference in style between passages which seldom have more than one enjambment to a stanza, and often none at all, and passages which average two or more run-on lines to a stanza is very marked.

Furthermore, because of its intricate organization, the Spenserian stanza discourages revision. The necessity of finding three and four useful rhymes

[1] "The *Cantos of Mutabilitie:* Further Considerations Bearing on the Date," *PMLA*, XLV (1930), 704–11.

makes changes in the last six lines particularly difficult unless the revision amounts to a complete re-writing. The rhyme scheme establishes a rigidity, especially at the end of the line, which would preserve the original phrasing and cadence, even when the narrative content of the line has been changed, as when the line, "Till him Chylde *Thopas* to confusion brought" (III, vii, 48.4) became, "And many hath to foule confusion brought."

As a result of this rigidity of stanza form, the poet would be likely to transpose and reorganize by stanza units, re-writing as little as possible, since re-writing involved the creation of a whole new stanza or a process of very clever and laborious patching. Probably it was easier to write a new stanza than to make important or extensive changes in the content of an old one. Therefore, where early writing is preserved in the poem, it would be likely to be preserved without enough revision to affect the enjambment ratio. Lines might be smoothed up, compounds inserted, and even the rhymes improved, as in the cases cited in chapter xii, without altering the syntax sufficiently to affect the phrasing at the ends of the lines.

Another result of this stanzaic unity and integrity is that the use of run-on lines may be significant not only as in blank verse for passages of considerable length but also for relatively small units, since the frequency of enjambment tends to be fairly uniform throughout a narrative unit.[2] This relative uniformity throws into relief the variation from unit to unit of the narrative. The variation is also emphasized by the frequent agreement in enjambment ratio between two parts of a narrative which are closely related, and yet which I have called two episodes instead of one. For example, see 209 and 210, or 114 and 115, where the practical identity in enjambment ratios suggests that these pairs of episodes were written as a continuous whole. Another example of this uniformity is provided by 102, the fight between Redcrosse and Error. This episode has a total of 22 stanzas and 26 enjambments. If we arbitrarily cut it in two in the middle, we find that each half has exactly 13 enjambments. With such evidence of uniformity of practice at a given point in the composition of the poem, it is hard to doubt a correlation between the time of composition and the enjambment ratios.

Unfortunately, there are few passages the composition of which we can date on external evidence, and none of these is early in the 1579–89 period, so that we lack points of reference. There is a seventeenth-century anecdote which describes Spenser as reading the account of the Cave of Despair to Sidney,

[2] For illustration, let us examine the first six episodes in I, i–ii. Letting each digit stand for the number of enjambments in a stanza, the stanzas can be represented by a series of numerals ranging from 0 to 4, as follows:

101—002132 ratio 6.75
102—0010113122220231112100 ratio 7.615
103—110223122221123311141121312432321 ratio 4.95
104—00123 ratio 7.5
105—3231321212113411 ratio 4.645
106—323111142022011212 ratio 5.4

Such passages as 101 and 104 seem too short for the ratios to have any significance. The difference between 103 and 105 and 106 is not great enough to seem significant, but 102 stands out from the other passages as having more *0*'s and no *4*'s.

presumably in 1579–80, but the story has too little authority to be useful for our purpose, although the passage shows a relatively low (7.1) ratio of run-on lines.[3] The 1596 ending of Book III, with the related opening of Book IV, constitutes a passage which it is natural to assume was written after 1589, and in both parts of this passage the run-on lines average two to a stanza (ratio 4.5). An almost identical ratio is shown in the passage in Book VI in which Colin sees the Graces dance about his lady—a passage so closely linked in subject matter with the *Amoretti* and *Epithalamion* that we naturally associate it with them and assume that it belongs to the same period of composition. These passages would seem to give us a normal ratio of about two enjambments to a stanza for Part II.

The figures for the Mutability Cantos support that conclusion. They show a variability as follows:

701	The revolt of Mutability. vi, 1–36	4.32
702	Diana abandons Arlo hill. 37–55/	4.5
703	The trial of Mutability. vii, 1–27, 47–59	5.906
704	The pageant of the seasons. 28–46	3.886

As we would expect, the philosophical exposition shows a slightly higher ratio of end-stopped lines, and the brilliant and fluent pageant of the seasons is marked by an increase of enjambment. But the contrast in enjambment ratios between the philosophical, narrative, and descriptive writing in this passage is by no means great.

Most of the second instalment shows a normal "mature" ratio of about two enjambments to a stanza (4.5), but there is definite evidence of a tendency to tighten up the structure of the verse, reversing the tendency of Books I–III. This tendency is apparent in the Burbon episode in Book V, which refers to events of the late summer of 1593, and which was probably written in 1595. The episode has an enjambment ratio of 6.1.

In order to gain a general view of the situation, let us summarize the evidence in a table. Throughout the six books and two cantos the majority of the stanzas show a ratio of enjambment between 6.9 and 4.5. But in each book there are episodes showing ratios above and below these limits. It is the shifting proportions of these groups which is significant for the present study (see Table 1). The progressive decrease in the number of stanzas with enjambment ratios below 6.9 is uniform in the first three books but not in the second three. If it represents a progressive development in Spenser's technique, then the condition of the second instalment probably indicates the incorporation of old material in Books IV, V, and VI.

The tendency toward the use of more than two enjambments to a stanza (above 4.5) is not progressive in the first instalment in the same way as is the decrease in low enjambment ratios. There are only 27 stanzas of that kind

[3] The story is told by John Aubrey, *Brief Lives*, ed. A. Clark (Oxford, 1898), II, 248. It appears in an elaborated form in the "Life" prefixed to the 1679 edition of Spenser's *Works* and was reprinted by Hughes. Todd, in his "Life," prefixed to the *Works* (London, 1805), I, xxxiii, points out that Spenser was already acquainted with Sidney some time before he published the *Calender*, so that this cannot be a true account of his *introduction* to Sidney.

in the first two books, as against 240 in Book III. Then the structure of the stanza was tightened up again in the second instalment, either intentionally or accidentally. The explanation probably lies partly in the use of old matter in Books IV–VI. It will be noticed that Book VI, the book most clearly written after 1590, is nearest to Book III in the proportions of high and low enjambment.

The development of the technique of the Spenserian sonnet seems to throw some light on the problem of enjambment in the second instalment of the *Faerie Queene*. The metrical similarity between the sonnet and the Spenserian stanza is obvious, and it would be almost inevitable that the technique of one would affect the other when the poet was writing both alternately. Now the seventeen dedicatory sonnets, printed at the end of the first part of the *Faerie Queene*, and almost certainly written in 1589–90, show a ratio of one

TABLE 1*

Book	Enjambment Ratio		
	7.0 or Less	6.9–4.5	More than 4.5
I	249	350	19
II	191	484	8
III	33	404	240
IV	110	436	51
V	127	349	73
VI	71	356	125
VII	0	61	55

* A few introductory stanzas which are not closely related to what follows have been omitted from the totals.

enjambment to each 4.4. lines. That is, the ratio is practically that of the revised ending of Book III and the opening of Book IV. But the *Amoretti* have the much tighter structure of one enjambment to 7.08 lines.[4] If we accept the usual dating of the sonnets as written between 1590 and 1595, then we must conclude that about 1590 the usual fluidity of Spenser's verse was about one run-on in 4.5 lines but that between 1590 and 1596 he substantially decreased this ratio, probably in accordance with a change of theory such as led him to introduce feminine rhymes in his second instalment.

I believe this reduction in enjambment was the result of a conscious intention, because the long practice in writing his stanzas must have produced a habit of mind which moved easily in that pattern. The end product of this development is evident in Book III and in such late additions to that book as the Timias and Belphoebe matter (4.1, 4.5, 5.0) and the closely related epi-

[4] Of the 88 sonnets, 49 have either one or two enjambments each (28 have two, 21 have one); on each side of this norm, 14 have three and 13 have none. Just 12 sonnets show an unusually large proportion of run-on lines; 6 have four, 5 have five, and 1 has six. These are scattered through the body of the sonnets, four in the first 10 (Nos. 2, 4, 6, 10) and four in the last 10 (79, 81, 82, 85). The other four are 45, 48, 58, and 71.

sodes describing the birth of Belphoebe and Amoret (3.3, 3.8). The deduction about Book III of which we can be most sure is that it was put together in haste out of materials, especially those which concern Britomart, which had been quite recently written. All considerations seem to point to a gradual increase in the use of enjambment from the inception of the poem until 1590 and to a conscious effort to decrease the enjambment in the second instalment.

Other factors in the use of run-on lines, besides those of practice and policy, are hard to detect. Within episodes there is, of course, a certain amount of variation essential to the flexibility of the medium. But the nature of the material does not seem in any marked degree to have controlled the use of enjambment. The procession of the seven deadly sins in Book I has a very low enjambment ratio (except in the description of Envy), while the very similar procession of the seasons in Book VII has a very high ratio. The same principle holds true for descriptive and narrative passages. In the early books rapidly told narratives, like that of the Dwarf in I, vii, 19–28, and Phedon in II, iv, 16–36, have low enjambment ratios. But the same kind of story in VI, xii, 1–10, has a high ratio. There may have been a tendency to shorten the phrasing (producing more end-stopped lines) in passages where great excitement is indicated, as in VI, x, 32–37, when Calidore rescues Pastorella from a wild beast, or in VI, xi, 25–35, where he is told of the disaster which has befallen Pastorella. But, in general, the nature of the subject matter seems to have had surprisingly little influence on the enjambment ratio of an episode.

On the other hand, there is often a striking similarity in the enjambment ratios of widely scattered episodes belonging to certain narrative and character groups. For example, there is a marked tendency toward similar enjambment ratios in passages, from Book II to Book V, which involve Braggadochio. He appears in the following episodes:

205	Braggadochio steals Guyon's horse and meets Trompart and Archimage	5.333
206	He encounters Belphoebe	7.568
332	He figures in the seduction of Hellenore	6.428
412	He attempts to recover the false Florimell	7.0
505	He takes part in the tournament	7.312
507	Guyon's horse is recovered, and Braggadochio is punished	9.0

In the third of these episodes he plays a minor part, and the participation of Britomart makes it evident that if the narrative was an old one, as its tone suggests that it was, it must have been revised for its present place in the poem. The first episode is the only real exception to the rule that wherever Braggadochio appears the enjambment ratio drops to 7.0 or less. Two things should be taken into consideration in connection with this episode. In the first place, the recovery of Guyon's horse (507) cannot be older than the theft of it, unless the account of the theft has been re-written. In the second place, if old matter were being fitted into a new situation or into a new narrative sequence, the chief changes would naturally be made at the beginning and end. If we subtract the first and last stanzas from 205, it develops that the enjambment ratio for the remainder of the passage is 7.0. The first stanza has three enjambments, and the last stanza has five; no other stanza has more than two. The first stanza is linked by its subject matter more closely with the preceding than with the following matter, and the last stanza describes the flight of Archimage and serves as a causal link with what follows. If these two linking stanzas were added later, then the rest of the episode belongs with the rest of the Braggadochio matter, which seems to have been early writing.

The Braggadochio stories are light in tone and approximate Ariosto's sardonic humor. We might expect the informal tone of this subject matter to produce a more informal handling of the stanzaic structure. But Shakespeare in his early plays shows a similar tendency to stiffen his verse in humorous passages, often with the use of rhymed couplets. Later he tended to drop into prose, but that medium was not open to Spenser. Some may argue that Spenser's practice merely illustrates his inability to handle humorous passages, but it is at least equally probable that the humorous passages were written early, before his mind acquired the habit of thinking freely in his complex stanzaic pattern and in units of phrasing larger than the single line.

The tale of the Squire of Dames in Book III, which I have argued was a survival of part of the earliest narrative of the poem, has an enjambment of 7.411—a very unusually low ratio for Book III. I pointed out in my discussion of Book II that in that book the part of Archimage is curiously fragmentary, as if a story had been planned which did not survive the final revision of the book. Archimage appears in the first episode in Book II—an episode which continues his story from the close of Book I. It should be noted that the close of Book I and the opening of Book II have very similar enjambment ratios (7.56 and 7.45). Spenser may originally have intended to carry Archimage and Duessa along as the enemies of each knight in turn, since he gives them so large a part in the opening of Book II. But after the opening of this book Duessa is supplanted by Acrasia, and Archimage makes three brief appearances in connection with the plot to steal Arthur's sword. The first of these appearances is 205, which I have just discussed, another is 215 (ratio 7.0), and the third is 218 (ratio 5.79), where he plays only a minor part in what is probably not a piece of early writing. The last appearance of Archimage is in Book III, where he is mentioned in a short linking passage as in pursuit of Britomart. No explanation is ever offered for that situation, which evidently represents some unfulfilled intention.

In general, Archimage, like Braggadochio, is associated with passages showing a low enjambment ratio, except for his very first appearance (103), where the description of him is borrowed from Ariosto but has been modified by presumably later borrowings from Tasso.

Spenser drew upon Ariosto throughout the process of composition of the *Faerie Queene*, but his chief borrowings seem to fall into two stylistically distinct groups. Besides the stories of Braggadochio and Trompart and of Archimage, important parts of the story of Florimell and the knights of Maidenhead and such isolated tales as those of Phedon and of the Squire of Dames show low enjambment ratios. On the other hand, practically all of the story of Britomart and some parts of Florimell's show high ratios of enjambment such as approximate Ariosto's own practice of running the phrasing over the end of the line in every third or fourth line.[5] This situation supports the theory that Spenser had two chief periods of Ariosto imitation: one early, when he was trying to write in Ariosto's humorous and somewhat scandalous vein, and a much later one, when Britomart was created and much was added to the story of Florimell.

Indeed, the story of Florimell, since it belongs to both kinds of Ariosto imitation, may be taken to illustrate one phase of Spenser's method of developing a narrative. According to both my analysis of the narrative and the enjambment test, the chief events in her story were written quite early in the history of the poem. The three chief episodes—her flight from Faery Court, Marinell's courtship, and the tournament at her wedding—all have less than one run-on in seven lines. These episodes constitute all the essential parts of the Florimell story except the account of how she came to be imprisoned. This necessary element in the story involves a whole train of episodes showing ratios from 6.0 to 3.4. The general pattern for the whole is the story of Ariosto's Angelica, but the condition of the narrative indicates that Spenser added to it from time to time. He has also made three further elaborations which do not derive from Angelica's adventures. These are the attack on Marinell by Britomart, the story of Florimell's girdle and the tournament held for it, and the creation and adventures of the false Florimell.

Evidently, in elaborating and complicating his story of Florimell, Spenser followed the authentic method of the romances, where story after story was added to an elementary core, and where some of the core often disappeared, or was replaced, in the process. It is a method which can be studied in the two versions of Sidney's *Arcadia*,[6] and we need have no doubt that this accretive process came as naturally to Spenser as it did to Sidney.

The evidence that Florimell's story has been dismembered and rearranged is clear enough. Miss Janet Spens[7] has pointed out that Florimell's flight occurs the day before Marinell is wounded by Britomart, and yet we are told that the occasion of her flight was the news that Marinell had been wounded. The two accounts of her lost girdle are contradictory, and the two tournaments, one for her girdle and the other at her wedding, duplicate each other to such an extent as to suggest that they are two versions of the same original. Finally, there is a very striking dislocation of narrative which leaves her in the cave of Proteus for a full book before she is rescued. Evidently her story has not only been added to from time to time but has also been broken up to meet the requirements of Spenser's changes of plan.

When to this change of plan and consequent rearrangement is added the change of names which the poet apparently sometimes employed to shift an episode from one character to another, it does not seem possible to trace his steps in the maze. But we can gain some conception of his method of working from the materials I have presented. We must recognize the existence of the

[5] In Canto I Ariosto has a run-on ratio of 4.4. In Canto III, which Spenser imitated so closely in III, iii, the ratio is 3.3, and Spenser's ratio in the corresponding canto is 4.2. I have depended for my figures for Ariosto on the edition of the *Orlando Furioso* published at Venice (1582) by Domenico & Gio. Battista Guerra fratelli.

[6] See chap. viii, n. 8.

[7] *Spenser's Faerie Queene* (London, 1934), p. 20.

next two episodes are borrowed from two different episodes in Ariosto. The ninth episode is a linking passage which joins 4 and 16, both apparently examples of older writing. But the link need not be as old as the matter it connects. The next four episodes include all of the House of Pride, except the procession of the seven deadly sins (111) and the tournament between Redcrosse and Sansjoy. The account of the sins may go back to the lost *Pageants* or to some of the dream-vision material of the 1580 period and may be introduced as a unit to ornament the passage. The fight between Redcrosse and Sansjoy (113) echoes both Tasso and Ariosto, as well as the *Iliad*, the *Aeneid*, the Psalms, and Chaucer—all in the compass of eighteen stanzas. Such a wealth of echoes suggests to me that the poet worked over the passage more than once, having different models uppermost in his mind at different times rather than all at the same time. In this case a fight between two knights may have been transferred from one situation to another, and the House of Pride, which seems otherwise to be a late creation, need not have been the original setting.

The Ariosto-like ending of Canto vi (118) not only borrows the episode from Ariosto but makes use, for the only time in this book, of Ariosto's method of ending his cantos in the middle of a story. We can hardly imagine that this bad joint was allowed to stand through several revisions of the book. On the other hand, if it was added in the final revision, the two episodes which belong with it (116 and 117) but which seem to be of older composition may have been revised to make an introduction for it.

Even in the account of the visit of Redcrosse to the House of Holiness, although the rest of the episode shows a low ratio of enjambment, the visit to the hermit who shows Redcrosse a vision of the New Jerusalem, a passage imitated from Ariosto, has a much higher ratio of enjambment. Except for this one passage, the freer use of run-on lines is confined to the first half of the book. It is observable only in passages imitated from Ariosto, and it seems at least possible that it represents a revision of the book made in the second period of Ariosto imitation, when Spenser was combining his early moral allegory with later romance materials and also working in what he could of his early imitation of Ariosto.

The way in which the enjambment test sorts out the various elements in the story and shows consistency in series of episodes which belong to the same thread of narrative suggests that Spenser developed his books by inserting new episodes at various points, as in the case of the House of Pride, and occasionally by fully revising old matter, as in the description of Archimage. Probably he also occasionally changed the order of events. The almost identical enjambment ratios of such closely related episodes as 110 and 112, 114 and 115, and 122 and 123 seems to dispose of any argument that the ratio was consciously varied from episode to episode.

The correlation between the Ariosto imitation and the frequency of run-on lines is a very interesting phenomenon, and one which, I believe, has a bearing on the sequence of composition of the *Faerie Queene*. There is no trace of an early humorous imitation of Ariosto in Book I, unless it is in the rescue of Una from Sansloy by the satyrs, an episode which might originally have been a part of the lust-chastity theme; but if the nine episodes which have "mature" enjambment ratios represent additions made when Book I was put in substantially its present form, about 1586–87, the influence of Ariosto on the newly added material reflects the poet's preoccupation with the *Orlando* during the period when he was creating Britomart.

The evidence of late additions to Book I has an interesting bearing on the probable length of the early illustration of holiness and also on the probability, or improbability, of a connection between the early version and the *Faerie Queene*. According to the enjambment test, the older parts of the book are almost entirely confined to the more formal allegories, while the newer parts mingle allegory with imitations of Ariosto's narrative. The same situation is apparent in Book II and in the first section of Book V and lends support to a theory that the early illustration of the cardinal virtues was a fresh start and not a development of the early, humorous emulation of Ariosto which came eventually to be amalgamated with it.

Only ten episodes in Book II, totaling 275 stanzas, show less than three run-on lines to two stanzas (ratio 6.0), as compared with eighteen episodes, 449 stanzas, in Book I. Whereas in Book I the bulk of the episodes fall in this division, in Book II the bulk of the book shows more than a 6.0 ratio. The balance has shifted. The ten episodes in Book II are as follows:

201	The link with Book I, in which Archimage sets Guyon upon Redcrosse. i, 1–34	7.458
202	Guyon finds Amavia and her babe. 35–61/	6.0
206	Belphoebe comes upon Braggadochio and Trompart. iii, 20–46/	7.568
	Sts. 22–31 description of Belphoebe . . 5.294	
	32–34 Vergilian imitation 0.0	
207	Guyon conquers Furor and Occasion. iv, 1–15	6.38
208	He hears Phedon's tale. 16–36	7.826
213	Guyon visits Phaedria's isle. vi, 19–26	9.0
215	Guyon meets Atin. Pyrochles is saved by Archimage. vi, 38–51/	7.0
217	Guyon visits the Garden of Proserpine. vii, 51–66/	7.584
221	Guyon and Arthur visit the Castle of Alma. ix, 17–60/	7.452
222	The chronicle of British kings. x, 1–69	6.21

Three of these episodes come too close to the arbitrary dividing-line to be significant (202, 207, and 222). The other sixteen episodes in Book II show between 5.8 and 3.8 as the ratio of run-on lines, leaving only seven episodes with ratios below 7.0. These seven include the independent tale of Phedon, the episode of Belphoebe, and the opening link with Book I, all of which have already been discussed. The remaining four are scattered passages, of which the Castle of Alma is the longest and most interesting. The whole account (ix, 17–60/) shows a ratio of 7.452, but upon examination the composition proves to be very uneven:

Sts. 21–27, 31–32	the description of the body	16.2
28–30	the digestion	3.0
33–44	the affections	5.7
45–58	the mind	9.0

According to this analysis, the descriptions of the body and the mind belong to an old piece, worked over to fit its present use by the insertion of the passages on the digestion and the affections. The later writing mentions Guyon and Arthur, while the passages on the body and the mind are very formal and make no mention of the two heroes.

In contrast to this irregularity within a long episode, it should be noticed that, as in Book I, closely related parts of the same narrative sometimes have practically identical ratios, as in 209 and 210 and also in the three parts of the Cymochles story (211, 212, and 214). Therefore, we can hardly attribute the situation in the Castle of Alma to a normal or usual tendency toward variation.

Book III has only three episodes, totaling 33 stanzas, showing an enjambment ratio below 7.0, and these three—the two opening episodes introducing Britomart and Florimell and the tale of the Squire of Dames—have already been discussed. Two others—the seduction of Hellenore and the closing canto containing the Masque of Cupid—have ratios between 6.0 and 7.0. I have already given reasons other than the enjambment test for thinking that both of these were written some little time before they were fitted into their present places in Book III.

The last three books have 110, 127, and 71 stanzas, respectively, below 7.0. But the possible significance of these passages is complicated by the evidence that Spenser tightened up the structure of his stanzas in the second instalment. Some passages, like the Braggadochio stories, and the continuation of Chaucer's *Squire's Tale*, seem like survivals from a body of early writing upon which Spenser drew wherever he could. The exceptionally low enjambment ratios of the exemplary episodes in the first section of Book V seem to support strongly the theory that Spenser began a book on justice early in his career of writing Spenserian stanzas. But the equally low ratios of the episodes describing the retreat of Timias and his reconciliation with Belphoebe (423, 424) and of the related Timias episodes in Book VI (610, 611) are puzzling, unless we suppose that the poet had on hand a story which he found it possible to fit to the allegory of Ralegh's disgrace with almost no revision.

We certainly cannot use the enjambment test as a unit of measure upon which to base a chronological rearrangement of the 185 episodes which make up the poem. But, on the other hand, it does afford interesting corroboration of the narrative evidence about the inner history of the composition. The ratio of run-on lines is by far the most important test so far worked out for determining the period of composition of a passage or series of passages. But other features of Spenser's style need to be thoroughly investigated in order to secure further evidence of changes in technique during the progress of the composition.

APPENDIX III

SPENSER'S USE OF COMPOUND WORDS

Spenser's use of compound words has been advanced as evidence of the date of composition of the Mutability Cantos. This feature of the poet's style has been studied by Professor F. M. Padelford and Dr. W. C. Maxwell, who find that the use of such words diminishes from Book I to Book VI.[1] Book I has four and one-half times as many as Book VI. The decrease is not regular in the last three books, however, as the following summary shows: Book I averages one compound in 39 lines; Book II, 64; Book III, 78; Book IV, 106; Book V, 73; Book VI, 148; and Book VII, 73.

The infrequency of compounds in Books IV and VI contrasts with the fairly consistent practice in Books II, III, V, and VII. Book I is distinct from the other books, set off by its frequent use of compound words as it is also by its infrequent use of past participial rhymes.

On the basis of an assumption of seriatim composition, the authors of this study draw the following conclusions:

> The poet freely coined such words in the *Amoretti* and *Epithalamion*, written in 1593–4 while he was at work upon the later books; and in the *Prothalamion* written in 1596, after the completion of the sixth book, adorned his verse with such mellifluous epithets as '*sweet-breathing Zephyrus*' and '*silver-streaming* Thames' and with such a daring creation as Venus' '*heart-quelling* sonne.' There can be only one explanation: Spenser had come to regard words of this character as more happily accommodated to lyrical than to narrative verse. That he had not changed his feeling about the artistic merit of compounds as such is evidenced by the fourth hymn, in which they occur with greater frequency than in any other poem except the *Muiopotmos*, that most delicate of Spenser's compositions. The sublimity of this hymn is clearly responsible for the frequency of the compound words and refutes any notion that the poet had come to regard them as intrinsically cheap and tawdry [p. 507].

I think it was not so much that the poet came to regard compounds as "more happily accommodated to lyrical than to narrative verse" as that they constitute a very special type of ornament which required intensive work on the phrasing of the verse. Therefore, they occur most frequently in those poems and passages over which Spenser labored most assiduously. That would explain their great frequency in the first book, which I believe was completely revised more than once, and in the shorter pieces. They are less frequent in the running narrative which has not been worked over, since they only occur there as happy accidents, spontaneous felicities of phrasing. On the other hand, experience and practice at such creation would certainly increase the frequency of these "accidents."

[1] "Compound Words in Spenser's Poetry," *Journal of English and Germanic Philology*, XXV (1926), 498–516.

Aside from Book I, compounds occur at a rate of one or less to seven stanzas, even where they are most frequent. Moreover, they could be introduced in a process of revision much less extensive than any involving the rhyme scheme or the phrasing at the end of the line. Therefore, since we have reason to believe that Spenser revised assiduously, we cannot regard the occurrence of compounds as of primary significance in determining the period of composition of any particular passage. Spenser used them even in the *Shepheardes Calender*, where the rate of occurrence is one in 105 lines, almost exactly the same rate as that in Book IV. In the *Muiopotmos*, the *Amoretti*, and the *Fowre Hymnes* the rate of occurrence is from two to four times as great. But except for Books I, IV, and VI the poet's practice shows uniformity rather than progression. The very infrequent use of compounds in Book VI may be due to its pastoral character or to its rapid composition. But, at best, the appearance of several compounds in a passage can be regarded as evidence of careful composition or of revision but hardly as an indication of the date of composition.[2]

[2] The authors of this study (p. 507 n.) regard the compound verbal adjectives and participles as more original than the nouns and adjectives, and they list the frequency of their appearance separately, as follows: I—51; II—82; III—111; IV—162; V—108; VI—187; and VII—102. It does not seem likely that Spenser grew less original, but it does seem probable that he polished the last four books less thoroughly than the first two.

INDEX